THE
TEACHER'S
Complete & Easy
GUIDE TO THE
INTERNET

Ann Heide   Linda Stilborne

Supported by: Ingenia Communications Corporation
Technical advice: Craig McKie

Trifolium Books Inc.
http://www.pubcouncil.ca/trifolium

This book is dedicated to Karen Kostaszek and the SchoolNet Support Group at Ingenia Communications.

Trifolium Books Inc.
238 Davenport Road, Suite 28
Toronto, Ontario, Canada M5R 1J6

Trifolium's books may be purchased in bulk for educational, business, or promotional use. For information please write: Special Sales, Trifolium Books Inc., 238 Davenport Road, Suite 28, Toronto, Ontario, Canada M5R 1J6.

Credits
The Glossary at the back of this book was reproduced with the permission of Unisys Corporation. The cartoons on pages 39, 74, 94, 119, 234, 235, 237, 238, 240, 241, 242, and 243 were also produced from the Glossary with the permission of Unisys Corporation. The "Time" activity on page 51 was reproduced from *The Educator's Guide to the Internet* with permission from Addison-Wesley Publishing Company: The Alternative Publishing Group.

Canadian Cataloguing in Publication Data

Heide, Ann, 1948-

The teacher's complete & easy guide to the Internet
Includes bibliographical references and index.
ISBN 1-895579-85-6

1. Teaching –Computer network resources. 2. Education–Computer network resources. 3. Internet (Computer network). I. Stilborne, Linda. II. Title. III. title: The teacher's complete and easy guide to the Internet.

TK5105.875.I57H44 1996   025.06'37   C96-930280-0

Printed and bound in Canada
10 9 8 7 6 5 4 3 2 1

Editing & production coordination: Francine Geraci
Text design & layout: Jack Steiner/Joan Wilson
Cover design: Blair Kerrigan
Cartoons: Scot Ritchie (pages 85, 107)

Acknowledgments

The authors and publisher would like to thank the Unisys Corporation for granting permission to include its excellent Glossary entitled *Information Superhighway Driver's Manual: Key terms and concepts that will put you in the passing lane* in our book. Special thanks to James B. Senior and Michael Heck of Unisys Corporation for providing us with all the material we needed on such a timely basis, and to Jim Chiponis for his delightful cartoons.

We thank these educators and friends who took the time to provide valuable reviews: Lynn Barkley, Anthony Czerneda, Roberta Dykstra, Dale Henderson, Maureen Kelly, Janet Killins, Ron Miller, John Rising, and Mary Kay Winter. We thank the Lafayette County School District for sharing their Acceptable Use Policy with all of us on the Internet. Lastly, the many teachers who shared their ideas with us on the Internet are warmly thanked for their important contributions.

About This Book

The Teacher's Complete & Easy Guide to the Internet, as our title states, will show you what the Internet is all about. We explain the Internet at an introductory level and provide lots of ideas for using it in the classroom. Here are some of the many questions this book will help teachers answer.

- **What impact is the Internet having on learning?**
  See Chapter 1, which explains what the Internet is, why teachers might want to start using it, and how it's changing the teaching/learning process.

- **How can I get connected to the Internet?**
  Since no one solution will be workable for every teacher or every school, Chapter 2 identifies issues and options that teachers will need to explore before "hooking up."

- **How are teachers in the early, middle, and higher grades using the Internet for student projects?**
  You'll find ideas throughout this book, but see especially the *Project Ideas* features that appear in Chapters 3, 4, 5, and 6. These contain specific curriculum-related activities for each grade level.

- **How are teachers dealing with controversial and unacceptable material on the Internet?**
  Student security issues (such as acceptable use) are a major issue with teachers and with parents. Chapter 3 discusses acceptable use policies (AUPs) and offers practical guidelines for safe and productive online learning. (See also Appendix A, which contains a sample AUP.)

- **What are the basic tools and resources available on the Internet?**
  Chapters 4 through 7 describe specific Internet tools such as e-mail, the World Wide Web, Gophers, FTP, telnet, MOOs, and Cu-SeeMe.

- **How can I connect with other teachers on the Net?**
  See Chapter 4 for a discussion of e-mail, as well as suggestions for listservers (discussion forums) and newsgroups of particular interest to teachers.

- **What is the World Wide Web?**
  The World Wide Web provides multimedia access to the Internet, and is currently the hottest place for teachers and students to be! Chapter 5 explains the Web and introduces such key terms as HTML, URLs, browsers, and more.

- **Where can I find curriculum-related information on the Internet?**
  Chapters 4 through 7 direct you to specific curriculum-related resources. As well, Appendix B includes an extensive list of

excellent educational resources that can be found on the Internet (including *The Teacher's Complete & Easy Guide to the Internet* Web site!).

- **How are schools publishing information on the Internet?**
  See Chapter 5 for examples of school Web sites maintained by kids, for kids.

- **What strategies can help me bring the Internet into my classroom?**
  Before you can use the Internet with your students, you'll need to explore it yourself! See the *Getting Started... with* features in Chapters 4 through 7 for step-by-step exercises and strategies aimed at teachers new to the Net.

- **How can I gain access to libraries and other online information services?**
  You'll want to check out Chapter 6 (Gophers) and Chapter 7 (FTP, telnet, and Hytelnet), which tell you how to make use of these resources.

- **Where can I get information on technological planning?**
  See Chapter 8 for resources that can help administrators and teachers meet the continuing challenge of implementing technological change.

- **How can I get my classroom involved if funding is limited?**
  Funding is another challenge for integrating the Internet into the classroom. Chapter 8 also offers practical suggestions for enlisting corporate, government, and community support to make the Internet a reality in your school.

About This Book's Features

We have designed *The Teacher's Complete & Easy Guide to the Internet* in a way that we think will make good sense to teachers. We explain all the basics on how to use the Internet and provide practical tips and project ideas that will help teachers turn the Internet into a useful tool for the classroom.

Here are some of the exciting features of this book:

Getting Started... with. We're aware that you need to gain a level of comfort with new technology before launching into class projects, so we include structured learning exercises specifically designed to help teachers master basic concepts and skills.

Project Ideas. We think this is one of the most exciting features of this book! These take you step by step through a range of Internet projects that you can use in the classroom. Projects are included for all grade levels and for varying levels of connectivity. You'll be able to implement some of these with just a basic Internet connection.

A Sampling of... Great Internet Sites. Our "site samplers" identify many of the very best educational sites currently on the Internet. We've also provided space for you to add your own personal favorites, as your list of exciting educational resources on the Internet continues to grow.

| HINT   Scattered throughout the text, these highlight extra suggestions for learning about the Net and using it effectively.

Teaching Tips. These time-saving tips will help you and your students make the most of your time online as you integrate the Internet into your classroom.

Tech Talk. These are technical points that are not essential, yet are useful to know about. If a particular point seems obscure at first, you can highlight it and return to it once you've gained more experience. It's not necessary to understand everything all at once. In fact, we hope this guide will continue to be useful to you over the long term.

Teacher Quotes. Our teacher quotes (most of them culled from the Internet!) offer practical hints and insights into the value of this technology for learning. We hope you'll find these as exciting, motivating, and helpful as we did.

Glossary. Check the back of the book for an excellent glossary of Internet terms from the Science Learning Network.

Acceptable Use Policy. Appendix A shows you how one school has addressed the issues of student safety and acceptable use of Internet access.

Curriculum Links: Online Resources. Appendix B lists many, many links that will lead you to resources in your specific teaching area. We include everything from Arts and Language Studies to Environmental Studies and Special Needs. The list is designed to help teachers link the Internet to practical learning outcomes. Even teachers who are already familiar with the Internet will find this extensive list of curriculum resources invaluable.

How to begin?
We suggest you read Chapter 1 first because it gives an overview of the ways that the Internet can be used in the classroom.

Chapters 2 through 8 offer down-to-earth instructions on "how to" that you can explore in whichever order works best for you. Use the Table of Contents and the Chapter Goals to help determine which chapters will be most immediately useful to you. Some teachers may want to focus initially on using electronic mail, while others will prefer to start by sampling some of the curriculum resources on the World Wide Web.

Our most important goal in designing *The Teacher's Complete & Easy Guide to the Internet* has been to try to make it work for individual teachers. Thus, we have relied on the suggestions, ideas, and experiences of teachers like yourself. Their input has helped us to identify many issues that need to be addressed for the Internet to be successfully implemented in schools. We welcome your comments and suggestions about sections of this book that you have found particularly useful.

If you have ideas you would like to share with others, please send them to

Trifolium Books Inc.
238 Davenport Road, Suite 28
Toronto, ON M5R 1J6

Or, e-mail your suggestions to Trifolium's president at **trising@io.org** .

"I am proud to be able to use the Internet as a way of speaking to people all over the globe to help provide quality education to my future students! We've only just begun!"

Cheryl Janik, Elementary School Teacher, currently a graduate student in the Elementary Education Program at the University of New York at Buffalo.

About the People Behind This Book

Ann Heide, author. As a consultant for her school board, Ann has helped hundreds of teachers incorporate technology into their classrooms over the last five years. It was only two years ago that Ann stopped relying on school board equipment and bought her first computer, "one with all the bells and whistles." Since then, she has been exploring how the Internet can be used as a tool for classroom use. She has also co-written two books on bringing technology into the classroom (*The Technological Classroom: A Blueprint for Success,* Trifolium Books, 1994, as well as the book you're now holding). Ann loves assisting teachers in meeting the challenges and opportunities of technological change; this book is just one more way she's doing it.

Linda Stilborne, author. Linda, who has taught at elementary, secondary, and college levels, came to computers only reluctantly "in the days of arcane operating systems and unfriendly software." She maintains that her background in language arts and poetry was invaluable in helping her decipher cryptic software manuals. For her, computers are just a tool; they become meaningful only when they enhance personal interests and pursuits. Her biggest online thrill so far has been finding new information on Charles Dickens over the Internet.

Ingenia Communications Corporation, sponsors. Ingenia is a young, dynamic organization begun by a group of engineering students and friends, volunteering to develop Canada's National Capital FreeNet. Subsequently, Karen Kostaszek, Ingenia's president, had a vision of linking K–12 schools across the country using the Internet. From this concept SchoolNet was begun. Ingenia's support of this book reflects their vision of having teachers, administrators, and importantly, children, wired.

Craig McKie, an Ingenia associate and professor of sociology, is also an avid techie; his technical support has been greatly appreciated. It was Craig who provided our fabulous Appendix B (Curriculum Links: Online Resources).

Trifolium Books Inc., publisher. Trudy Rising, president, became a high school biology and chemistry teacher just a few years after Sputnik went into orbit. Her partner, Grace Deutsch, started out as an editor. Because of their interest in producing educational resources, both took positions in the educational publishing industry. By 1991 they had amassed some 25 years' combined experience in educational publishing, and embarked on their own venture in order to produce high-quality resources for educators. Computer literacy eluded them, however, until their technoweenie children recently brought them both kicking and screaming into the twenty-first century.

Francine Geraci, *editor and production coordinator.* Francine began in publishing when typesetting was still done in Linotype "and you could feel the raised letters when you brushed the galleys with your finger." Now she edits books onscreen, updates clients via e-mail, and supervises disk-to-film production of printed materials. Francine does not miss the good old days of manual paste-up, when she often walked around with waxed bits of galley stuck to the bottom of her shoe.

Jack Steiner, *designer.* Jack remembers delivering a job to a client ten years ago, bearing an armful of finished artboards rustling with tissue-paper overlays. When the production manager showed him another designer's streamlined electronic output, he went out and bought a computer the next day. Jack admits there was a significant learning curve "until I realized that designing and drawing with a computer just meant learning another medium, not much different from learning to use a T-square or a pen."

Contents

Introduction

"Professionally, I see the chance to help my students experience the world outside rural Kansas. I see the chance to share ideas in forums I never thought possible; to gather information that's not in any local library, and to help others who might never have found the answers to their questions without such a wide base to draw from. Teachers often feel isolated. The Internet makes us a community that doesn't have to meet at any set time in a world that seems over scheduled already."

— HEDDI THOMPSON, TEACHER, CHASE COUNTY ELEMENTARY SCHOOL, COTTONWOOD FALLS, KS, USA

This book is for any teacher who wants to learn more about how to use the Internet in the classroom. It is especially for teachers who approach the Internet with reluctance and perhaps with a touch of skepticism about its value in the classroom.

Educators who have begun using the Internet as a learning tool know the critical role it can play in linking students to the world of telecommunications and information technology. Others are excited by the vastness of the information resources on the Internet. More than anything, teachers who have begun to explore the Internet with their classes are thrilled by its potential as a communications tool.

Communication in the form of electronic mail or student publishing on the World Wide Web helps to break down the isolation of the traditional classroom and facilitates reading, writing, and language development in a context that students find relevant and real.

Your guide
The Teacher's Complete & Easy Guide to the Internet is intended to help you, the teacher, experience the excitement that the Internet can bring to your classroom. It explains key concepts and helps you learn to use basic Internet tools. It also tells you where to find some of the best educational resources on the Net. Most importantly, it will help you to discover how the Internet can help your students learn.

The global village

We read and hear a great deal these days about how the world is shrinking. Traditional political, economic, and social boundaries are being redefined almost daily. As we search for common values and a common understanding, we develop an appreciation for the complexities of managing a world of profoundly different cultures and social structures.

Education will be the key to resolving economic and cross-cultural problems, and it is the younger generations that will need to find solutions. We are all aware that we have a responsibility to provide today's students with the tools they will need to succeed in a workplace that is increasingly information based. These tools will certainly include knowing how to use computers. Even more important are the personal and social skills that must be developed.

A central skill

Central to these skills is the need for students to develop a sense of personal responsibility. We feel strongly that the Internet is a powerful force for helping them do just that. It brings to the classroom educational opportunities in which students take responsibility for their own learning. Students expand their horizons by learning how to communicate, how to collaborate, and indeed, how to learn.

Teachers who understand that the world is changing also understand that classroom learning needs to change in response. Schools must play an integral role in bringing about the necessary social adjustments as we move from an industrial to an information-based economy. The Internet will be a vital tool for bringing about such change. It is increasingly clear that we as teachers must think about the impact that telecommunications can have on education and respond in positive ways to it.

The opportunity

A major challenge is that much of this technology is new to almost everyone. Even seasoned "Internauts" are still struggling to improve the technology and sort out the technical, political, and pedagogical issues. Major improvements need to be made to our telecommunications infrastructure to accommodate increasingly complex applications, such as multimedia and video-conferencing. Then there are the serious social questions, such as, "Should there be complete freedom of information on the Internet?" Educators must play a part in helping to resolve some of these issues. We have a unique opportunity to ensure that knowledge and understanding, rather than power and greed, are the forces that will steer the growth of the information highway.

A team approach

As you and your class become familiar with the Internet's many resources, learning can become a team effort in which everyone is encouraged to share knowledge, skills, and new discoveries. A team approach to learning is one of the things that makes the Internet fun for students. One innovative geography teacher has even involved her class in designing learning units for other classes—including establishing learning outcomes and evaluating learning. A team approach also allows students to become active in their own education and reinforces the value of personal responsibility.

The three keys to keeping this dynamic environment manageable are

- committing enough time to become reasonably familiar with Internet tools
- seeking out others who can help when you get stuck
- moving slowly enough to make sure that you understand each stage before moving on to the next.

You are about to embark upon an adventure that will change the way you teach and the way your students learn. It will also change the ways in which you—and they—see and respond to the world. It is our hope that *The Teacher's Complete & Easy Guide to the Internet* will help to make this adventure a mutually exciting and satisfying one.

Ann Heide
Linda Stilborne

If you live in a country where the grade levels K–12 are not used, please note the following approximate ages of students at each grade level. This chart will permit you to see readily which projects in the book are at the appropriate level for your own students.

kindergarten (K)	grade 1	grade 2	grade 3	grade 4	grade 5	grade 6
ages 5–6	ages 6–7	ages 7–8	ages 8–9	ages 9–10	ages 10–11	ages 11–12

grade 7	grade 8	grade 9	grade 10	grade 11	grade 12
ages 12–13	ages 13–14	ages 14–15	ages 15–16	ages 16–17	17–18

Ten tips for Internet success :-)

Here are some approaches you and your students can use to get started quickly and avoid common pitfalls. Many of these suggestions are based on the idea of sharing expertise. This is the best way to master the Internet. Take advantage of what other teachers, students, administrators, and the broader community can offer to help you to bring this technology into your classroom.

1. **Find a learning partner,** possibly another teacher in your school who also wants to learn about the Internet. You can compare notes on resources and encourage each other. (If you find yourselves complaining to each other, find a different partner!)

2. **Sign up for any local courses** that promise to help you learn more about the Internet and its tools. Your school may be willing to fund such a course, particularly if you agree to share some of what you learn with your colleagues. (Hint: Taking a course with a partner is also a good way to ensure you don't miss key points.)

3. **If you know someone who is using the Internet,** ask him or her to help you get started. If other teachers in your school have experience using the Internet, offer to help them manage an Internet project.

4. **If your school does not have Internet access,** get your own account. Shop around for a service provider until you find one who is willing to provide help with the installation. If possible, seek out Windows- or Macintosh-based access, since these bring you the best of the Internet's marvelous graphics.

5. **If you know of any student technowizards at your school,** ask them to help with such tasks as installing a modem. As you may have discovered, many students (particularly those in the upper grades) are already knowledgeable about the Internet, and are eager to share what they know.

6. **Visit your local library** and see what books and resources they have on the Internet. Your librarian is probably already using the Net, and may be willing to provide help and advice.

7. **Once you're online, seek out online tutorials** and resource tools. (This book suggests some helpful sources.)

8. **Don't try to master everything at once;** take time to explore. In particular, give yourself ample time to learn before beginning a classroom project. If you spend even thirty minutes a day learning something new, you'll be amazed at what you've mastered in a month.

9. **Once you're comfortable with electronic mail, join one of the educational listservs** such as INCLASS or Kidsphere. (See Chapter 4 for more information about these.)

10. **Although Net browsers let you keep track of resources on line, keep a small notebook or card file** of some of the interesting resources you find. A personalized, computer-based card file or database is great for quick searching.

Hope you find our hints helpful! We will provide useful tips throughout this book.

Chapter

The Role of the Internet in Today's Classroom

❝I asked my daughter, 'What would be the number one thing you would want us to teach you if you were heading off for college today?' Her answer was immediate: 'Teach me to use the Net!'**❞**

— JOHN DALTON, TEACHER, JENNIFER MERCHANT TAIPEI AMERICAN SCHOOL,
    TAIPEI, TAIWAN

Marshall McLuhan, the communications visionary of the sixties, said that new technologies are always used to do the old job—that is, until some driving force causes them to be used in new ways. It can be argued that, so far, this has been our experience with computers in education. Today there are computers in schools, but as yet they have not significantly changed the nature of teaching or of learning. And for most of us, this is not a problem. Computers can deliver learning in novel ways, but they still fall far short of delivering the kinds of school experiences we want for our children. With the advent of the Internet, this situation could change, and very quickly. Again, it was McLuhan who captured the concept that is now the driving force behind the Internet—as well as behind an impending revolution in education. The concept is that of the *global village*.

This chapter looks at the Internet and its potential to bring about revolutionary social change.

Chapter goals

■ To consider the role of the Internet in education
■ To introduce some specific Internet tools that teachers can use
■ To examine some practical ways in which the Internet can help students learn

The Internet today

The Internet is an extensive network of interlinked yet independent computer networks. In less than two decades, the Internet has gone from being a highly specialized communications network used mostly for military and academic applications to a massive electronic bazaar. Today, the network includes

- educational and government computers
- computers from research institutions
- computerized library catalogues
- businesses
- community-based computers (called *freenets*)
- a diverse range of local computer bulletin boards.

Anyone who has an account on one of these computers can send electronic mail throughout the network and access resources from hundreds of other computers on the network.

Because of the free-wheeling culture of the Internet and its overall lack of structure and external controls, it is tempting to dismiss it as a novelty. Those who take time to learn about it soon discover, however, that the Internet is actually a microcosm of our society. Most of what happens in the real world is in some way reflected on the Net. On the Internet you can find libraries, radio programs, and shopping malls. You can meet friends, take courses, subscribe to magazines, and obtain medical or gardening information. The Internet can be a source of news, a forum for dialogue with other people about current events, a place to find out about government activities and about jobs. For kids, the Internet offers pen-friends (known as *keypals*), learning resources, a place to share their thoughts and ideas, and even a place to publish their own stories and pictures.

While all this is interesting, the availability of so much information and so many opportunities to share and communicate with people at a distance may not at first appear to be sufficient justification for schools to spend the amounts of money needed to link classrooms to the Internet. This chapter discusses some of the reasons why the Internet is an increasingly important tool for educators and shows how telecommunications technologies have the potential to transform the ways in which teachers teach and students learn.

Technology and education

In fact, the Internet offers only a bare suggestion of the role that telecommunications will ultimately play in the lives of today's students. Yet, the skills they will require to navigate this environment can be learned today. It is generally agreed that in the twenty-first century, technology will be pervasive. Futurists predict that by the end of this century, approximately two-thirds of all work will involve some form of computerized information. It is therefore important that all students today learn to access, analyze, and communicate electronic information effectively.

It has been suggested that if someone who died one hundred years ago were to visit North America in the last decade of the twentieth century, the only thing that would be recognizable would be the schools. Although technology has radically changed factories, offices, banks, and hospitals, most of our classrooms might appear unchanged.

There has been change, of course. Teachers know that the whole philosophy of learning has changed radically in recent years. As a result, both the way students are taught and the kinds of skills they acquire in today's classroom are very different from the methodology and curriculum of a decade ago. In fact, schools *must* change continually to accommodate the society in which they operate. For example, junior kindergartens, school lunch programs, resource teachers, and sex education—all unheard of fifty years ago—are commonplace today. Because information technology is currently the driving force in our culture and in our economy, it is time to incorporate it into the curriculum in a meaningful way.

There are a number of reasons why some teachers have been less than enthusiastic about bringing the Internet into the classroom. These reasons include

- the apparent complexity of the Internet
- the lack of telephone or data lines in schools
- the lack of both time and training opportunities for teachers.

As well, sometimes there is a lack of administrative support, and occasionally, colleagues may resist a teacher's attempt to explore new methods. There is also the problem that—at least at first glance—the Internet may seem to be dominated by technowizards who appear to be more concerned about what the technology can do than about how it can improve the teaching and learning processes.

Teachers are also justifiably concerned about students' accessing unacceptable content on the Internet. One consequence of this free-wheeling culture is that unsavory elements co-exist on the Internet alongside the many valuable learning opportunities. Parents, teachers, and administrators all share the fear that a student may be harmed or, at the very least, may simply waste time unless access to the Internet is closely monitored. For these reasons, some school boards may be reluctant to adopt the Internet in their schools.

These are all real problems, but they are problems that must somehow be overcome. The Internet—or, more precisely, the broader world of computers and telecommunications, of which the Internet is only a part—is restructuring society.

The phenomenal growth of the Internet is one indicator of the impact that this technology will ultimately have. For the past six years, the Internet has doubled in size each year. That means that each year, there are as many new people connecting to the Internet as there are existing users. Currently, the Internet is able to connect more than 27.5 million people in 159 different countries.

At the very least, the Internet is a powerful vehicle for communication. It is also a phenomenon that challenges some of our assumptions about how the world works. Consider the following examples, which signal the reality of the new global village. Via the Internet:

- A North American company can hire programmers in countries as distant as India or Russia.

- Within minutes of the 1994 earthquake in Los Angeles, people around the world were able to obtain first-hand accounts of the event. Because telephone calls to Los Angeles were not possible, the Net became a critical means of relaying information to and from the disaster area. In one poignant case, a family asked anyone within the disaster zone to check on their grandmother, whom they could not reach. Within a couple of hours, a response was posted on the Internet: "I couldn't get through to your grandmother, so I went to the apartment building and found her. The building didn't hold up very well, but your grandmother did. She's fine."

- A small bookstore owner in Nova Scotia, Canada turned his business around virtually overnight by tapping into the global marketplace. Currently, there are twenty to thirty million potential consumers on the Internet who can purchase everything there from pet food to automobiles. Each month, more than 1500 new companies connect to the Net.

- Large companies are increasingly involved in collaborative research with other companies to develop new products in a rapidly evolving marketplace. Global competition and multinational corporate ventures are fueling the need for Internet connectivity and an increasingly sophisticated telecommunications infrastructure.

Education is also taking its place in the global village.

- There are now hundreds of distance education courses available over the Internet. A high school in Oregon offers anyone with Internet connectivity the opportunity to acquire a diploma through distance learning. Some school districts, particularly those serving rural populations, are investigating delivery of elementary-level classes.

- Twelve thousand children from nine countries compete with one another in track-and-field events without having to leave their own schoolyards. This one-day event, which is billed as a "virtual" Olympics, is facilitated by the Internet.

- Recently, students from ten different schools across Canada were simultaneously linked with one another for an online interview with Canada's Justice Minister who was visiting Egypt at the time. This event is just one example of the real-time experiences made possible by the Internet.

Through the computer, students can converse with other students in remote classrooms. With video-capture technology, students can participate in a dynamic fashion in events as they happen around the globe.

During the 1994–95 school year, students across the United States carried on a continuous dialog with scientists journeying to Antarctica.

> "I've never seen a project that was so alive with the breath of what it means to do the work of science…"
>
> *Parent of a middle schooler from New Jersey, USA talking about Live from Antarctica*

In another example of an electronic field trip, students can join NASA scientists on board NASA's Kuiper Airborne Observatory as it flies at 41,000 feet to study planets, stars, and galaxies with its infrared telescope. Through telecommunications, the walls of the classroom recede and learning about the world becomes more immediate, personal and real.

Time for a change

Technology consultant and award-winning teacher Alan November describes the necessary changes to our schools in terms of changing "job descriptions":

> "… the job descriptions of everyone in school will fundamentally change because of the [information] highway. Students will move from working in the test-preparation business to building information products that can really be used by 'clients' around the world. For teachers, perhaps the most difficult job change will be that we'll no longer be at the center of learning for our students. We'll become brokers—connecting our students to others across the nets who will help them create and add to their knowledge in a way that one teacher alone could only dream of."
>
> *Quoted by Thérèse Mageau (1994, May/June), "Will the superhighway really change schools?" Electronic Learning, 13(8): 24.*

Some teachers might raise an eyebrow at November's unconventional views, but others would insist that the reality he envisions is not far off. Classroom use of the Internet is already a reality. One set of figures indicates that between 1991 and 1993, educational use of the Internet grew by an astonishing 23,000 percent, and that much of this growth was in elementary and secondary schools. By December 1994, there were nearly 200 elementary and secondary school Internet servers. By July 1995, this figure had increased to 450, and by February 1996, there were more than 2500 schools

Figure 1-1
New models for learning

Old model	New model	Implications for learners
Teacher centered	Learner centered	Students are empowered as learners
Passive absorption	Learner participation	Student motivation is enhanced
Individual work	Team learning	Team building skills are developed; learning is enhanced through sharing
Teacher as expert	Teacher as guide	Framework for learning is more adaptable to a fast-changing world
Static	Dynamic	Resources for learning (textbooks, existing knowledge base) are replaced by an online link to the real world. Resources can be adapted to immediate learning needs
Prescribed learning	Learning to learn	Development of skills for the information age

from forty-three different countries with their own home page posted on the World Wide Web. The Free Educational Electronic Mail Network (FredMail), which began as a bulletin board exchange in 1984, is now accessible through the Internet and has grown to include roughly 10,000 classrooms a year, comprising more than 300,000 students.

It is often the case that, at least initially, people approach new technologies with the thought that these are somehow replacing something more familiar. Sometimes this perception proves to be true. Television has in large part replaced radio, just as the car has replaced the horse and buggy. We may worry that the Internet has the potential to replace the textbook, the school library, and ultimately, the classroom teacher. Undoubtedly the role of the classroom teacher will change, but teachers will not become redundant. In fact, the best guarantee that teachers, and not technology, will be at the heart of the classroom of the future is to ensure that we as the teachers of today master new tools for learning, such as the Internet. With access to the Internet, the classroom becomes an even greater cooperative learning environment in which the teacher provides focus, guidance and inspiration.

Figure 1-1 outlines some of the shifts between the old and the new models of learning, together with their implications for students.

Keys to using the Net

As with any learning venture, success depends on mastering the basics, and then gradually expanding knowledge through practice. Although the Internet is a huge and ever-expanding universe of information, the good news is that you don't have to know it all.

For teachers, the key to using the Internet successfully is to learn to use a few basic tools—and then to focus on using a few key educational resources.

This chapter briefly describes some basic Internet tools. Subsequent chapters will discuss each of these in detail. The paragraphs that follow are intended to give a preview of some of the ways that you can access educational resources over the Internet. With the exception of the World Wide Web (described below), most of these applications are possible even on an outdated computer with a relatively slow modem connection.

E-mail

Electronic mail, or e-mail, is probably the most common Internet application, as well as one of the most powerful. Electronic mail allows you to send and receive messages over the Internet. Using electronic mail, you can communicate with anyone else who has an Internet address. You can also send messages through "gateway" services to other systems, such as bulletin boards or CompuServe. Many classroom projects may use electronic mail, which provides an opportunity for interactions with students and teachers around the globe.

In addition, through electronic mail you can join worldwide discussion groups. There are literally hundreds of discussion groups for educators on the Internet. Favorites among elementary through secondary school teachers include Kidsphere, an international discussion group for teachers; Edtech, which focuses on the use of technology in the classroom; and Kidlit-L, a discussion group that explores children's literature. There is also a wide range of discussion groups with a specific curriculum focus. Such groups include **K12.lang.art**, for language arts education; **k12.ed.soc-studies**, for social science teachers; and **k12.ed.life-skills**, for school counselors.

You will be amazed at the number of projects you and your students can undertake using e-mail. Chapters 3 and 4 provide a wealth of examples and ideas.

FTP

FTP stands for *File Transfer Protocol*. This process is used to transfer files across the Internet. FTP can be used to transfer all kinds of files from a remote computer to the local computer where your own account resides. Resources available through FTP include educational software, text files of sample lesson plans, electronic books, research reports, and graphics files. Using FTP you can quickly bring many useful resources into the classroom. Canada's SchoolNet is one example of an FTP site that offers resources specifically for teachers.

Telnet

Telnet is a way of connecting to a computer at a remote location and using that computer as if you were actually at that remote site. Although telnet is not used as commonly as it once was, it is still important to know about. You might use telnet to get to another site such as an online library catalog located at a university. When you telnet to a remote location, you basically use the telnet command and provide the Internet address of the location you wish to access. Once you reach that location, you complete the logon information. The Big Sky Telegraph bulletin board, which serves as a clearinghouse for many school telecommunications projects, is accessible through telnet.

Gopher

Gopher is an Internet tool that allows you to go to hundreds of sites on the Internet using a straightforward menu structure. You can maneuver your way through the Internet simply by selecting items listed on a menu. Gopher is one of the most valuable tools on the Internet for accessing information, particularly if you do not have a graphical (i.e., Windows or Macintosh) connection to the Internet. The initial basic services available on the Internet were e-mail, telnet and FTP. When Gophers arrived, they greatly simplified the process of accessing information and downloading files to a local computer. AskERIC, NASA Spacelink, and SchoolNet are popular Gopher sites with a wealth of educational resources.

World Wide Web

The World Wide Web, along with special software called Web browsers (such as Netscape or Mosaic) provides point-and-click access to text, graphics, sound, and occasionally video files, often integrated around a specific topic. The World Wide Web provides easy access to a vast array of information. A Web page can be a "clickable" children's book, an online museum exhibit, an art gallery display, a government information resource, a lesson from a distance learning course, a weather map, or even an interactive frog dissection. Increasingly, Internet applications that have traditionally been separate and distinct are now all accessible through the World Wide Web. Newsgroups, FTP sites, and even online "chat groups" are all available through the Web. For many teachers, the Web is the real focus of the Internet, to the point where some people have come to think (erroneously) that the Web and the Internet are synonymous. The World Wide Web also provides a great opportunity for schools to publish their own information.

Using the Internet successfully will depend on teachers' understanding of exactly how it relates to the classroom. Figure 1-2 (page 14) suggests some of the ways in which the Internet can be tied to teaching and learning.

HINT References to the World Wide Web are sprinkled throughout this book. You'll recognize these because they start with **http://** . We'll explain how to access these sites in Chapter 5.

Figure 1–2
The Internet in the class-room

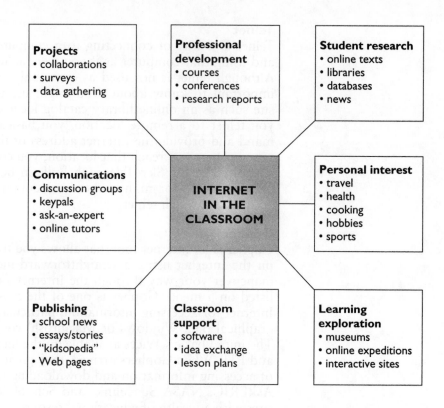

Projects • collaborations • surveys • data gathering	**Professional development** • courses • conferences • research reports	**Student research** • online texts • libraries • databases • news
Communications • discussion groups • keypals • ask-an-expert • online tutors	**INTERNET IN THE CLASSROOM**	**Personal interest** • travel • health • cooking • hobbies • sports
Publishing • school news • essays/stories • "kidsopedia" • Web pages	**Classroom support** • software • idea exchange • lesson plans	**Learning exploration** • museums • online expeditions • interactive sites

Each Internet tool has a specific function, and most teachers exploring the Net will want to become familiar with all of them. For teachers, these tools can be used to provide students with exciting opportunities to access and interpret the world around them. Teachers in a traditional classroom often have to create an artificial world, from whatever resources are available, to create learning opportunities that capture some dimension of the real world. But such resources have always been limited, and the classroom environment has never been quite "real." By becoming familiar with a few basic Internet navigation tools, teachers can bring the real world into the classroom. Following are some examples of typical Internet learning activities.

Learning through connectivity (e-mail)

Possibly the most powerful feature of the Internet is its potential as a communications tool. Students delight in being able to connect with people around the world. A fairly simple educational activity using electronic mail involves linking individual students with their counterparts in other places. Sometimes class groups are linked, enabling them to interact and share ideas with a group of students of comparable age; sometimes individuals are linked as keypals. This is an excellent way for students to learn about life in other countries, to develop and improve their language skills, and to share their thoughts on contemporary issues and problems.

> "When the earthquake happened in San Francisco, we read about tidal waves in kids' swimming pools, earth movement in soccer fields, and kids being thrown down stairways—kids' perceptions of what it was like to be in an earthquake. When the Berlin Wall came down, we had classes in Berlin that were giving us day-by-day reports on what it was like to be there. When the Gulf War was going on, kids in Saudi Arabia's schools talked about the crocheted gas mask backpacks that their mothers made."
>
> *Margaret Riel, Consultant, AT&T Learning Network*

Being able to see world events at the same level of detail at which ordinary people actually experience them is one way that students can discover the basic humanity they share with people around the globe.

Students can also use e-mail to involve other classes in a project. One seventh grade class recently used e-mail to conduct a survey. They wanted to know how much time other students their age spent watching television, so they designed an electronic questionnaire and distributed it to other students over the Internet. This project provided students with an opportunity to learn about gathering and analyzing data. The project was also an interesting way to explore an important social issue.

A somewhat younger group of students used e-mail to find out about food resources around the world. Through a single e-mail account, they requested that students in other countries send them messages about what foods were native to their area. The responses they received provided the basis for developing a classroom map on which foods from various regions were displayed. Being able to interact with other students around the globe in this way brings a new and exciting dimension to learning.

In yet another learning application, electronic mail can be the vehicle through which students in distant classrooms can collaborate on research reports, story writing, and electronic publishing. They can also compete with one another to solve math problems, history quizzes, and "scavenger hunts," and they can share knowledge and observations in group projects. In one cooperative project, students analyzed the quality of rivers in their area and compared the data that they collected with data gathered by other students in their state. In another project, students reported on when various wildflowers started to bloom in their area, with data being collated centrally.

Finally, electronic mail connectivity is a powerful tool for accessing experts and tutors. Purdue University in Indiana operates an online writing lab (OWL) which provides some excellent writing resources as well as human writing coaches. Along a similar line, the Canadian-based Writers in Electronic Residence has professional writers reviewing student writing samples. Other programs link students with scientists and researchers to help with class projects and units of study.

Learning through online resources

As classrooms are able to connect to Gopher sites and Web resources, learning can become an endless adventure. Not only are there substantial text-based resources on topics ranging from planets to politics, but a wide range of resources is available for electronic field trips involving pictures, text, sound, and sometimes interactivity. Here is a sampling of some recent online exhibits sponsored by museums and other educational institutions.

- Honolulu Community College offers a fascinating dinosaur exhibit that features pictures, textual information, and an opportunity to take a narrated tour of the exhibit.

- The Institute of Physics in Naples offers an exhibit of some early instruments used to study physics. Specialized exhibits of this type abound on the Internet, and many of them are exhibits that few people would have a chance to visit otherwise.

- The Smithsonian Institute makes available its exhibit, *Oceans of the Earth*. Students visiting the exhibit electronically can learn about fascinating sea creatures and about how the oceans affect climate. Teachers can download video clips from the Undersea Flyby or access educational resources such as the *Killer Whale Teacher's Guide*.

- At another exhibit sponsored by the French Ministry of Culture, students can learn all about the discovery of a Paleolithic painted cave. The University of California at Berkeley sponsors the Online Museum of Paleontology with exhibits on geology, fossils, and pre-history. A computer server in Oxford, England provides a gateway to these and many other museum sites.

- Classes can visit the Louvre and other art galleries as well as photography exhibits, such as a recent exhibit of the works of photographer Ansel Adams. Students can download graphics and incorporate them into their own printed or electronic reports.

- At Questacon, Australia's hands-on Science Center, students can explore current exhibits, read about intriguing science discoveries and applications, practice problem-solving skills with something called Puzzlequest, and actually try experiments online. Like many resources on the Internet, these are available at no cost, apart from the cost of basic connectivity.

In addition to Web sites, which offer multimedia and interactivity, there are a great many less exciting but equally useful text-based resources available on the Internet. These include online books, magazines, references sources (such as an online dictionary and table of chemical elements). Selected news features, back issues of popular magazines, and full-text encyclopedias are increasingly available on the Net. Extensive archives of historical topics and online documentation of current events provide a depth and breadth of learning resources unmatched by anything previously available in even the best-equipped schools. The Internet is a very good resource for students researching current events, science, or social science topics. In addition, many discussion groups publish basic information about their area of interest. From these resources students can obtain information on topics ranging from pet care to astronomy to ballet. While the Internet falls somewhat short of having information about "everything," it is a substantial information resource. In most communities, it is a welcome supplement to the generally limited resources available in a local library.

Figure 1-3
Hands-on learning from Questacon, Australia

Learning by becoming involved

Perhaps one of the most rewarding ways to use the Internet in a classroom is actually to participate in a real-world adventure. An interesting example of how this can happen is the MayaQuest project. This was an online experience through which students could interact with archeologists investigating the ancient world of the Maya. The project took place in 1995–96. It enabled students to follow a team of researchers on a trek through southern Mexico and northern Central America. Students and teachers could participate in this project in many different ways.

A major component of the project involved the researchers regularly posting on the Internet narratives of their experiences in which they described not only details of the ruins they encountered, but geographical conditions and local customs in the areas they visited. In addition, photographs of the journey could be viewed online or downloaded and printed. Newsgroup discussions allowed students to pose questions to the researchers as well as offer their opinions on just about everything, from whether or not the researchers should consider eating in restaurants (not exactly an authentic Mayan travel experience!) to where the team might head next.

In addition to the teaching resources on the Maya that were made available, students themselves could test their learning by participating in an online Scavenger Hunt. The Scavenger Hunt presented them with questions designed to help them review what they had learned about the ancient Mayan civilization and to think deductively about some of their discoveries (see page 19). The project culminated with satellite broadcasts of video footage from the expedition, and classrooms with appropriate equipment could access this video over the Internet. The material gathered from the project is now a resource base for information about the Maya—and a wonderful example of the new learning experiences in which students using the Internet can actually participate in scientific research.

Learning to learn

An important development in current thinking about education is that we now acknowledge the need for students to develop skills for lifelong learning. The Internet is an ideal mechanism for encouraging students to assume responsibility for their own learning. In accessing the diverse range of learning resources on the Internet, students become active participants in their quest for knowledge. They learn to define their learning needs, to find information, to assess its value, to build their own knowledge base, and to communicate their discoveries.

MayaQuest Scavenger Hunt

This scavenger hunt will inspire children to learn about the region and its rich Mayan culture. It will also give them the necessary background to form their own theory as to why the ancient Mayan civilization collapsed, and to draw parallels to today's world. To find answers to the following questions, students can conduct their own research and can follow the expedition. We encourage participants to share and discuss their ideas in the MayaQuest discussion forum. At the conclusion of the expedition, the MayaQuest team members will post their answers.

1. Find three sites where ancient environmental abuse is apparent. What shape did it take? (clear-cut forest, slash-and-burn agriculture, pollution) In what century did it start occurring? Why did it happen?

3. Find three sites where there is clear evidence of warfare. What does it look like? (fortresses, violent scenes on glyphs) Where are they located? Are they pre-classic, classic, or post-classic?

4. Find evidence of modern-day warfare. What does it look like? How has it affected the surrounding environment and the lives of the people?

5. Find three sites where there is evidence of ancient overpopulation. What is the evidence? Are there any other related signs? (cut rain forests, smaller skeletons)

6. Find three examples of modern-day overpopulation. How are overpopulated cities affecting rural areas? social tensions? the environment?

7. Find three clues that ancient natural disasters occurred. (collapsed temples, stelae scenes depicting disasters...)

8. Research the remains of a modern-day natural disaster. What sort of damage did the last hurricane that hit the coast leave? Have there been earthquakes? What happened to the homes? Did people flee or rebuild? Did sickness or social unrest follow? What did the event do to the environment?

9. Find three Mayan stories or myths. These must be collected from village elders. They will be transmitted in Spanish and English. What clues do they hold about ancestors of modern Maya?

10. Read the interviews with the presidents of Honduras, Belize, Mexico, or Guatemala. Give your reaction to their comments.

"By going online, students can delve into special libraries, develop relationships that dissolve the barriers of age and distance, and share the enthusiasm of experts who love their careers. Over the Internet, pupils from different schools and backgrounds work together on projects and publish their results for thousands to view. Together, they are opening a window onto a vital world that might otherwise exist only as a flickering two-dimensional image on a television screen. As a result, many educators are rethinking the three traditional 'Rs' and adding resources and relationships to reading, writing, and 'rithmetic."

"The Internet Style of Learning." http://io.advanced.org/ThinkQuest/i-style html (January 8, 1996)

Incorporating the Internet into classroom learning gives students significantly more opportunities to structure their own learning than are available in traditional classrooms. Years ago, in the days of the one-room schoolhouse, it was assumed that there was more knowledge inside the schoolroom than outside. Today, there is much more knowledge outside the classroom. Moreover, given the diversity of learning styles, it is difficult if not impossible to "repackage" the world of knowledge to suit individual learner needs. More and more, the role of the teacher is to facilitate learning, not to prescribe it. Learning becomes an evolving process rather than a prescribed set of tasks, and the teacher's relationship to the students shifts from that of an all-knowing authority to that of a facilitator, a counselor, and a guide.

Almost any educational endeavor that is enriched by geographical diversity can be carried out on the Internet, but for teachers, there are other benefits as well. Teachers equipped with a computer, modem, and a phone line can tap into hundreds of project ideas on the Internet. Online discussions expand a teacher's network of colleagues to include teachers from around the world. This is especially important for teachers in small schools or in rural communities who may not otherwise have the opportunity to interact with teachers in their area of specialty. The Internet is a source for electronic books and journals, for educational research, and for professional development opportunities in the form of conferences and courses.

With patience and persistence, anyone can learn to use the Internet. This chapter has identified some of the potential obstacles for classroom teachers. But as long as teachers appreciate the ways in which telecommunications technology can enhance education in the classroom, they will undoubtedly find ways to overcome the roadblocks and help to pave the way for learning in the twenty-first century.

> "To have students who are explorers, we need teachers who encourage exploration. To deal with the Information Age in and out of the classroom, we need teachers who can teach students how to manage information through available technologies and who can aid students in turning information into knowledge."
>
> *Nancy Hechinger & Melissa Koch (1993), "Beyond the lightbulb." Technos: Quarterly for Education and Technology, 2(1): 23.*

Summing up

This chapter has examined some interesting ways in which teachers are using the Internet. The chapters that follow will present many more examples of classroom Internet use. The best way for teachers to ensure that the Internet is relevant and meaningful in their own classroom is to become familiar with a range of its resources. This builds confidence in developing original projects and ideas.

The next chapter discusses how teachers can get connected to the Internet.

Ann Heide and her colleague, Dale Henderson, planning an Internet class project.

Chapter **2**

Getting Connected

"I think that the way to a teacher's heart is through the students. I doubt any teacher who sees the interest, the motivation, the skills, and the excitement in her or his students can long resist taking what, here in Quebec, we call 'le virage technologique'—'the technological turn'"
— CHRISTIANE DUFOUR, TEACHER, SMALL SCHOOLS NETWORK, PQ, CANADA

In order to access the many wonderful things the Internet has to offer, you need a computer, a modem, and a connection to the Internet. Because so much of a teacher's work is done after school hours, you are likely to find that you want to be connected to the Internet from both home and school. Once you have a connection, you will use the Internet for much more than schoolwork. You can find the latest news, take an online course, get up-to-date travel information, or communicate with colleagues, friends, and family.

If you are in the fortunate position of having Internet access through an already established school- or system-based infrastructure, getting connected may be as simple as turning on your computer and clicking on an icon or selecting from a menu. If not, you will need to deal more directly with the hardware and software required to get connected, whether at home or at school. Your school will be faced with such questions as: How many phone lines, computers, and modems do we need? Where should these be located? Who will monitor students as they use the Internet?

This chapter explores several different kinds of Internet connections. Although each school has different needs and resources, examining the various models described in this chapter will help you with the technological decisions.

Chapter goals

■ **To examine options for connecting to the Internet**
■ **To help decide the right kind of connectivity for you**
■ **To determine what you need to get connected**

What is a connection?

Remember that the Internet isn't a place or a thing; it is a network of computers linked together. You want to become a part of this global communications network in order to communicate with others and gain access to resources and information. Although approximately twenty million people use the Internet in some fashion, many have limited access, and many others use only e-mail. For educational purposes, you want to take advantage of the full range of resources available. The kind of connection you establish determines, to a great degree, both the type and format of the information that you and your students can access. This, in turn, affects learning outcomes for students. In order to plan for your integration of Internet resources into the curriculum, consider the kind of connection that will best suit your needs and the costs of the equipment and services that are required.

If your school is already connected, you can skip the next couple of pages. Still, it's useful to know how the connection works and why certain things may be possible while others aren't. Your students will certainly want to know! Or, you may wish to consider upgrading your existing connection, particularly if it is limited to text-based viewing, in order to benefit from the Internet's excellent graphics.

Types of connections

There are many ways of connecting to the Internet. The most popular ways are:

- dialing into a large computer that is on the Internet
- joining an online service such as CompuServe, America Online, Prodigy, or GEnie
- connecting your computer directly to a local area network (LAN) whose server connects to an Internet host
- establishing a SLIP/PPP connection (described below) with an Internet service provider.

These methods are called indirect connections because only the host computer is directly connected; your computer isn't really "on" the Internet. You use your computer to communicate with the host computer. Although you can access the Internet only when connected through your host, your host remains online at all times. The last method simulates a direct connection because when you dial in to your service provider, your computer temporarily becomes a location, or node, on the Internet. Anyone with a computer, modem, and phone line can get a SLIP/PPP connection for a fee. The ultimate state of Internet connectivity is a direct link from your school's LAN to the Internet, in which the server becomes an Internet gateway. Each kind of connection has specific advantages and disadvantages. The following pages explain in greater detail all these ways of connecting.

Dialing into another computer

Many people get indirect access to the Internet by using a modem to dial in to a large computer that is itself on the Internet. Your computer becomes a terminal that communicates with the host computer. Community freenets (discussed later in this chapter) allow Internet access of this kind. When you log on to the central computer, you use its programs to navigate the Internet. You'll probably be limited to a text-only interface, but you will still have access to lots of information. The computer you are dealing with will undoubtedly have programs for such things as mail, FTP, Gopher, and telnet. There may even be a program called Lynx, which provides text-based access to the World Wide Web. In this situation, you must often use a special program to transfer a file from the host computer to your computer. For example, if you wanted to look at a picture file from NASA, you would have to

- connect your computer to the host by dialing in through your modem
- transfer the picture file to your own computer
- view the file using an image viewer on your own computer.

This kind of file transfer is necessary any time you want to view pictures, graphics, or movies from the Internet. Despite its limitations, this type of connection is a good starting point for teachers and students just beginning to explore the potential of the Internet in the curriculum.

Joining an online service

Commercial services such as CompuServe, America Online, Delphi, GEnie, and Prodigy offer online banking, shopping, dating, entertainment, and connectivity to the Internet. Using these services in schools where students spend many hours online can be expensive, but they have been designed to be user friendly. Most of these services offer their own interface to the Internet which can help reduce the learning curve for teachers and students. America Online offers a wide variety of educational resources, such as live classes, homework assignments, contests, awards, conferences for teachers, and complete graphical Internet access. Classroom Prodigy is a special version of the Prodigy online service designed for use in schools. It includes a bulletin board, craft ideas, an online encyclopedia, an art gallery, quizzes, current events, creative writing exchanges, and more. The Microsoft Network is an online service built into Windows '95. You can join directly using a modem and your Windows '95 software. The Microsoft Network offers full access to Internet facilities and e-mail, with different pricing plans from which to choose.

Commercial services vary in cost, and several cost options are available. For example, you might pay between $10 and $20 (US) per month for five hours of online time, or get a nine-month subscription with twenty-five hours of online time per month for about $400 (US). For specific details, contact the services directly. Be sure to ask which services are offered, as some offer only e-mail and may add personal message charges. Others may add surcharges for specific features. Some commercial services currently do not provide complete access to the World Wide Web, but this situation is likely to change in what has become a very competitive market. The best advice is to devote some time to exploring each service before joining. Look for current articles in computer magazines such as *PC World* or *MacUser* comparing the most recent offerings of the major commercial providers. Here are some of the best known.

America Online	(800) 827-6364
CompuServe	(800) 848-8199
Delphi	(508) 323-1000
GEnie	(800) 638-9636
Microsoft Network	(206) 882-8080
Prodigy	(914) 448-8000
Scholastic Network	(800) 473-2500

Joining an online service is the easiest way to connect to the Internet, but it may not be the cheapest or the most inclusive. However, these companies are competing to make complete access for consumers easy, cheap, fast, and reliable.

HINT America Online provides a good organizational framework that makes it easy to find what you want:

ESH	The Electronic Schoolhouse
TIN	Teacher's Information Network
KOOL	Kids Only Online
Internet	Internet Connection
Reference	Links to Internet resources

Connecting through a LAN

Large organizations such as universities and corporations purchase high-speed, high-volume direct connections to the Internet. They make use of these connections by developing ways in which hundreds of their users at a time can share that single high-speed central connection. Users may be physically dispersed throughout many buildings in laboratories, offices, and classrooms. Everyone is then connected by some technical means to a central server which controls the Internet connection.

This LAN is Your LAN
This LAN is My LAN
From Cali...

Similarly, in many schools, all the computers in the school are connected on a local area network (LAN). By connecting a modem to the LAN, every computer on the network has Internet access. This is a complex way of connecting to the Internet, and explaining it in detail is beyond the scope of this book. However, since your school may be connected this way, you may wish to understand how it works.

The number of users is limited by the number of phone lines going out of the school. One phone line allows only one user at a time, despite the fact that all the computers theoretically have access. To allow for many simultaneous users, an expensive piece of equipment called an IP router is substituted in place of the modem. A high-speed data line, such as an ISDN (*Integrated Services Digital Network*) line, replaces the ordinary phone line. An ISDN line provides speeds four to six times as fast as those of a standard 14.4 kbps modem. This line can connect the school's LAN to a commercial Internet provider or to the local college or university Internet server. Alternatively, a LAN can be directly connected to the Internet in such a way that the services of an Internet provider are not required. The LAN's server becomes an Internet gateway and your school an Internet site with its own domain name. For example, if you are from Cedarhill School, your address could be yourname@Cedarhill.edu. This type of direct connection is initially expensive and labor intensive to set up. It also requires a technically knowledgeable site manager to maintain the gateway and user accounts and to troubleshoot.

Whether through a direct or indirect connection, all computers on the network can access the Internet at any time. As a "resident" on the Internet, you can receive information in a graphical format, provided you have the appropriate Internet software, as described in the chapters that follow. This is obviously of great benefit in schools. Figure 2-1 illustrates how a LAN configuration differs from a single-computer connection to the Internet.

HINT For a comparison between direct dial-up options for LANs in schools, read "Internet Access for Educators: Options, Solutions and Costs" by Bob Avant and Keith Rutledge (gopher://SJUVM.stjohns.edu/00/educat/nebraska/neb-inf-0022.nebraska).

Despite the obvious complexity and expense of installing and maintaining an Internet connection through a LAN, most large schools have or will select this option because it provides such generous and complete access for students and teachers.

"Our school has a large lab of sixteen computers directly connected to the Internet. The library has its own network, which is hooked into our Internet pipeline. Our goal is to have one computer in every room directly connected. The staff has already trained in Net use and has access to the lab for that purpose."

Jamie Boston, Librarian, Birch Lane Elementary School, Davis, CA, USA;
quoted in Classroom Connect, May 1995

Figure 2-1
It's much more complex to connect a local area network to the Internet than a single computer.

A SINGLE COMPUTER CONNECTED TO THE INTERNET

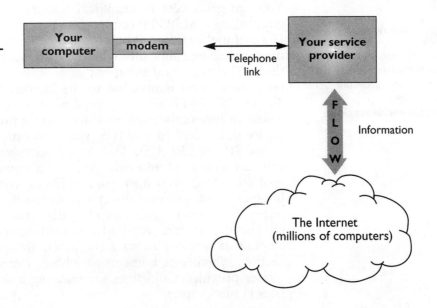

A LOCAL AREA NETWORK CONNECTED TO THE INTERNET

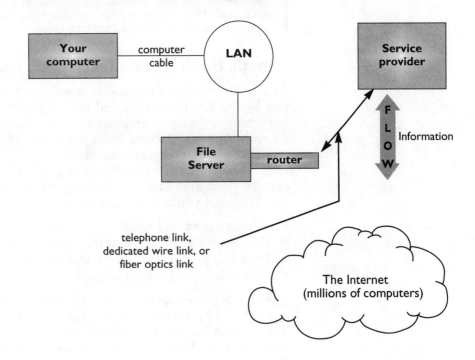

Establishing a SLIP/PPP connection

You can get access to graphical resources in addition to text by establishing a SLIP/PPP connection. You will see the acronyms SLIP (*Serial Line Interface Protocol*) and PPP (*Point-to-Point Protocol*) used interchangeably, although there are subtle differences between them. The important thing is that a SLIP/PPP account gives you a temporary direct connection to the Internet from home or school. To get a SLIP/PPP account, you'll need to sign up with a company called an Internet service provider. Service providers charge a start-up fee in the $30 to $50 (US) range plus monthly charges, usually about $10 to $30 (US). The service provider will supply the basic software you need and help you to get connected if you run into problems. Once you have your SLIP/PPP connection, you can run Internet client software directly from the hard drive of your computer. This means you can use either the simplest or the most advanced software available, according to your needs and the amount of memory in your computer. To open your Internet connection, whether at home or at school, you simply dial in to your service provider. Guidelines for selecting a service provider appear later in this chapter.

> **HINT** Although a SLIP/PPP account is generally more expensive, this is the type of access you will require if you want to want to work in a Macintosh or Windows environment. This type of access will also require a faster modem (no less than 9,600 baud). Most service providers can offer an alternative type of connection for users who are not Windows or Macintosh based.

What's the best connection for me?

At school, the type of connection will probably be determined for you by the administration and the computer support staff. What's important is that you understand what you and your students can do with the type of connection you have. Thus, good communication with your colleagues is essential.

If you want to use the Internet from home, you'll have to explore some alternatives. Choosing the best connection method is not difficult if you ask yourself these questions:

- What services do I need?
- Do I want a graphical interface, or will text-only meet my needs?
- How many hours per month will I use it?
- How much am I willing to pay?

For a beginner, direct dial-in access via a SLIP/PPP account with a good service provider is the best way to get a feeling for the Internet and its potential. If this isn't affordable, find out if family members have Internet access through their business that you can share by dialing in to it from home. If a community freenet is available, this is a completely free way to begin. Another simple way to get online is to purchase one of the "in a box" products found in bookstores and computer stores. Although this can be a relatively painless way to connect, the publishers will likely not connect you to the least expensive Internet service. Be especially wary of long-distance charges involved in accessing these services. You might begin with them until you're up and running, and then shop around among the commercial online services to see what they offer and at what cost. Once you are on the Internet, however, there are no long distance charges; you can access sites around the world at no extra cost!

If your school, school board, or district has a LAN connection, find out from the site administrator if you can get Internet services by dialing in from home. You will need instructions on how to dial in and how to run the programs available there. You'll also need some specific software, described later in this chapter, for your home computer.

If you can't get access through a LAN, yet you're ready and eager to have full access to "surf" the Internet and "cruise" the World Wide Web, it's time to get your own SLIP/PPP account from a service provider. This is the most complete option for those who have developed some expertise and are prepared to invest some time and money.

Demystifying the modem

You need a modem to access the Internet. The modem may be attached to your personal computer or to the LAN through which you are communicating.

Modems for sale today routinely pass 14,400 bps, and the most recent pass double that number. They can be internal or external. Most new computers come with an internal modem already installed. External modems can be connected to your computer by a cable. Modems are no longer expensive to purchase; most are in the $100 to $200 (US) range. The faster the modem, the more expensive it will be. If you have a slower modem, 2,400 bps or 9,600 bps, you can still access the Internet, but you will be limited in what you can do and everything will take longer. Generally, modems come with a detailed manual describing how to install and use the product. If modems and communications software are completely new to you, try to get help from someone who has experience installing one. The manufacturer often provides 1-800 help service, and your dealer can also help you to get started.

Most, but not all, modems for sale these days are fax modems. If there is only a small price increase for the fax feature, it's well worth it. A fax modem is very useful because it allows you to send

Tech Talk

Modems are classified according to the speed at which they transmit data. Modem speeds are expressed as baud rate, e.g., from a relatively slow 2,400 baud (or bps, bits per second) to 28,800 bps (also expressed as 28.8 kbps, kilobytes per second).

and receive faxes directly from your computer screen. You can write a letter to a parent and fax it immediately—no paper is required.

Be aware of development in the area of cable modems. With a cable modem, you gain access to the Internet through your local cable company. These modems are currently more expensive than telephone modems, and thus are not widely used. Nevertheless, telecommunications through the connection that currently brings you television programs is very convenient, fast, and powerful.

HINT While you will want to purchase a reasonably fast modem (9,600 baud or greater), not all computers currently offer connectivity at faster speeds. Most vendors will offer at least 9,600 bps, but connections through a bulletin board or local freenet may not. Your access provider should specify the speed at which to set your modem for connectivity.

What computer do I need?

You don't need a particular type of computer to connect to the Internet, nor do you need to reserve a computer solely for this purpose. Chances are you'll be using an existing school or home computer that you also use for daily tasks such as word processing and desktop publishing. Old, low-memory machines such as an Apple IIe or 286 PC will do the job, but very slowly. In general, if you are using this type of equipment, you will be limited to low-volume, text-oriented activities. Don't expect your students to be able to access the multimedia features of the World Wide Web. They may also become frustrated at the slow pace at which the screen display changes when commands are issued. With instructional time at a premium, many teachers are understandably reluctant to have students spend an hour locating a small amount of information that might have been obtained more easily from a book, video, or phone call. On the other hand, if your learning goals relate to communicating with e-mail or simply learning to use text-based Internet menus, older technology is adequate. However, if your students have more sophisticated computers with Internet access at home, you may find them less than enthusiastic.

If you are buying a new computer, consider an IBM-compatible multimedia 486 PC or Pentium, or a Macintosh. Such attributes as the amount of available RAM (*Random Access Memory*) and the size and speed of the hard drive inevitably have an effect on your computer's performance on Internet tasks. As a general rule, you will need eight to sixteen megabytes (Mb) of RAM. As the Internet rapidly expands its offerings, we will need faster, more powerful computers with more storage space to take full advantage of its multimedia features. In other words: *Buy the best machine you can afford, and don't be disappointed when it becomes rapidly outdated.*

HINT If you intend to use the graphics-oriented World Wide Web, you will need a multimedia computer with a video card and a monitor that has enough resolution and color capability to render the images accurately. This generally means that you should have a video adapter card with 1 Mb or more of video memory and an SVGA monitor. External speakers and/or headphones are required for sound and features such as Web-phone.

It's wise to stick with the type of computer, either PC or Macintosh, that is prevalent in your school, since each type requires its own brand of Internet software. Most people don't want to buy, install, or learn to use two different species of hardware and software.

What software do I need?

To dial in to an indirect connection, you need only basic communications software on your computer. Most new computers come with a communications package, and all modems come with software. Works packages such as ClarisWorks and Microsoft Works include communications software, or you can purchase a separate package such as Procomm or Crosstalk. Many shareware programs, such as Telix, are also available at little cost. Once your modem has connected to the host, you use the host's software for your Internet navigation and tasks. This software usually includes Pine, Elm, or Mail (for electronic mail), telnet (to connect to other computers), FTP (to get files from other computers), Archie (to search for files on other computers), Gopher (to browse through other computers and get files), and Lynx (to navigate the World Wide Web using text).

With a direct connection, on the other hand, your computer is part of the Internet and the network applications you need must run on your own computer. Which Internet services you can use depends upon what software you have on your computer. You need two types of software—the first to establish your connection and the second to navigate the Internet. Your service provider or your school computer expert should handle all this for you, but here's a very brief explanation.

The Internet's computer language is called TCP/IP (Transmission Control Protocol/Internet Protocol). TCP/IP software lets your computer "talk" to other computers on the Internet. In other words, it governs the way packets of information are broken up, packaged, labeled, transmitted, and received. Once your Internet connection is open and the TCP/IP software begins to work, you are ready to navigate.

At this point, you may need a separate program for each Internet task—e-mail, FTP, telnet, Gopher, World Wide Web, etc. Fortunately, many software packages include all these tools. Alternatively, you can choose to use Netscape or another Web

Tech Talk

For accessing most online services, set your communications software for 8 data bits, 1 stop bit, and no parity. The abbreviation for this is 8,N,1 or 8N1.

If you're an advanced Internet user, you may be the person installing and configuring TCP/IP software. In the Windows 3.1 and NT environment, obtain a shareware program called Trumpet Winsock. In the Macintosh platform, you will need a copy of the program called MacTCP (which is included in System 7.5 and later operating systems) and SLIP/PPP software such as MacPPP or InterSLIP. In order to configure your TCP/IP software to work with your SLIP/PPP connection, you'll need to get the following information from your service provider:

- your login user name and password
- the access phone number you'll be using
- your Internet Protocol (IP) number, which is the address of your machine

- the IP address of the domain name server you are assigned to use
- the IP address of the gateway machine used to handle e-mail and Usenet newsgroups
- the maximum packet size to use in your connection
- any other technical information, such as subnet mask address, that your service provider wants you to use.

You'll also need this information if you plan to create a dial-up connection to your own Internet service provider using the built-in TCP/IP feature of Windows '95. The help menus provided within Windows '95 will walk you through this process step by step.

browser alone to access a range of resources such as FTP, Gopher, and the World Wide Web, though some applications such as telnet require special configuration. A number of companies now offer Internet suite software. These are software packages that bundle together a selection of tools that you can use for different Internet functions. A typical Internet suite might include a mail package, a newsreader, a Gopher client, FTP retrieval software, and a Web browser. The Internet Chameleon and Emissary are examples of suite packages. Most service providers have FTP sites that give away all the software you'll need. You'll find out much more about specific software and what it can do for you in the chapters that follow.

Selecting a service provider

A service provider is a company that charges a fee to provide Internet access either through a direct SLIP/PPP connection or an indirect commercial online service. Look for lists of service providers in computer magazines, business magazines, Internet books, phone books, and newspapers. There are a large number of providers available, and they offer a wide variety of subscription plans. Once you register with a provider, you are assigned an Internet address, like a phone number, which others use to communicate with you. If you've ever had to change your phone number, you know how inconvenient *that* is. The same is true of your Internet address, so selecting a reliable, stable provider from the huge number available is important. Consider the following factors.

HINT These Web sites contain indexes of service providers worldwide.

YAHOO   http://www.yahoo.com/Business_and_Economy/Companies/Internet_Access_Providers/

THE LIST   http://thelist.com

HINT You can find out about a range of Web browsers (and suite software packages) at a Web site called the Consummate Winsock Apps List at **http://cwsapps.texas.net/** . You can obtain the latest Net-scape browser from **http://home.netscape.com/home/**

For Mactinosh Internet software, go to **http://www.macatawa.org/~mthomas**

Services offered

What do you want to do on the Internet? What do you want your students to be able to do? Make sure the service offers the Internet features you want. Are Gopher and Archie available? Does the system support World Wide Web? Will you be limited to certain newsgroups or the amount of e-mail you can send or store?

Cost

For many users, this is the first consideration. Ask for detailed fee schedules, and spend some time examining and comparing different packages. Usually, the charge depends upon what services you use and the amount of time you spend online. Many services have a flat-fee monthly rate for a given number of hours and surcharges if you exceed the designated limit per month. Others charge a basic fee plus an hourly rate based on the exact amount of time you spend online. Thus, one provider's rate might be better for people who spend a lot of time online, but not as good as another's for those who spend less time. Reasonable cost is nice, of course, but as with many other things in life, you are likely to get what you pay for from an Internet service provider.

Access

Access relates to cost if there is no local number for the service you want to use. Find out how you would connect—via a local call, a long distance call, or a 1-800 number. Long distance charges can add up quickly. Don't assume that a 1-800 number is free, either; you'll pay for it through a surcharge. For home or school use, a local number is best. If you travel frequently, find out if the provider has local numbers in other major cities. Many do. Access also relates to the number of lines and modems the service has. How often will you get a busy signal when you dial in? You can ask the provider for their user-to-line ratio, and you can ask others who use the service if they ever have trouble getting connected.

HINT The number of phone lines that an Internet access provider controls is very important. Ideally, a provider should offer an account/line ratio of not more than 10 to 1. Commercial vendors should also offer at least 14,400 baud access, but be aware that rural phone lines don't always accommodate higher speeds.

Customer assistance/technical support

This might be the most important factor for beginners and even experienced users. Find out the answers to these questions.

- Does the service provider supply some help documentation?
- Do they staff a help desk?
- During what hours is assistance available? (evenings? weekends?)

- Is there an extra monthly charge for help?
- When you call, do you get a machine or a person?
- How quickly do they respond to requests for help?

The best way to get an honest, unbiased answer to these questions is to talk to someone who uses the service.

Track record
New service providers are popping up everywhere these days. It seems almost everyone wants to get into cyberspace! Some of these companies will be short lived for a variety of reasons. Others may suffer from technical problems that cause their system to shut down more frequently than you would like. A history of reliable service can be a sign that a provider is here to stay. Look in computer magazines and periodicals for Internet provider performance surveys, and talk to colleagues and friends who have been on the Net for awhile.

Software
What software will you need to do what you want to do? Access providers should give you a package of software (on a diskette with clear instructions for loading) that will give you all the basic tools you'll need on your desktop for using e-mail, FTP, Gopher, and the World Wide Web. Some providers will tell you that it's all available on the Net—but unless they tell you exactly how to get it, choose another service. If you are already an experienced user, however, you don't need to let the choice of starter software be a deciding factor in your decision. When you connect to a commercial online service, you may need a special software package. Sometimes this is an added cost, and you might prefer to use your own communications software. Check with the provider to find out if your software will work.

Freenets

Freenets are community-based computer bulletin boards designed to provide local residents with a forum in which to share community information. Freenets exist in many urban communities in North America. The greatest advantage of freenets is that they are free! It's easy to join a freenet. You just dial in on your modem, log in as a guest, and follow the online instructions to register. After a few days, you'll be given your own login and password. If your school is located in a community with a freenet, you can get Internet access anytime, twenty-four hours a day, through the freenet. If your school is located outside the local calling area of the nearest freenet, however, you will have to pay long distance charges. If your community doesn't yet have a freenet, be patient: many more community freenets are in the process of being established. The limitations of freenets include

- a one-hour time limit, in many cases
- limited services, such as FTP
- limited mailbox size
- difficulties in establishing a connection, owing to a shortage of lines
- lack of appropriate educational content.

Thus, a freenet won't be an ideal solution. But it might get you started and provide a gateway to the Internet.

Most freenets presently offer only text-based access to Internet resources. You navigate the system with simple keyboard commands. The average freenet allows you e-mail and Gopher services. Some also offer telnet, though its use may be limited. Keep in mind that the main purpose of freenets is to serve the community, not to give free Internet access, so they won't be the ideal solution for most schools. In the near future, we can expect that many systems will add graphical (SLIP/PPP) access so that users can access the World Wide Web, but they are likely to charge a fee for this.

Freenets are very busy places. It's often difficult to get online during peak hours. Many freenets suggest optimum times to make a connection, in order to keep stress on the system to a minimum, but it's unlikely that these times will fall during school hours. It may take thirty or forty dialing attempts to get a connection at a heavily used freenet, especially during the daytime or early evening. Rapid, automatic redialing is a very desirable feature in your communications software! The consequence of this heavy freenet traffic is that you cannot assume a connection can be made at the exact time a student needs it, making curriculum integration tricky. Knowing this, however, you can build flexibility into classroom projects. As you read on, you'll get more ideas in this regard.

> "One student each week takes on the task of getting us connected to the freenet. He or she comes in before school begins and dials in on our classroom computer. By the time the class arrives, we are connected and ready to check our e-mail."
>
> *Debbi Wensley, Teacher, St. Gregory School, Ottawa, ON, Canada*

A freenet is a good vehicle for teaching students simple Internet navigation and manners. However, for purposes of using advanced Internet tools, you'll need to obtain higher-quality services than are available on a community freenet.

Without public support, the freenet system may not survive, so make a donation to your community freenet if you use it frequently. Students could have a bake sale or a garage sale to raise funds.

Models for schools

The Rolls Royce model: all computers in the school connected
Imagine that your students can access the Internet whenever they

What can you find on a freenet?
- community events
- links to schools, colleges, and universities
- links to public libraries
- links to government agencies and resources
- weather reports and forecasts
- Internet access
- educational projects through Canada's SchoolNet and America's Academy One
- special interest discussion groups

Ask your local library for a list of freenets, or ask a friend with Internet access to connect to **gpx.lis.uiuc.edu** and get the file **/pub/netinfo/lists/freenet.list** .

need to from any computer in the school. All the computers are connected to a LAN, which in turn is connected to the Internet. This kind of flexibility allows students virtually unlimited access to information and the ability to communicate worldwide. Information passes quickly in text or graphical form over a high-speed, dedicated data line. In every unit you plan, you can include a component that requires students to use the Internet. They can e-mail peers and experts in different fields, Gopher search for information, and telnet to remote sites to find particular documents. They can download pictures, video clips, and sound clips to include in their multimedia projects. Any project described in this book is easy to manage—the possibilities are endless.

The standard sedan model: Internet terminals in various locations in the school Some schools have several phone lines, each with a modem-equipped computer, located around the school. In this case, school equipment dedicated primarily to Internet use might include

- two or more computers with modems
- two or more dedicated phone lines
- communications software (which often comes with your computer, and much can be obtained free of charge from the Internet itself)
- Internet access through a service provider, commercial online service, or even a community freenet (costs will vary, according to your choice).

Although students may have to leave the classroom, they can still have easy Internet access provided that the number of terminals is adequate for the student and teacher population of the school. Other schools have several modems but are limited to only one phone line. If your class is online and another unknowingly tries to connect, you'll be disconnected in the midst of your work. To avoid this inconvenience, you can obtain an inexpensive "line-in-use" indicator light from your local hardware store, although some modems don't draw down the line enough to activate the light.

In our experience, we see most terminals located in the school library/resource center and the computer lab. This configuration allows each class structured Internet use for an hour or so per week but makes it difficult to integrate activities into the curriculum in a seamless, natural way. This model also works best with older students, where teacher supervision is not an issue. With younger students, the most useful location for a terminal is in the classroom. You'll need to plan for individuals or pairs of students to move freely to wherever the terminals are located at the times that they need them. The cooperation and teamwork of all staff members helps to make this work. A schedule might be needed, especially in larger schools, so that all classes get a fair share of time. You'll also have to arrange for someone to be available to assist these students as they work, especially at first. Often, the librarian or computer teacher can be available. Parent volunteers and student experts are also invaluable.

If you are fortunate enough to have phone jacks in each classroom throughout the school, you might consider putting one or more modem-equipped computers on carts and creating a rotating schedule for their use. Modems on wheels allow access in the classroom, where you can use the technology most effectively to meet your educational goals. Depending on the type of connection you have, students may be able to access graphics or may be limited to text only. You can plan your Internet activities accordingly.

> "The Internet becomes a valuable tool when it is accessible to the greatest number of students. It is difficult to find a location (when you have only one shared phone line) to allow all students supervised access. The computer room is supervised only when there is a class in attendance; the library is run by volunteers on a part-time basis. Each classroom needs its own access."
>
> — *Debra Killen, Teacher, Chelsea School, Chelsea, PQ, Canada*

The economy model: one computer, one modem, one phone line

This is an excellent, inexpensive way to get started. All you need is

- a computer
- a modem
- a dedicated phone line
- communications software (which often comes with your computer, and much can be obtained free of charge from the Internet itself)
- Internet access through a service provider, commercial online service, or community freenet (costs will vary, according to your choice).

The installation of a dedicated phone line in your classroom or school library is often the biggest hurdle. Your school's parent council or a local business might be willing to cover installation costs or monthly charges. (Chapter 8 provides some ideas for obtaining funding.) If you have to depend on using one of the school's existing lines, you'll probably be limited to after-school connections, since most schools need all their lines during school hours. In this case, students can compose their e-mail messages during class, and you can send them after school. In one school, the after-school computer club has the task of sending and receiving e-mail twice each week and distributing it the next morning.

> "We used school funds to purchase a modem and hooked it to the existing computer in the classroom. When I approached the parent council, they were excited about the idea and immediately agreed to install a dedicated phone line in the classroom and pay the monthly phone bills out of the profits from their fund raisers."
>
> — *Bob Benning, Principal, Convent Glen Catholic School, Orleans, ON, Canada*

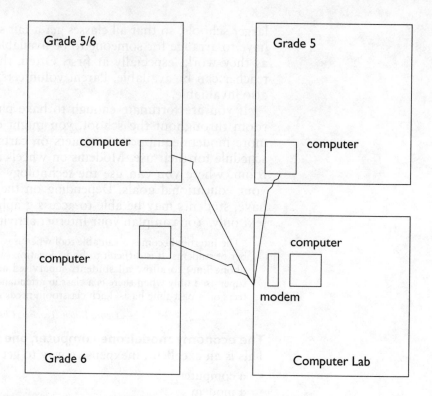

Figure 2-2

In this pod of Grade 5 and 6 classes, phone cables were strung across the ceiling into each classroom and left hanging down near the modem. When the scheduled daily Internet access time for each class arrives, a student simply slips into the computer lab and plugs the class's phone cable into the modem.

Because only one computer can access the Internet at a time, curriculum integration is somewhat limited. Whole-class e-mail projects are a good way to take advantage of this setup. By pairing students at the computer and using cooperative learning groups, you can also maximize usage. Hopefully, every student would get an opportunity to use the Internet in a classroom project at least once each term. Figure 2-2 illustrates an example of how, with a little creative stringing of phone cable, more than one class can share a single connection.

Summing up

There are two things we can say for certain about the Internet: it will keep on growing, and the number of ways to access it will become even more varied. The information highway is open, and the traffic is getting heavy. Before you set out on your Internet travels, figure out exactly where you want to go and how best to get there. You'll find that the journey is well worth the effort—the Internet is an educational resource of incalculable value.

Project Ideas

Cybernauts Only

Learning outcomes
- Students will participate in an Internet club.
- Students will exchange messages with keypals.
- Students will explore World Wide Web sites and share their findings.

Grade level: All

Getting started
- Invite students to join an "Internet Club."
- Establish a time for weekly meetings.
- Select a general topic for meetings, such as space, animals, weather, or countries.

Developing
- Have students select more specific subtopics, identify some World Wide Web sites, and set up bookmarks.
- Share sites at the next meeting.
- Compile a list of sites for school use.
- Have students exchange electronic messages with keypals to get more ideas for their topics.

Extending
- Have students compose messages offline, on another computer, and bring their messages on diskette to the weekly meetings, where they can upload them.
- As responses are received between meetings, you can simply print them for distribution at the next meeting.

Checklist for connectivity

You're ready to "surf" the Internet when you have

- a modem of sufficient speed to sustain your work (14,400 bps or faster), unless you are connected through a LAN
- a personal computer and monitor of sufficient resolution for the text and graphics
- activities you wish to carry out
- a telephone line or high-speed data line
- a connection to the Internet in one of the ways described in this chapter
- instructions from your service provider
- on how to make and sustain a connection
- software to use once connected
- your service provider's customer service telephone number, should problems arise.

3 Bringing the Internet into the Classroom

"In a world often over enamored of change for change's sake ... advocates of technology in our schools should have a compelling answer to the question, 'Technology for what?' The answer, we suggest, is twofold: to promote equal educational opportunity for all our children; and to raise the academic achievement of all children. Technology can advance both equity and excellence in education."

— DIANE RAVITCH (1993, JANUARY), "THE PROMISE OF TECHNOLOGY: EIGHT WAYS TO TAKE FULL ADVANTAGE OF TECHNOLOGY." *ELECTRIC LEARNING,* 50.

Educational technology will continue to advance at an everincreasing pace. As educators, it is our job to plan for and implement the use of technology in ways that are best for all our students. This means integrating Internet use into the curriculum in a meaningful way and incorporating it into current successful classroom practices such as outcomes-based education, cooperative learning, active learning, and student portfolios. Internet projects can provide an authentic context in which students develop knowledge, skills, and values. Knowing how to use the Internet is not an end in itself; rather, it is a gateway to lifelong learning.

> "I am involved in a totally online school ... the students dial up from their homes via modem, download their specified lessons for the day, then upload them to a computer or to the teacher of the class. There are also group discussions in the specified disciplines. I am currently examining their learning with standardized tests, and our faculty is amazed at thier progress. We even have parents now enrolled. I think it's the way of the future, and it's happening now."
>
> *Kevin Gerrior, Teacher, CA, USA*

Perhaps the easiest way to begin is to participate in an Internet project started by others that meets your educational goals. These goals should include the development of social and cooperative learning skills in addition to knowledge and task-related skills. As

Chapter goals
- To describe some ongoing Internet projects that invite participation
- To outline strategies for developing original projects
- To establish student procedures for accounts and use of Internet tools
- To examine issues of acceptable use

you and your students become more familiar with Internet tools, you can design your own project and invite participants from around your community or around the world.

This chapter describes some strategies both for joining and for planning projects. Helping students learn to use some basic Internet tools will be critical to their success. You will also want to make decisions about student accounts and establish some classroom routines for acceptable Internet use before you begin. These issues are addressed in the pages ahead.

Types of projects

As you investigate other teachers' projects in your reading and online explorations, you will discover a wealth of Internet activities to satisfy many styles of learning.

Learning through connectivity

- **Keypals.** This is the electronic equivalent to pen pals and is probably the most common of all school telecomputing activities. Group-to-group exchanges are easier to manage than person-to-person messages in terms of quantities of e-mail.

  "Our French classes are corresponding with students in the French Alps who are studying English. They compare lifestyles, pleasures, and problems they experience. The students use a teacher's e-mail address; they incorporate several students' letters into a single document as attachments. They have also sent pictures to France as attached files."

  Rick Pyles, Teacher, Tyler Consolidated High School,
  Sisterville, WV, USA

- **Global classrooms.** Two or more classes located anywhere in the world can study a common topic and share their learnings. Current issues relevant to students, such as environmental problems, school policies, disasters, or discrimination can generate interesting responses.

  "Several of my students have been using Internet Relay Chat to speak with people around the world. Social studies students listen to the nightly news for foreign events, such as the recent earthquake in Russia, and then try to contact individuals from the countries mentioned in the hope of hearing from people who are involved."

  Rick Pyles, Teacher, Tyler Consolidated High School, Sisterville, WV, USA

- **Ask-an-expert.** Specialists in a variety of fields make themselves available to students via the Internet. Some examples are Ask Dr. Math, Ask Dr. Science, Ask-a-Geologist, and Electronic Innovators in the Schools. Sometimes experts respond to postings from students; however, it is unwise to count on this.

"One team spent hours in libraries looking for documents on sundials. They found nothing. After posting a request for information on the Internet, they received recommendations from distinguished professors from several renowned universities. Even when expert–student collaboration is brief, it really boosts student morale."

Mathieu Dubreuil, Teacher, École Secondaire Dorval,
Dorval, PQ, Canada

Learning through online resources

- **Information collection.** Data can be collected from multiple sites and analyzed in the classroom. Students can gather information by conducting their own online surveys and election polls or by collecting weather statistics, comparative prices, or athletic records.

"As part of a unit on developing strategies for organizing information, my students have been researching the Titanic disaster. This subject lends itself both to factual reporting and to creative writing. Some kids are interested primarily in the technological or historical angle, while others focus on the human drama."

Marty Beilin, Teacher, Sandy Run Middle School, Dresher, PA, USA

- **Online field trips.** These can be as simple as students sharing information about their community or as complex as monitoring an expedition to reach the North Pole by dogsled. Museums, galleries, and other educational institutions offer text, pictures, sound, and sometimes even interactivity.

"My favorite project focused on virtual museum visits. These allow learners to experience the multimedia strength of the World Wide Web. The esthetic and other curriculum goals that can be enhanced by multimedia museum visits have great learning potential. My favorite museum listing can be found at **http://www.comlab.ox.ac.uk/archive/other/museums.html** ."

Robert Christina, Associate Professor, Oakland University,
Rochester, MI, USA

Learning by becoming involved

- **Electronic publishing.** Students can publish their original works in an online newspaper, poetry anthology, or magazine. In some cases, such as the Electronic Writers in Residence program sponsored by Simon Fraser University, peers or experienced authors offer constructive feedback.

"We shared students' writing among various schools in our province. Students had the opportunity to analyze and critique each other's writing. This was a great experience for them, since we are a small school and students don't often get the opportunity to see much writing by students their own age."

Jill Colbourne-Warren, Teacher, H.L. Strong Academy,
Springdale, NF, Canada

- **Information exchanges.** Many classes contribute to compilations of games, jokes, folk tales, music, holidays, or recycling practices from around the world.

"We have posted a project on the Internet that is called Local Hero. This project invites participants to share the story of a local hero with us. Each response was unique and contained an interesting story. Many different people from many different countries responded to our project, from Grade 2 students to university professors."

Bonnie McMurren, Teacher, Stony Mountain Elementary School, Stony Mountain, MB, Canada

- **Virtual events.** Students who participate at their local school in athletic events, read-a-thons, or collections can submit their results to a larger arena. This is a good way to overcome the isolation of some rural schools.

"A host school runs the virtual track meet. The students create and send out entry forms to the schools interested in being involved. A certain number of participants are allowed per event, with age and gender categories. A deadline is set as to when results are sent back to the host school (e.g., results for the high jump or 100-m sprint). The students of the host school then figure out the placings and send back some type of their results sheet."

Margot Alwich, Teacher, Lindsay Place High School, Pointe Claire, PQ, Canada

Learning to learn

- **Games and quizzes.** Students enjoy learning through interactive games that revolve around a curriculum topic. Such projects are extremely motivating to most students of all ages.

"The activity, Insect Wacky Facts, is quite simple. Participants are told about unusual or 'wacky' insect behavior. They must identify the strange creature, suggest an explanation for its behavior, and cite any sources consulted. Sometimes there is more than one 'right' answer. Bob [the online science teacher] then writes back, giving supplementary information in a straightforward, or sometimes tongue-in-cheek, way."

Christian Dufour, Teacher, Small Schools Network, PQ, Canada

- **Problem-solving activities.** Similar problems can be presented to students in various locations; or, two or more classes can take turns presenting problems for peers in other locations. Teams of students use telecommunications technology to plan strategies, discuss progress, share results, and solve problems collaboratively. They might even produce a joint final report.

"A group presents a complex task as a challenge or contest. Participants attempting to complete the task e-mail requests for specific help as needed. For example, a math problem may be posed and the solution is required to be described in words; or, a physics experiment may be explained and the distant students are asked to repeat the experiment within a defined error tolerance."

Shelley Martin, Student, Department of Graduate Studies, Carleton University, Ottawa, ON, Canada

- **Social action projects.** When students focus on a real-life problem rather than on the technology used to communicate, the Internet truly becomes a tool for learning. Students electronically brainstorm solutions to world issues and often get involved in awareness projects or fund raising as a result.

> "The PLANET Project (People Linking Across Networks) involves a consortium of many large Internet-accessible educational networks. ... During the first months of operation, PLANET participants wrote petitions to the United Nations to protest conditions in Yugoslavia, brainstormed ideas about how to address the starvation and political unrest in Somalia, and planned for and carried out fundraising efforts to ... help purchase rope pumps for villages in Nicaragua that do not have access to clean water."
>
> *Judi Harris (1994), Way of the Ferret: Finding Educational Resources on the Internet, p. 149.*

Joining an existing project

Once you start looking around, you'll be delighted by the number and variety of projects that students can join. Some are specific to a particular age or grade level, while others are more general. All you need to get involved in an interactive Internet project is access to Internet e-mail. As discussed in Chapter 2, you can get this easily through a commercial service such as CompuServe, America Online, or Prodigy, through a local Internet service provider, or through your community freenet. Once you are online, look for forums, conferences, or special interest groups related to education. You can also subscribe to one of many listserv groups, which are discussion groups interested in a specific topic (Chapter 4 discusses listservs and how to subscribe). When you subscribe to one of these mailing lists, you receive all messages posted by other subscribers around the world.

When reviewing the many available projects, look for one that is consistent with the learning outcomes you have in mind for your students. You might begin by selecting a curriculum-specific project that focuses on process writing, geography skills, or science. Consider simple projects before trying more complex ones: you might begin by participating in a survey, exchanging writing samples, or responding to keypal requests.

> "Getting students online can be frustrating at first because everything is new—the hardware, the software, and all the tools of the Net. But don't get discouraged. Make sure you know some good resources that will help the kids get started."
>
> *Sholom Eisenstat, Teacher, Earl Haig Secondary School, Toronto, ON, Canada*

As your students become more comfortable with the technology and see what is possible, they will be eager to get involved in more sophisticated projects, such as tracking an expedition or working cooperatively with others to address an environmental problem. Once you are involved in a project, learning outcomes that you had not anticipated are likely to emerge. Be sure to document and assess the skills and values your students develop as they proceed.

The chapters that follow provide many examples of exciting projects that you and your students can enjoy together.

> **HINT** For teachers interested specifically in science and math projects, the National Internet Projects in Mathematics, Science & Technology Education Web site has many links to project directories and specific projects. Use your Web browser to access this site at
> **http://www.ncsa.uiuc.edu/Edu/MSTE/oldfiles/national projects.html**

Planning your own project

After you have participated in an online project or two, you might feel ready to initiate your own Internet project. Regardless of what instructional medium you are using, student learning must be well planned, with specific purposes and goals. A successful project does not require a networked school; all you need is one computer, a modem, a phone line, and a well-organized teacher. In planning projects using the Internet, follow basic unit design steps as you would with any other instructional project, and add the features unique to the online environment.

teaching tip

If you're not yet online and want some idea of the types of projects available, look in periodicals such as *The Computing Teacher*, *Electronic Learning*, and *Classroom Connect*.

Figure 3-1
**Sample project from the
IECC Projects database**

```
To: iecc-projects@stolaf.edu
Subject: Project: "CULTURAL EXCHANGE PROJECT"
Request from:
_____

Name: Bunnie James
E-Mail: jamesc@mail.firn.edu
Institution: C. W. Norton Elementary School
             (primary)
Location: Gainesville, Florida USA
Summary: CULTURAL EXCHANGE PROJECT
Other Comments:
_____

Invitation to Join******Cultural Exchange

Teachers of Students ages 6-9

   You are invited to submit an application to
join our Cultural Exchange project. During the
1995-1996 school year we will be communicating
by e-mail and exchanging cultural boxes with
three schools from around the globe. This is our
second year doing this project.  Our first
attempt was very successful and was a lot of
fun. Students will exchange information via
e-mail and will later exchange cultural boxes
full of photos and local geographical/cultural
information.
   To receive more information or to apply send
the following information to:

jamesc@mail.firn.edu

****************************************************
```

Step 1: Select a topic

A teacher's choice of topics is usually controlled by curriculum set in place by the school or school system. Working within these guidelines, involve your students as much as possible in selecting a topic, giving them scope to pursue their own related interests. If you are planning to invite participation from others, give your project a snappy title that reflects its process or its content goals: "Fast Food Flash," "Great Gourmet Gastronomy," "Taming the Tube." Your students will enjoy creating novel project names.

Step 2: Establish learning outcomes

Effective use of the Internet in education requires standards and outcomes for student learning. Without specific learning outcomes for Internet-based activities, students will lack direction and focus, and will be overwhelmed by the sheer quantity of information available to them. Learning outcomes define the criteria by which to measure both student progress and teacher effectiveness in using the Internet as a tool. Learning outcomes related to Internet use in the classroom fall into two broad categories:

- those associated with the knowledge, skills, and values of the curriculum unit (e.g.. "Students will describe regional, national, and global environmental problems related to the use of technology and investigate ways of sustaining life in the future")
- those related to effective use of the technology itself (e.g., "Students will send e-mail letters to peers in other part of the country").

Whether learning outcomes are teacher-selected or designated by the core curriculum, keep them foremost in mind as you plan your Internet project. Ask yourself the following questions:

- What learning outcomes do I want the students to achieve?
- Are these outcomes clear, specific, and measurable?
- Am I trying to fit the outcomes to the technology, or am I using the technology as a tool to meet the outcomes?
- To what extent will Internet use assist students in achieving the desired learning outcomes?
- Could these learning outcomes be achieved just as effectively or more effectively using other methods?

Step 3: Investigate other projects

Examine other teachers' successful projects and identify the common elements that contributed to their success. Look for situations that parallel your own in terms of anticipated learning outcomes, student ability, access to computers, time available, and teacher experience. Find a good project that has already been tried, and then improve it by customizing it to suit your own needs. Some of the keys to successful Internet projects include

- clearly identified student learning outcomes
- lots of lead time (six to eight weeks) for participants to join the project
- realistic timelines for beginning, ending, and accepting submissions
- specific information describing the project (goals, location, grade level, timelines, contact person, number of desired participants, what you will do with responses)
- results shared with all participants.[1]

Have students working on the same project use the same diskette. Several letters, poems, or reviews can be combined into a single document as pages 2, 3, 4, and so on. This ensures that teachers don't spend unnecessary time getting students' material onto one diskette (or retyping).

> "For a successful cooperative project, be clear about your objectives, be sure the students understand the purpose, plan how you are going to manage the project, and be sure to follow through on your commitments to others."
>
> *Connie Mark, Teacher, Pearl City, HI, USA*

Step 4: Select and design activities

What kinds of projects are possible given the type of Internet access you have? What kinds of projects suit the learning outcomes you want your students to achieve? What kinds of projects will be comfortable and manageable for you?

Step 5: Decide teaching/learning strategies

The number of computers with Internet access readily available to you will be a determining factor in the way you structure your project. As well, let your own comfort level with the Internet guide, but not restrict you. The teacher learns along with the students. Watching adults learn can be helpful to children. It can also be an opportunity for some students to take on a leadership role.

> "I find that working on the Internet with students is a great motivator. It really changes the teacher–student relationship when you learn together."
>
> *Sharon Lewis, Teacher, Red Deer, AB, Canada*

- **Whole-class activities.** If you're a beginner, start with a teacher-directed whole-class activity, especially if you have a limited number of computers with Internet access. Corresponding with another class either locally, nationally, or internationally is a good way to introduce students to the Internet. E-mail can be integrated into just about everything: reading, writing, social studies, science, second language learning. You can use e-mail as a vehicle for teaching both curriculum-related skills (such as letter-writing, devising questions, or improving punctuation) and Internet-related skills (such as addressing, formatting, and sending e-mail, and online etiquette). Once students have mastered electronic messaging in the group setting, they will be able to use it individually as a tool for other assignments.

You don't have to limit yourself to e-mail. The Project Ideas feature on page 51 shows how the Internet may be used for information gathering. This whole-class activity is appropriate for young students, and focuses on science and mathematics outcomes.

Not only is whole-class instruction an effective means to learn the basic skills of Internet use: it is also an appropriate forum for exploring such topics as

- sources of information found on the Internet
- accuracy of information found on the Internet
- copyright issues
- security issues
- acceptable use.

For whole-class activities, assign a student or pair of students to do the actual online computer task, and then have them report to the class.

- **Cooperative learning activities.** In a well-structured, active learning environment, the Internet can become one of a number of tools that a group of students (or one or two members of each group) can use for a specific purpose. In such a setting, student experts emerge and peer tutoring happens naturally. Most Internet projects involve a great deal of learning offline. This might involve manipulating graphics or information files that have been gleaned from the Internet, or developing e-mail messages in a word processing package for uploading later. It can also include posting new findings on a bulletin board, or tracking responses to a questionnaire on a graph or map. Each student in the group can play an important role, yet all need not have access to the Internet.

Computer networks allow us to look at cooperative learning in a new way. Students can learn to work in teams in which the members of the team are separated by distance. This reflects the reality of our changing world of work. Before getting involved in a cooperative Internet activity, you can simulate this situation using your school's local area network. For example, while one team member gathers observational data about reptiles in the science lab, another might research the topic in the library, and another might scan drawings and diagrams in the multimedia room. Team members communicate strictly via computer.[2] Following this experience, students will be eager to try collaborating with others in more distant places.

The Project Ideas featured on pages 52–53 is a cooperative learning activity for middle-school students. In it, each group explores the literature of indigenous people.

"When student teams work in collaboration with other schools (virtual grouping), they know that the other group is counting on them and that they have to trust them."

Mathieu Dubreuil, Teacher, École Secondaire Dorval,
Dorval, PQ, Canada

Project Ideas

It's About Time

Learning outcomes
- Students will use Gopher or the World Wide Web to access information about time zones around the world.
- Students will compare time zones around the world.
- Students will view a demonstration of the Earth's rotation.
- Students will describe activities occurring simultaneously in different time zones.

Grade level: 2–4
Getting started
- Choose several major cities around the world.
- Locate them on a world map.
- Record your local time from the classroom clock, to the nearest hour.

Developing
- Have a student connect to Local Times Around the World. You can access this site via the Gopher at Austin Hospital, Melbourne, Australia (through All the Gopher Servers in the World) or through the World Wide Web at **gopher://gopher.austin.unimelb.edu.au** .
- Record the current time, to the nearest hour, of the cities you have chosen.
- Mark these times on the world map, using push pins, post-it notes, or tape.
- Discuss the relationship between the times and locations of the cities.
- Use a light and globe to demonstrate the rotation of the Earth.

Extending
- Have students select five cities around the world and describe what a peer of their age living there might be doing right now.
- Arrange a real-time online chat with a class (or a friend or relative) in a different time zone.
- Compare what the two classes are doing at a certain time of day.

Adapted from The Educator's Guide to the Internet (2nd ed.), Virginia Space Grant Consortium, 1995.

Project Ideas

Myths and Legends

Learning outcomes

- Students will use the World Wide Web to find myths and legends from indigenous people.
- Students will read the literature of indigenous people in their own country and around the world.
- Students will prepare a report about a group of indigenous people.
- Students will dramatize a myth or legend.
- Students will find common themes in the stories and draw conclusions about human needs and feelings.
- Students will rewrite a myth or legend in a modern setting, and publish their stories.

Grade level: 5–8

Getting started

- Divide the class into five cooperative learning groups.
- Have groups gather myths and legends from library books, interviews with family and community members, storytellers, videos, books from home, and the World Wide Web.
- The following World Wide Web sites will be useful:

KidPub
http://www.en-garde.com/kidpub (search all KidPub stories for "legends")

Indigenous People's Literature
http://kuhttp.cc.ukans.edu/~marc/natlit/stories.html

Links to Folklore, Myths and Legends
http://www.ucalgary.ca/~dkbrown/storfolk.html

Developing

Have each group select a story from one group of indigenous people and complete the following tasks.
- Show on a world map the location from which the story comes.
- Briefly describe the culture.
- Read the selected story to the class.
- Dramatize the story.

After each group completes its report, look for common themes in the stories. Discuss what conclusions can be drawn about human needs and feelings across cultures and time.

Extending
- Have each group post their story beside the world map, with a string to connect it to its country of origin.
- Have each group rewrite its story in a modern setting, reflecting the values of their own culture.
- Publish the modern stories on the World Wide Web at one of your students' favorite sites, your school's site, or one of these:

KidPub
http://www.en-garde.com/kidpub/

Australia's OzMail
http://www.ozmail.com.au:801~~reed/global/mythstor.html

- **Individual activities.** You'll need a lot of student access if you expect all students to engage individually in an Internet activity as a mandatory course requirement. However, many schools are fortunate enough to have all their computers online. To be fair, ensure that all students have mastered the basic skills of Internet use, have attained a certain level of expertise through practice, and can get help when they need it. One of the great strengths of individualization, of course, is that no two students learn in exactly the same way. While one may approach an information search in a step-by-step manner, another may prefer to "surf" through a variety of sites. There is no right or wrong way, as long as the final goal is achieved within the specified timeframe.

> **HINT** If you have a computer with Internet access in your classroom, use it as a learning center that students access as one component of a unit. For example, in a study of whales, allow each student an opportunity to find the answers to specific questions about whales using the World Wide Web whale watching site (http://www.physics.helsinki.fi/whale/). Visit the site yourself first to compose your questions.

In the next Project Ideas, senior students make individual use of the Internet for research. (Viewing of images requires graphical access to the World Wide Web or .gif viewing software. These are discussed in detail in Chapter 5.)

Project Ideas

Periodic Research

Learning outcomes

- Students will use the World Wide Web to obtain information on an element of the Periodic Table.
- Students will formulate and ask a question of a chemist using e-mail.
- Students will prepare a brief tutorial to share their findings with classmates.

Grade level: 7–12

Getting started

- Discuss the Periodic Table and examine the chart.
- Have each student pick an element to research using the Internet. (In Grade 7, each student might 'adopt an element'; in higher grades, each student or group might focus on a specific property, such as the element's most important reactions.)

Developing

- Suggest the following sites for students to begin their research:
  http://www.cchem.berkley.edu/Table/index.html
  http://www.rpi.edu/dept/chem/cheminfo/chemres.html
  http://rampages.onramp.net/~jaldr/item03.html
  http://www.chem.ucla/chempointers.html
  http://kuhttp.cc.ukans.edu/cwis/reference/Misc.html
- At some point during the research, have students access the **sci.chem** Usenet newsgroup or contact a local scientist with an e-mail question about the element being studied.
- Have students prepare an interactive tutorial based on their findings. Encourage the use of multimedia authoring software (e.g., PowerPoint, Hyperstudio, Corel Show) that allows them to download and import text and graphics obtained from their Web search.

Extending

- Have students present their tutorials to the class, to small learning groups, or use them as individual modules.

Step 6: Define roles of participants

It's important to decide which staff will take a leadership role in initiating, managing, and monitoring a project. The most common method is for the adventurous and innovative teachers to be pioneers and then to encourage others. If you are eager to get involved in a project, brainstorm with interested colleagues and assign tasks according to individual strengths of the team members. For example, classroom teachers might look after overall organization and student groupings; the computer resource teacher might schedule computer use and manage technical problems; selected students might act as Internet researchers and resource people; parent volunteers might supervise and assist individual students as they work; and the librarian might print a variety of the best projects and display them in the library.

Step 7: Plan a timetable

Students need large blocks of time for Internet use. If you have explored the Internet at all yourself, you know how fast time goes. It is very frustrating to get to the site you've been searching for only to find that there is not enough time left to download the information you want. It is also difficult to predict how long it will take to get to a particular site, or even if you can get there when you want to. Thus, it is inadvisable to create rigid timeframes. Involve your students as much as possible in establishing realistic time limits for the completion of projects, and try to keep your timetable flexible. By observing carefully, you can identify students who are off task and those who are using their time wisely. Have students keep a list of any sites they have used, with a brief description of their contents. If all are working on the same topic, share findings at the end of each computer session. This fosters collaboration and saves time for everyone. By the end of the term, you will have developed an excellent resource package. Don't forget to build in time for sharing the finished products, whatever form they take.

> "Be patient. Don't be discouraged. Things may not go as planned: they may go a lot slower, or they may not go at all. It's all part of the learning experience."
>
> *Sharon Lewis, Teacher, Red Deer, AB, Canada*

If you teach in a setting where subjects are strictly segregated, team with another teacher. Your two subject areas can complement each other (e.g., language and history; math and science), and students can devote time from both classes to the project.

If you are initiating a collaborative project, set definite starting and ending dates, and announce these when you call for participation. If you expect submissions such as data or student writing, set realistic deadlines and stick to them, but set timelines that are broad enough to allow flexibility. One teacher may see your project idea and think that it's great, but may need to pass it on to another. This takes time. It also takes time to gather and compile student input and prepare students to begin.

> "In cooperative projects, be clear on your expectations from other schools. If they lack the time to meet all project requirements, perhaps they can participate to a lesser degree."
>
> *Sharon Lewis, Teacher, Red Deer, AB, Canada*

Step 8: Incorporate evaluation

How will you evaluate the student learning outcomes you established for your project? How will you evaluate the usefulness of the Internet as a tool, perhaps even the primary medium, for your project? Teacher, peer, and self-evaluation are all appropriate tools in an active, student-centered, technology-enhanced classroom. Develop checklists (see Figure 3-2) and rubrics (see Figure 3-3) of observable performance indicators to use as assessment criteria. Use observational data, teacher–student conferencing, and a portfolio of work samples for formative evaluation. End your project with a tangible product such as an oral presentation, written report,

Figure 3-2

SAMPLE TELECOMMUNICATIONS SKILLS RECORD SHEET				
OUTCOMES	JANICE	ABDULLAH	GUY	SARAH
1. Student understands network concepts				
• describes how physical connections are made				
• identifies hardware components: server, terminal, modem				
• uses terminology: user ID, password, account, logon, logoff,				
online, upload, download, e-mail, attachment, netiquette				
2. Student accesses and uses local bulletin board				
• logs on and off				
• reads e-mail				
• sends e-mail				
• reads conference mail				
• uploads a file				
• downloads a file				
• uses appropriate netiquette				
3. Student accesses and uses Internet services				
• logs on and off				
• navigates the main menu				
• sends and receives e-mail using Eudora				
• retrieves information using Gopher				
• retrieves information using Netscape				
• creates and uses bookmarks				
• uses a search tool (e.g., Web Crawler) to locate information				

Figure 3-3 **Sample rubric**

OUTCOME	LEVEL 1	LEVEL 2	LEVEL 3
Students will select appropriate technologies and use them effectively for a variety of purposes.	Uses a range of technology as suggested by the teacher for purposes within the school.	Uses a broad range of technology as suggested by teacher and peers for purposes both within and outside the school.	Selects appropriate technology independently and uses it competently for both academic and personal purposes.
Students will use an extensive range of media texts as sources of information.	Uses a range of media texts; discusses content and expresses personal opinions about the material.	Uses a broad range of media texts to acquire information; uses material to clarify and extend point of view.	Uses sophisticated media to locate and analyze specific information related to social, political, economic, and cultural issues.

video, or student/class portfolio that can be used for summative evaluation purposes.

Step 9: Share your plans with parents

Let parents know what you're planning and indicate that you would welcome their suggestions and assistance. This is a good way to identify contacts in your community who are knowledgeable about this new technology. You'll probably find that they will offer to help in a variety of ways, such as donating equipment, advising you of useful Internet sites or spending time helping students.

> "When our school's old modem finally bit the dust, I made a point of mentioning to my students that we could really use a modem, especially if their parents had upgraded their modems at work. Within a week we received three working modems. We were back online in no time!"
>
> *Chris McQuire, Teacher, Pope John XXIII School,*
> *Nepean, ON, Canada*

Teaching students how to use Internet tools

Many students today know what the Internet is all about, but younger students may know the language without truly understanding how the Internet works. Consider inviting a guest speaker from your community to provide an overview, or do a quick introduction yourself.

> "I tell my kids that the Internet is an international network of computers, connected to each other by modems and telephone/fiber optic cables. I explain the different machines that are connected over the Internet, such as the servers, which 'serve' people the information they need in many different ways: mail servers, file servers, Gopher servers, FTP sites, and HTML file servers, or Web sites. This is easiest to do with a diagram. I then explain the various tools available across the Internet, and how students should use these tools depending on what they are looking for and where they wish to go. My lab has TurboGopher, Fetch, InterNews, Eudora, and Netscape on each computer. Although each program works differently, all navigate the international

network of computers to help people trade information. I explain that the WWW is just a small subset of the Internet, specifically the patch of Internet traffic conducted and controlled by HTML. ... My third to sixth graders seem to 'get it' just fine."

Sally Grant, Teacher, Sewickley Academy, Sewickley, PA, USA

Your students need both direct instruction and skill-building activities to learn how to use the Internet and its tools effectively. Explain, demonstrate, and illustrate each skill you expect them to use in their project. Then provide exercises and allow time for them to practice before expecting them to use the skill independently.

"... the first time you introduce students to The Weather Underground, you might lead them step-by-step to the site, show them how to locate the current temperature of a given city, then how to successfully leave the site. Next, you might have them attempt to return to the site on their own and locate weather conditions in a city of their choice. You might allow teams of students to compete in scavenger hunts to locate information. All of these activities help students practice the needed retrieval skills. Once they know how to retrieve the information, then they will be ready to put the available information to real instructional use."

Patricia Ross (1995, February), "Relevant telecomputing activities." The Computing Teacher, 28–30.

Direct instruction

There are several expensive tools available that facilitate whole-class direct instruction. You may be fortunate enough to have access to one of these in your school. An LCD (liquid crystal display) tablet, used on an overhead projector, allows projection from the computer onto a large screen for whole-class lessons. Alternatively, a TV/video cable can be used to display your computer screen onto a larger TV screen. Lanschool is a computer program that enables a teacher working at one computer in the lab to lock all the student computers to show only what is on the teacher's computer. Students can take notes as the teacher goes through material. (Teachers can also use Lanschool to "peek" into what students are doing on their computers when they are working on projects.) On the other hand, direct instruction may require that students gather around a single computer, if that's all you have. Rather than try to show thirty students at once, you could divide the class into groups of four or five and have a student expert, helping teacher, or parent volunteer assist with the instruction.

"The grandfather of one of my students was wonderful! For six weeks during our whales unit, he came every morning. He worked with pairs of students, helping them to find information about whales and to contact scientists. By the time the unit was complete, everyone had used the Internet and we had many great resources to share!"

Joanne Dillon, Teacher, Elmridge School, Gloucester, ON, Canada

The technical skills necessary to navigate the Internet cannot be taught in a vacuum. Introduce and practice each skill only as it is needed to accomplish a curriculum task. For example, an isolated lesson on how to do a Gopher search is soon forgotten if students are not involved in a related activity. However, teaching that same lesson while students are engaged in researching earthquakes provides them with a valuable tool to use immediately for a specific purpose.

You don't have to teach the whole group yourself. Identify student leaders in each class, train them, and let them teach others. Everyone benefits from this experience. Explain and discuss the learning outcomes you expect in these roles. Look for students who have leadership skills and will attend the school for a few years to come. Get a long-term commitment from them. Some schools award bonus marks or course credits for such services. Having one student teach another is also an authentic evaluation tool, since the ability to teach a particular skill is a demonstration of how completely it has been mastered. You can use cooperative learning strategies to take advantage of the strengths of the technowizards in your class by distributing them among the groups to act as leaders during the technology-related parts of the project.

> "Using library visit times and moments from planning periods, we showed small groups of students the basics of using Ottawa's freenet, Usenet newsgroups, and resources retrievable by Gopher. A morning group would watch like hawks as the demonstration unfolded. By the afternoon, the new group knew what to do, mysteriously having learned—during recess—from the other group."
>
> *Doug Walker (1995, January/February), "Making an Internet project work."*
> *Multimedia Schools.*

Some of the many Internet courses and tutorials available on the Internet itself are appropriate for student use. These are discussed in Chapter 8.

Practice activities

Games, simulations, and scavenger hunts allow students to have fun while practicing skills. You can design your own practice activities or take advantage of those you find on the Internet itself. Here are some specific sites.

ftp://ftp.cic.net/pub/hunt/
Hunts and answers are available for every grade level and on several educational topics. Choose the questions or answers subdirectory.

gopher://schoolnet.carleton.ca:419/11/Virtual.School/recess
Internet scavenger hunts for elementary through secondary students.

HINT You can simulate a World Wide Web experience using WebWhacker software from the ForeFront Group. WebWhacker allows you to download a series of Web pages, including text and graphics, connected by links, thus creating a module on your own computer. Your computer needs lots of hard drive space to store these Web pages, but this is a useful technique for those with limited Internet access. A thirty-day evaluation copy of Web Whacker can be obtained from the ForeFront site at

http://www.ffg.com/whacker.html

"Don't overwhelm your students by creating projects that are too big or that have too many parts. Take a couple of preparatory weeks practicing how to use a browsing tool such as Netscape or any multimedia software before launching the project. Then, make sure you've identified the main ideas and reviewed how to take notes."

Terrie Gray, Teacher, Chico Junior High School, Chico, CA, USA

Learning together

Some school systems have initiated training sessions or courses that include teachers, students, and parents. The groups could be mixed or handled separately, but all learners gain expertise at approximately the same rate. Working as a community reinforces the goal of lifelong learning and breaks down some of the traditional barriers between home and school.

"I created a system that targets entire school families for Internet training to 'jump-start' as many educators, students, and parents as possible. I bundle teacher training, student training, and parent training into a five-part, ten-hour series I call the Internaut Academy. I cover Net basics, classroom management, and other practical issues, and rotate the teacher, student, and parent sessions in order to maintain equity among the groups. Ten hours is enough to launch people in individual directions."

Mike Abbiatti, Teacher, Woodlawn High School/Louisiana State University,
Shreveport, LA, USA

The change process

Integrating the Internet into regular classroom use will be a continuing challenge, and every experience won't be a success. Change is a journey, a nonlinear trip loaded with uncertainty and excitement. Educational experts in implementation and the change process state that

- change takes place over time
- change involves anxiety
- change involves learning new skills through practice
- successful change involves pressure

- the people who must implement the change need to see why the new way works better
- problems are our friends
- connection with the wider environment is

- critical for success
- both top-down and bottom-up strategies are necessary
- every person is an agent for change.

Students with special needs

The Internet is highly motivating for most students, and it can be used to implement and complement proven strategies in working with students with special needs. It can free the special student from a history of negative experiences with more traditional education and provide control and autonomy that may previously have been missing.[3] The Internet can open up the world to the student who is confined by socioeconomic or physical limitations. The multimedia technologies of the World Wide Web are powerful tools for meeting the needs of learning-disabled students and those with specific auditory or visual needs.

Teachers can individualize Internet activities to suit special-needs students by giving them a specific task to do online, such as searching an encyclopedia to make a list of the ten biggest cities in the world. Cooperative learning strategies support them as they participate in the regular program. Cooperative learning doesn't have to be limited to students within the class, as telecommunications links students throughout the community and the world. Cooperative problem solving, information exchanges, and pooled data analysis involve and engage all students as peers. One of the advantages of electronic communication is that gender, race, age, and physical characteristics are invisible. In online communication, we focus on what people say in their writing, not how they appear.

> "I became aware that my students of low socioeconomic status had a harder time dealing with computers than those who had computers and video machines at home. We need to expose kids to technology at an early age in school. When pairing kids for computer use, I try to place them with kids at their own level, rather than with a more capable student who might unknowingly 'take over'."
>
> *Heddi Thompson, Teacher, Chase County Elementary School, Cottonwood Falls, KS, USA*

Here are some further strategies for students with special needs.

- Provide a learning partner or buddy to assist the student who has difficulty reading, following instructions, or staying on task.
- Encourage parents to use the Internet at home with the student, if possible.
- Provide opportunities for individual electronic mentoring. For example, Electronic Writers in Residence is an online project in which students submit original writing to professional writers, teachers, and other students and receive personal feedback.
- Use Internet resources such as learning games, puzzles, scavenger hunts, and simulations for skill development.

You might want to check out some Internet resources associated with special needs, such as the following.

Windows '95 includes Accessibility Options for users with special needs, e.g. Filter Keys to ignore brief or repeated keystrokes or slow the response rate, High Contrast to use colors and fonts designed for easy reading, and Show Sounds to display captions accompanying sounds.

http://www.eskimo.com/~user/kids.html
A convenient starting point for gifted students, their parents and educators to access Internet and other resources.

http://fohnix.metronet.com/~thearc/welcome.html
This home page provides links to support groups, reading lists, other disability-related sites such as dyslexia and autism, parenting information, assistive technology and software, and funding sources.

http://www.chadd.org/
An extremely well-organized site that provides resources and links related to children and adults with Attention Deficit Disorder.

http://schoolnet2.carleton.ca/~kwellar/snehome.html
This site lists Internet services specific to parents, teachers, schools, and professionals, individuals, groups, and organizations involved in the education of students with special needs. Many links to further resources.

gopher://burrow.cl.msu.edu:70/11/msu/dept/deaf
A large Gopher database devoted to Deaf Education. It includes lesson plans and articles concerning deaf awareness.

listserv@ukcc.uky.edu
E-mail to this address. Type SUBSCRIBE DEAFBLIND <your name> to join this deaf-and-blind discussion list.

listserv@sjuvm.stjohns.edu
E-mail to this address. Type SUBSCRIBE CEC-TAM <your name> to join a discussion list for technology issues relating to exceptional children. Type SUBSCRIBE AUTISM <your name> to join the discussion list for issues relating specifically to autism.

handicap.shel.isc-hr.com
FTP to this address, a very large site dealing with all sorts of issues related to disability.

"The primary value of using the Internet in my Learning Disabilities classroom is the willingness of my students to do their own research because the Net is (a) up to date, (b) does most of the labor for them (compared with looking through books and magazines), (c) is interactive through the e-mail contacts they make, and (d) is still a novelty with them."

Gayle Fields, Learning Strategist, Queen Elizabeth Junior/Senior High School, Calgary, AB, Canada

"Adults often worry about socioeconomic, gender, and other issues regarding computer use, but the kids I see in my open-access lab don't show any of these problems. The experienced kids help the new ones, the gamesters defer to the workers, the girls and boys work in absolute equality, the age range in the lab is representative of the school, the Black–White ratio is also representative, and those students who have computers at home help the rest who don't have them. These concerns may stem from adult perceptions or preconceptions of young people rather than from observation of real kids at work. But maybe I'm just fortunate to have worked with an unusually great bunch of kids all these years."

Elizabeth S. Dunbar, Teacher, Baltimore City College,Baltimore, MD, USA

Student Internet accounts

Accounts and passwords are for your protection, to ensure that someone else will not log on as you and misbehave using your identity. Ideally, all staff members should have their own accounts. If your type of Internet connection permits it, giving each student an individual account is also a good idea. When students use generic logins and passwords, it's difficult to trace misbehavior and track student usage. On the other hand, when individual students are given the responsibility for acceptable use, you can monitor and track usage. Find out how much control your school's system provides over student access. In some schools, teacher accounts give staff full access to all Internet resources, while student accounts allow access only to certain sites and/or to certain navigation tools. When students require more than what is available, they need only ask a teacher to assist them.

Some teachers have only a personal account, and don't mind students using it after establishing guidelines for acceptable use. If the computer is in your classroom, it's easy to monitor, and if you work with younger students, you can be sure that someone will "tell" if classroom rules are broken. Naturally, those who abuse the privilege lose the privilege.

> "Students using the Internet should be instructed never to give out home addresses or phone numbers. We use our school address. Personally, I prefer to give my e-mail address to people whom I don't know, rather than my home mailing address."
>
> *Dean Christie (1995, May 23), "Re: Just to point it out," Kidsphere.*

Security

Every computer connected to the Internet needs a virus protection program of some sort. A good one will pick up any bugs in software downloaded from most sources. Another useful policy is for each student to be restricted to one personal floppy disk each. This way, when students are using computers for school work, such as gathering information for a research project, they save their work on their own disk. Keep these disks in school so that you have control over what gets loaded onto any computer.

Whether you connect directly to the Internet or rely on your service provider to safeguard your security interests, be aware that you are exposing your network activities, online files, and electronic communications to some degree of risk from the "outlaws" of the Internet. The good news is that Internet sites geared to school use have been spared the kinds of attacks you read about in the press. While your school site is unlikely to be of great interest to computer intruders, they remain a possible threat, if only as a nuisance. A successful intrusion can result in theft of files, malfunctions in your system, installation of new and bogus user accounts, the generation of e-mail messages in your name, or the storage of alien files on your system. It is unlikely that you personally will wish to become part of your system's defense service; that is best left to your service provider and your school's system administrator. Nevertheless, keep the following principles of defense in mind, and teach them to your students.

- Choose your password carefully. The best passwords contain at least six characters combining letters, numbers, and symbols. They should be random and meaningless, yet simple to remember.
- Don't let anyone see your password. If you must write it down, don't identify it as such, and don't leave it near your computer.
- Be aware of oddities in your system that you notice but cannot explain, such as your e-mail account filling up with hundreds of new messages from the same source.
- If you do have a problem while online, sever your connection. (When in doubt, pull the plug!)

> **HINT** One good strategy for choosing a password is to model it after a memorable phrase. For example, "A bird in the hand is worth two in the bush" lends itself to the password Bhw2iB.

Restricting student access

Parents and teachers are understandably concerned about the appropriateness of some of the material available online. The media have made us well aware of online pornography, violence, and racism. Most schools that are now online have taken precautions to keep inappropriate material out of the school setting. Some use special hardware and/or software to limit student access, while others rely on strict acceptable use policies and close adult supervision.

Software solutions

NetNanny, SurfWatch, and CyberSitter are examples of software designed to protect children on the Internet. At the discretion of parents and schools, they monitor and block inappropriate sites and subject matter. A password-protected on/off switch gives the ability to allow or prevent access. In addition to preventing access to pornography, hate literature, and bomb- and drug-making formulas, you can prevent addresses, phone numbers, and credit card numbers from being sent out on the Internet. These software babysitters screen and block both incoming and outgoing commands and content. For example, if you enter the word "bomb" in your NetNanny dictionary and someone sends the latest pipe bomb recipe via e-mail, the terminal will shut down when the file is accessed. If you are running SurfWatch and someone tries to access http://www.playboy.com, a colorful "Blocked by SurfWatch" dialog box appears. If you try to access the newsgroup alt.sex, it says, "No messages in this group." Even if your students drag SurfWatch into the trash and try to empty it, SurfWatch becomes an invisible file elsewhere on your hard drive, working still. Even if they rename it and put it somewhere else on the hard drive and reboot, it still boots when the computer is started. For more information about such products, visit the following Web sites.

NetNanny
http://www.netnanny.com/netnanny/home.html

SurfWatch
http://www.surfwatch.com

CyberSitter
http://www.solidoak.com/

CyberPatrol
http://www.microsys.com/CYBER/

Internet Filter
http://www.xmission.com/~seer/jdksoftware/netfile.html

SafeSurf
http://www.safesurf.com/

Free trial versions of CyberSitter are available for download from Solid Oak Software's CompuServe forum (GO SOLIDOAK), America Online, and via the Internet. A Child Safety Document is available at
http://www.compuserve.com/prod_services/consumer/childsfty.html

KidSafe sites
Some schools post a list of sites known to be safe for children, and these are the only sites that students are allowed to visit at school. Obviously, close supervision is required. Here is one such list.
http://ppc.westview.NYBE.North-York.ON.CA/WWW/wcss.html
http://mack.rt66.com/kidsclub/home.htm
http://www.ccnet.com/pegpoker/
http://www.klsc.com/children/
http://rdz.stjohns.edu/kidopedia/
http://www.freenet.ufl.edu/~afn15301/drsuess.html
http://www.portal.com/~rkoster
http://I-site.on.ca/Isite/Education/Bk_report/
http://www.netnanny.com/netnanny/

HINT A useful site for advice on general security and firewalls is

http://www.alw.nih. gov/security

http://www.eden.com/~greg/cb/index.htm
http://ppc.westview.NYBE.North-York.ON.CA/WWW/wcss.html
http://www.ucalgary.ca/~darmstro/kid_links.html
http://fox.nstn.ca/~puppets/activity.html
http://longwood.cs.ucf.edu/~MidLink/
http://robot0.ge.uiuc.edu/~carlosp/color/
http://www.pd.astro.it/local-cgi-bin/kids.cgi/forms
http://www.safesurf.com/wave/sskwave.html
http://www.primenet.com/~sburr/index.html
http://ipl.sils.umich.edu/youth/StoryHour/
http://www.wln.com/~deltapac/ocean_od.html
http://www.telescan.com/hdesign.html (Home Design) [4]

SafeSurf, a watchdog organization, has suggested a rating standard in which child-friendly sites identify themselves with HTML tags hidden inside the contents of their Web pages. Provided the child is using a SafeSurf browser, all tagless sites are invisible. For more information, visit SafeSurf:

http://www.safesurf.com/

HINT For a site that uses a question-and-answer format to help children learn to protect themselves in various situations, including on the Internet, visit

http://www.uoknor.edu/oupd/kidsafe/start.html

Firewalls

A firewall is a special-purpose computer that polices the flow of data between your school LAN and the Internet. A firewall can be implemented using a router, a device mentioned in Chapter 2, which connects two networks together. Like a security guard stationed at the main entrance to your school, a firewall monitors inbound and outbound traffic and can deny entry when it detects something suspicious. Firewalls can also be used to keep instructional and administrative areas of your work securely separated. Firewalls can be expensive, but they provide a high level of security. Many schools don't consider this level of security necessary because they have adopted and enforced an acceptable use policy that clearly delineates legitimate and prohibited uses of the school's Internet connection.

Acceptable use policies

"My main concern is that school boards and parents trust the teachers at the school to make the right decisions and teach telecommunications in a way that will guide, but not limit, student access."

Rob Darrow, Teacher, Alta Sierra Intermediate School,
Clovis, CA, USA

Despite strict supervision and control, however, you still can't *guarantee* that a student won't access something deemed inappropriate by teachers or parents. To protect the school and to reassure parents, implement an acceptable use policy. Most networks and bulletin boards have these. You will frequently see them referred to as AUPs. An AUP is a written agreement signed by students, their parents, and the teacher. It outlines the terms and conditions of Internet use. Some AUPs are instituted by school boards or districts. Others are school or even classroom specific. Find out if your school has an Internet AUP. If not, get together with interested colleagues and parents to develop one before allowing your students to access the Internet. (A typical AUP appears in Appendix A.)

A thorough AUP contains the following:

- a description of what the Internet is
- an explanation of how students will access the Internet at school
- examples of how the Internet will be used to enhance student learning
- a list of student responsibilities while online, which might address such issues as
  - privacy
  - morals and ethics
  - freedom of expression
  - legal constraints
  - safety
  - harassment
  - plagiarism
  - resource utilization
  - expected behaviors/etiquette
  - security issues
- the consequences of violating the AUP
- a place for student, parent, and teacher signatures.

Rather than simply send an AUP home for signatures, consider beginning the school year with a "cyberspace evening" to introduce the community to the Internet. Have students demonstrate some exciting Internet resources and projects. Talk to parents about how you plan to use the Internet in your classroom or school, and explain your AUP in detail. Stress that, with the privilege to use the Internet, students must accept the responsibility for acceptable use.

"Education is the key. We give a unit of Net Etiquette to each student and staff on the responsible use of the Internet account. You can find this agreement on our home page at
http://www.mvhs.fuhsd.org under resources ."

Peg Szady, Teacher, Monta Vista High School, CA, USA

HINT For more advice on acceptable Internet use, take a look at Child Safety on the Information Highway, available at

http://www.4j.lane.edu/InternetResources/Safety/Safety

If you're interested in joining an ongoing dialog with other educators and parents, you can subscribe to an e-mail discussion list called CACI (Children Accessing Controversial Information) by sending an e-mail message to

caci-request@cygnus.com

Acceptable use policies

Encourage parents who have Internet access at home to develop their own AUP with their children. A home AUP might include rules such as:

- I will not access areas my family and I have decided are off limits.
- I will not join an online service without checking first with an adult family member.
- I will not give out any information online about my home, family, or friends without asking.

- I will tell an adult if I don't feel right about something I see or read online.
- I will not download files without asking an adult in my family.
- I will tell an adult if someone I meet online suggests that we meet in person.

- I will tell an adult if someone I meet online pesters or insults me, or says things that bother me.

Dyanne Rivers (1995, May), "Peep shows and predators inhabit cyber-space too: Streetproofing kids for the info highway." Home and School, 23–25.

Sample acceptable use policies

If you now have Internet access, you might want to start by checking the acceptable use policies located at the following sites.

Gopher sites:

gopher.eff.org
6. Computers and Academic Freedom Archives and Info
18. Computer Policies from Many Schools

riceinfo.rice.edu
6. Search all Rice Inf
2. Jughead search for "Acceptable Use"

ericir.syr.edu
17. Internet Guides and Directories
1. Acceptable Use Policies/Agreements for K-12

nic.merit.edu
4. Internet Documents
2. acceptable.use.policies

FTP sites:
frp.eff.org/pub/CAF/faq/policy.best (best policies with critiques)
ftp.eff.org/pub/CAF/faq/policy (how to construct policies)

World Wide Web sites:
http://www.umich.edu/~sstrat/WhatOnWeb.html
http://www.pacificrim.net/~mckenzie
(school board policy vice aup)
http://www.ucalgary.ca/~mueller/hanson.html
http://www.usa.net/~pitsco/pitsco/accept.html
http://musie.phlab.missouri.edu/policy/copies (university AUPs)
http://www.voicenet.com/~crammer/censorship.html
http://www.lloyd.com/~pat/k12index.html (look at CoVis)
http://www.nmusd.k12.ca.us/Resources/Policies.html
(California K12)
gopher://gopher.PeachNet.EDU
gopher://gopher.eff.org:70/00/CAF/policies/README
(critiques of AUPs)
gopher://gopher.eff.org:70/11/CAF/policies
(critiques of university AUPs)
gopher://gideon.k12.mo.us (look under Technology 2000)
gopher://oldmine.ced.ca.gov (look under Technology)[5]

Responding to inappropriate material

The fact that your school has developed and enforced an AUP doesn't protect you or your students from possible violation from other less considerate Internet users. Though it's a relatively rare event, think about how you would respond if you or a student were to receive an e-mail message, for example, containing language or content that you deem unacceptable. It is then up to the offending student's school to take appropriate action, which might include the submission of a formal apology and suspension of Internet privileges.

> "I would treat [abuse of Internet privileges] much as I would treat a child who has been insulted on the playground or while going to or from school: I would counsel the child and try and deal with the offender.
>
> • I would counsel *all* children about the possibility of this kind of message, so that they are not caught off guard. They should know to report this kind of message immediately to the teacher, who should print the message right away and then forward it to a safe location for future reference.
>
> • I would ensure that all parents understood that this is a risk, but that the school doesn't sanction this behavior and that teachers try to prepare students to deal effectively with this.
>
> • I would write a message to the offending e-mail address, with copies to the system administrator and postmaster complaining about this behavior, with full details of how the student was affected."
>
> *Al Rogers, Executive Director, Global SchoolNet Foundation*

Curriculum resources for teachers

The Internet is a virtual gold mine of useful resources for teachers. These resources have been contributed by educators from around the world. You can find educational nuggets from A to Z:

- addresses, activities, almanacs, artists, artwork, authors
- biographies, books, book reviews
- case studies, conversations, comics, courses, current events
- diaries, dictionaries, discussions, dissections, drawings
- engineers, essays, exhibits, experiments
- facts, figures, film reviews, formulas
- galleries, games, glossaries, guides

- historical archives
- inventors, images
- journals
- kits
- labs, lesson plans, libraries
- magazines, maps, museums, music
- narratives, newsletters, newspapers
- opinions
- phone numbers, photos, plays, poetry, puzzles
- questions and answers
- reading lists, resource lists

- simulations, songs, sounds, stories, student worksheets
- tests, texts, tours, tutorials
- universities
- visual literacy, vocabulary lists
- writing exercises, workshops
- X-rays
- youth issues
- zip codes

HINT The Ontario Provincial Police have requested that a Web page be posted on the Govonca2 machine to assist in their search for any individual suspected of spreading hate on the Web. The Wanted Page is at http://www.gov.on.ca/opp/ . The address will be sent to Canadian police forces as well as the FBI. A reward of $2,000 to $5,000 is offered. Welcome to crimebusting in the '90s!

Summing up

Whether you're a teacher of science, history, languages, or technology, and whether you teach kindergarten or college, there is something to inspire and assist you on the Internet. Mining the Internet for these resources, however, can be time consuming. We've taken the time to list some excellent Internet sites for you. You can save time by trying out some of the Internet sites for curriculum development sources listed in Appendix B.

4

Communicating over the Internet

"I think the Internet has the potential to help students realize that they are an integral part of a living, global community. ... Students in minority cultures can appreciate anew the value of their own culture by seeing it reflected in the interests and questions of others.**"**

— SANDY MCAULEY, SECONDARY PROGRAMS CONSULTANT, BAFFIN DIVISIONAL BOARD OF EDUCATION, NWT, CANADA

The best way to learn about the Internet is to start small and to take one step at time. A very good place to start is to learn to send and receive electronic mail.

This is also an ideal starting point for classrooms that have minimal connectivity, such as a single account on the library computer. Through the Internet, with just a simple (even somewhat slow) modem connection and a very basic computer, teachers and students can connect to the world.

Electronic mail is the networking vehicle for many Internet inter-classroom projects. You can also use it to communicate with other teachers or subject specialists, to participate in educational discussion groups (listservers), and to subscribe to journals and request articles. You can even use electronic mail to search for and transfer computer files. Despite the many sophisticated tools for accessing information over the Internet, for many people, electronic mail remains the most useful application. This is probably because electronic mail is not about information. Rather, it is about human communication. It's a great place for teachers to get started using the Internet. Figure 4-1 (page 72) shows a typical e-mail message.

Chapter goals

- To provide an overview of electronic mail on the Internet
- To explain how to use electronic mail software in a graphical and non-graphical environment
- To describe how mailing lists work and provide some examples of lists that would interest teachers
- To explain how newsgroup discussion groups work
- To explore how electronic mail can be used in a classroom and provide some ground rules for e-mail projects
- To offer some examples of classroom-based electronic mail projects

Begin by sending messages to yourself to learn the ins and outs of your particular mail software. Try all sorts of variations, including sending attachments. Experiment with setting up a mailing list by entering your own address a number of times. The advantage to using yourself as a recipient is that you have immediate feedback on whether your procedure worked. After mastering a few basics, you'll be able to communicate electronically with other teachers.

Later, this chapter will explore in detail some of the ways in which teachers can use electronic mail for classroom learning. But first, let's take a broad look at how electronic mail works.

Figure 4-1
A sample e-mail message

```
Message 5/47 KIDSPHERE Mailing List


Date: Tue, 1 Aug 1995 14:41:47 EDT
Subject: Keyboarding Program
To: KIDSPHERE Subscribers
 <kidsphere@vms.cis.pitt.edu>
Errors-To: <kidsphere-request@vms.
   cis.pitt.edu>
Warnings-to: <kidsphere-
request@vms.cis.pitt.edu>
Reply-to: <KIDSPHERE@vms.cis.pitt.edu>

Date: Tue, 01 Aug 1995 07:19:10 +0100
From: twinter@ousd.k12.ca.us (Tony Winter)
Subject: Keyboarding Program

Hi Kidsphere,

  I am planning set up a typing program for
grades 4-6 this year in our computer lab and
classrooms. I have been trying to decide
between a typing software program . I am
considering three possibilities. These are:
Ultra Type, Type! (by Broderbund) and Type
to Learn (Sunburst). I'd appreciate your
recommendations (or other comments).

Tony Winter
Hepburn School
Maplewood, Ohio

* * * * * * * * * * * * * * * * * * * * * * * * * * * * * * * * * * * * * * * * * * * * *
```

Electronic mail: Overview

To send messages over the Internet, you will need (in addition to a computer that is connected to the Internet) your own Internet mail address and electronic mail software.

Internet mail addresses

If you have purchased an Internet access account from a local service provider, chances are you already have everything you need to send an electronic message. With an Internet account, you will receive, in addition to a place to log on to the Internet, an e-mail address on the Internet computer to which you are connecting. The messages that you send out will be identified with this address, and this is the address that others can use to communicate with you. An Internet e-mail address looks something like this:

bscott@uoregon.edu

The format used for addresses on the Internet is essentially:

username@hostname

The first part of this name is the user (you), commonly in some abbreviated form, and sometimes even as a number. The second part of the name (after the @ sign) identifies the location of the computer that uses the electronic mail account. Here are some more examples.

anita-gibson@admin.ubc.ca
kwilliam@dialog.com
r.bown@sheffield.ac.uk
library@badger.state.wi.us
nhenry@capaccess.org
12345.678@compuserve.com
meyer@educat.hu-berlin.de

If you look at an e-mail address carefully, you can often determine a bit about the location of the account. Following are some clues for reading an e-mail address.

- The final two or three letters in an address constitute the *top-level domain*. In the U.S. these are commonly descriptive domains that identify the type of institution where the address is located.

Domain	Type
.edu	Educational institution
.com	Commercial organization (used throughout the Internet)
.mil	Military site
.gov	Governmental office
.net	An Internet resource, such as an access provider
.org	Non-commercial organization

Domain

- In many instances, an Internet address will end with a two-letter designation for the country in which an account is located.

Domain	Country
.au	Australia
.ca	Canada
.de	Germany
.dk	Denmark
.es	Spain
.fr	France
.il	Israel
.jp	Japan
.ru	Russia
.uk	United Kingdom
.us	United States

- The .us (pronounced "dot U.S.") designation has traditionally not been used in favor of the basic descriptive domains for U.S. addresses, but is becoming more common as schools connect to the Internet. When the .us appears it is frequently used in conjunction with a two-letter state code. Here is an example of what an Internet e-mail address might look like for a teacher in Nebraska:

  mnichol@esu3.k12.ne.us

Once you can read e-mail addresses, you will quickly grasp the structure for other addressing conventions on the Internet. Besides electronic mail, addresses are used to identify a specific computer and/or application, such as a World Wide Web site. Here are some examples of other types of addresses you can find on the Internet.

gopher.powernet.nsw.gov.au   This is a Gopher address for PowerNet—Australian Schools Educational Network.

jupiter.cc.gettysburg.edu 4323   This is another Gopher address. In this case, the address includes a "port" number which tells your computer where to locate this particular Gopher on the remote machine.

sunsite.unc.edu   This is the location of a computer at the University of North Carolina.

listserv@uhupum1.bitnet   This is an address for a mailing list-server. You would use this address to subscribe to a mailing list that is run from this particular computer. The designation "bitnet" at the end indicates that this computer is on Bitnet (*Because It's Time Network*). Although you will still find people with Bitnet addresses, Bitnet was an older network for exchanging electronic mail, and many Bitnet addresses have been converted to Internet addresses that use the domain structure.

HINT Finding someone's e-mail address on the Internet can be difficult. The Four 11 database is a fairly comprehensive listing of Internet e-mail addresses. Before you use this service, you must provide your own e-mail address, which is then ad\ded to the massive database. Use your Web browser to access Four 11 at:

http://www.Four11.com/

The easiest way to obtain someone's e-mail address is to phone them and ask.

listproc@schoolnet.carleton.ca Another example of a mail server address. This one is run by SchoolNet.

192.58.107.230 This is also an address for a computer on the Internet. It's called an IP (*Internet Protocol*) address. All computers linked directly to the Internet are assigned an IP address. These addresses are used by the computer to locate other computers on the Internet. Every once in a while, you will see an address presented in its numerical form.

Electronic mail software

The ease with which you can compose and send messages over the Internet will depend on the particular electronic mail package you have access to. In a Windows or Macintosh environment, you will have a choice of user-friendly mail packages (such as Eudora Mail or Pegasus).

With a non-graphical account on a Unix machine, the software will be less "intuitive," but will provide you with the same range of basic electronic mail functions. A commonly used non-graphical e-mail package is Pine, which presents the basic electronic mail functions through a menu-based interface.

Most e-mail programs will allow you to
- send electronic mail to a specified address
- send one or more carbon copies
- reply to electronic mail sent to you
- forward electronic mail
- save messages to a file
- send enclosures or attachments
- automatically include a customized signature
- delete electronic messages.

Let's look at how these basic functions work for one commonly available package for both the Windows and Macintosh environments.

Using Eudora Mail

Sending an e-mail message

1. Click on the **Message** menu and select **New Message**.
2. Complete the **To:** field with the electronic mail address of the person to whom you are sending a message. The **From:** field will already include your own address as established in your configuration file. Use the tab key to move to additional fields in the header.
4. Type your message in the space provided below the address information.
5. Click on the **Send** button to send the message immediately.

HINT You may select to send a carbon copy and/or a blind carbon copy. You can also choose to send a file as an attachment. (See text.)

Receiving messages

1. Check for incoming messages by clicking on the **File** menu. Select **Check Mail**. Note that the system will check for mail when you first log on. It will also check for mail at regular intervals as designated in your configuration file.

2. The POP (*Post Office Protocol*) mail server will request your password the first time you request mail after logging on to the system. Input your password and click **OK**.

3. Incoming messages are downloaded into your **In Mailbox**. You can read your incoming messages by double-clicking on the message listed in the message summary.

4. When you have received a message, you have the option of forwarding it or replying to it. In either case, use the icon buttons on the summary screen. When the message is displayed, you can choose these options from the **Message** menu.

> **HINT** An upgraded version of Eudora called Eudora Pro is also available. This version is relatively inexpensive and makes available a number of slick enhancements, such as the ability to click on a Web site reference to bring the Web page into your browser automatically. Find out more from the Eudora home page at **http://www.qualcomm.com/ProdTech/quest/**

Saving messages

Save a current message to a file by selecting **Transfer**. Next, click on the name of the folder in which you wish to save the item. If you have not already established a folder in which to save your messages, you can do so by selecting **New**. You will be prompted for a new file name. Creating a folder allows you to establish a series of subdirectories, so that you can group together related messages without having to file them in the same file.

Deleting messages

You can delete a message from any folder by highlighting it in the summary and then clicking on the **Trash** icon. You can also delete a message by clicking on **Message** and then clicking **Delete**. Items are not actually removed from the Trash until you exit Eudora, or until you click on **Special** and manually empty the Trash.

Nicknames

Nicknames allow you to avoid having to type in a complete address each time you send a message. Instead, you can simply type the nickname, and the program will associate this with the correct address.

1. Select **Window** and click on **Nicknames**. To add a new nickname, click on New. You will be prompted for the nickname.

HINT Download new messages and disconnect from your server before taking time to read them. Reading and replying to mail offline helps reduce costs.

HINT You can learn more about Eudora from Peter's Eudora Page: **http://www.gildea. com/eudora**

Putting a name on the recipients list (address book) will let you bring up the name in a window for quick selection when mailing.

2. Once you have typed in a nickname, click **OK**. Next, place your cursor in the address box and type in the address of the person (or persons, if establishing a group mailbox) to whom you are assigning the nickname. Multiple addresses must be separated by commas.

3. When you have finished adding address information, close the window by double-clicking on the upper left-hand box. At the prompt, you can choose to save or discard the changes to the nickname list.

Signature files

Signature files are automatically appended to outgoing messages. They can lend distinctiveness to your messages. Many people choose to use humorous or thought-provoking quotes as part of their signatures. Some people also provide their phone number, address, and fax number.

1. Click on **Window**. Then select **Signature**.
2. Type in whatever information you wish to include as a signature.
3. Close the file by double-clicking on the upper left-hand box. Save any changes.
4. You can choose to exclude the signature on a specific message by manipulating the signature window (middle window just above the new message header) when a new message is being generated.

Attachments

This feature enables you to send files that have been prepared earlier in a word processing application. With a single Internet connection, the **Attachments** feature may be the easiest way to have your students send messages. It's best to avoid attaching messages that include word processing codes. You can prevent this by saving a file as a text-only (.txt or ASCII) file. Usually this just involves investigating the various **Save** options in your word processing package. With the text file format, you don't have to worry that the recipients will be unable to read your message because they don't use the same software as you.

Figure 4–2

Signatures lend a distinctive touch to messages and tell something about the sender.

```
Mary Lam, violinist (marylam@aol.com)
     _____  _____
    /     (_)     _____888
   ( {      _   %  _____$&$&$
    \_____( )_____/              888
```

1. To attach a document to an outgoing message, click on **Message**. Select **Attach Document.**
2. From the Windows **File** listing, highlight the document you wish to attach. Then click **OK**. The file names are automatically listed with attachments.
3. Binary files (such as word processed files) must be coded before being sent as part of an electronic mail message. Eudora offers BinHex and MIME (some versions also include UUencode) as options for sending files. If the receiver is using Eudora also, you can send the file using BinHex. Otherwise, choose MIME or UUencode. To select BinHex or other formats, use the third window across the top of the outgoing message.

Switches

Eudora provides a number of options that can be activated and de-activated using the **Switches** box. Switches appear under the **Special** menu. Refer to the Eudora manual for information on specific switches. Most of the switches should be left on their default settings. One setting that you may wish to alter from time to time is the **Immediate Send**. If you want to queue your messages before sending, this option should not be selected.

New messages will not be sent immediately. To send messages, select **File/Send Queued Messages.**

Using Pine

In a non-graphical environment, there is a range of software programs that are used to read and send messages. One of the most user friendly of the non-graphical electronic mail packages is Pine. Pine was originally developed for novice e-mail users. It was an attempt to improve on another commonly available mail package called Elm. (Pine stands for *Pine Is Not Elm*.) There are two key advantages to using Pine in a non-graphical setting:

• Pine uses a menu-based interface which makes it relatively easy to learn
• Pine can also be used to read newsgroups (discussed below), whereas most systems require a separate newsreader package.

Using Pine in this way can be a great advantage if you are making newsgroups available to your students, or wish to access them yourself. If Pine is not available on your local system, ask your access provider about the possibility of obtaining it.

If Pine is already on your system, you can access it by typing **pine** from your system prompt. (Do this after you have connected to your Internet service provider. Some access providers require you to access the mail software through an initial menu. In this case, select the appropriate menu option.)

Here is the main menu, or the first screen you will see once you have activated Pine:

```
?   HELP  Get help using Pine
C   COMPOSE MESSAGE  Compose and send a message
I   FOLDER INDEX  View messages in current folder
L   FOLDER LIST  Select a folder to view
A   ADDRESS BOOK  Update address book
S   SETUP  Configure or update Pine
Q   QUIT  Exit the Pine program
```

In Pine, you can highlight the menu item of your choice or simply type the single letter command for that option. A rule of thumb for using Pine is to read carefully the list of commands that will be displayed at the bottom of the screen. These commands indicate the choices available for any given function. Be aware that Pine Help is context-sensitive. This means that each Pine screen you use will have its own Help text explaining the choices available for that screen. Many first-time Pine users quickly learn to send and receive messages by following the screen commands.

Sending attachments
With Pine, there are two options for sending attachments. With either option, you will need first to have uploaded the file you want to attach from your computer to your access provider's computer. Your provider may have set up a process for doing this. The manual for your communications software should give additional information. (You may wish to ask a knowledgeable friend for help the first time you attempt this.) Once you have uploaded the file, you can specify the filename (including the correct directory specification) following the **Attachments** prompt in the header. Alternatively, you can include the text file in the body of your text. This second option is ideal when you want the file to be an integral part of the message or when you want to edit the file before sending. To include the correct subdirectories and filename automatically, use the ^T access (control key) to your file list. Then simply press **enter** to select. The file will automatically be listed as an attachment to your message.

Electronic mail in the classroom

Once you have familiarized yourself with the basic process of sending mail over the Internet, consider how you will actually use it in the classroom. The ideas in the following Getting Started... feature will give you a taste of how electronic mail can help you and your students obtain information.

Tech Talk

You will find that sometimes messages "bounce" (can't be delivered). When this happens, you'll receive a message from Mailer-Daemon or Postmaster. The subject line will start with "Returned mail." If you look carefully at the header information, you may be able to determine exactly why the message bounced. Host Unknown means that the computer address cannot be reached. Often that's just because of a typo which you may then quickly spot.

Another possibility is User Unknown. Again, this could be a typo—but it could also be that the person you are trying to reach is no longer at that location. Occasionally you might encounter network problems. For example, a server could be out of commission. Or, you might run into a "traffic jam." Some systems are set up to resend messages automatically over several days before giving up.

GETTING STARTED

with E-Mail

Exercises for teachers learning to obtain Internet resources

There are many useful educational resources, such as electronic newsletters, available through e-mail. The suggestions listed here are just a sample. These exercises will give you a chance to practice sending e-mail and will show you how quickly and easily resources can be obtained over the Internet.

Call up your electronic mail program and follow the instructions for obtaining any of the examples listed below that interest you. The requested materials will soon arrive in your electronic mailbox.

Exercise 1: To retrieve an electronic newsletter listing favorite educational sites of interest, send the following message to Rick Lakin.

> Mail to: majordomo@gsn.org
> Subject: <none>
> Message: subscribe infolist

Exercise 2: NetTeach News is a newsletter focusing on using the Internet in schools. You must pay to subscribe, but you can receive a free sample issue.

> Mail to: info@netteach.chaos.com
> Subject: <none>
> Message: request sample issue netteach news

Exercise 3: Classroom Connect is another useful publication dealing with classroom use of the Internet. Again, you'll need to subscribe, but you can obtain a sample issue.

Locate many resources for finding student keypals at the Pitsco Launch to Keypals/Penpals:

http://pitsco.inter.net/ pitsco/pitsco/ keypals.html

Mail to: connect@wentworth.com
Subject: <none>
Message: request sample issue

Exercise 4:   To obtain a free newsletter for educators involved in science, math, ecology, agriculture, home economics, or economics:

Mail to: ZLNQ31A@prodigy.com.
Subject: <none>
Message: request sample issue

Exercise 5:   To request a free monthly publication about CD-ROMs:

Mail to: CDRMAG@nsimultimedia.com
Subject: CD-ROM publication
Message: request to be added to mailing list
(Include a note on any topics that interest you.)

Exercise 6:   To find out how to access everything on the Net with just an e-mail account, send for Dr. Bob Rankin's helpful manual.

Mail to: mail-server@rtfm.mit.edu
Subject: <none>
Message: send usenet/news.answers/internet-services/access-via-email

Exercise 7:   *Interpersonal Computing and Technology Journal* (IPCT-J) is an electronic academic journal about technology and teaching. To obtain an article entitled "Teaching Languages with *NetNews*":

Mail to: listserv@guvm.ccf.georgetown.edu
Subject: <none>
Message: get cononelo ipctv2n1

If you like this resource, request a complete index of available articles by sending the message:

index ipct-J

to the same address.

Example 8:   Internet-on-a-Disk is a great newsletter for keeping up to date on electronic texts available on the Internet. It's aimed at teachers and contains much useful information on other school resources. Request from Richard Seltzer:

Mail to: seltzer@max.tiac.net
Subject: Internet-on-a-Disk
Message: request to be added to mailing list
(Back issues are available; see a copy of the newsletter for information.)

"E-mail is and will always be the most powerful tool for educators. While it's nice for my students to access information from Web sites, the real power is their being able to contact others in their search. For example, my fourth grade students will soon be looking for information related to gold prospecting. I have found Web sites that have good information, but more importantly, from these sites I've been able to contact gold prospectors who have enthusiastically agreed to field any questions my students may have."

Gary Quiring (1995, December 21), "Benefits of Web/E-mail," International
E-Mail Classroom Connections.

Listservers: Discussion groups via e-mail

Joining a listserver is an immediate way to connect with other teachers who are using the Internet. To join a listserver, you need only basic knowledge of how to send an e-mail message and specific information on how to subscribe to any given list.

What is a listserver?

Listservers are special-interest groups available through the Internet. Members post messages to the list owner, and Listserv software redistributes these to all members of a given discussion group. To participate, simply send a subscription message (**subscribe <listserver name> <your name>**) to the listserver address. Once you've subscribed, you will begin receiving messages from the list. You will be able to contribute your ideas and thoughts directly to the group, too, by using the group e-mail address.

Tech Talk

The term *listserver* is often abbreviated listserv. Listserv is the original program developed to handle mailing lists. Today, a number of other programs, such as Listprocessor, Mailbase, Mailserv, and Majordomo, can also be used to manage mailing lists. Because there are variations on the Listserv software, the commands that you send to a mailing list can vary. To find out which commands pertain to a given list, contact the listserv address and send a one-word message: <help> .

HINT Once you have subscribed to a listserv, you will receive important introductory information from the list owner. *Save this message!* It may be useful to print the message and keep it in a binder. Whenever you want to suspend your subscription, you will want exact information on how to <unsubscribe> .

Some discussion groups for educators

Here is just a sampling of discussion groups for educators that are available on the Internet. For a more extensive list, consult the outstanding collection of educational guides available from the Clearinghouse for Subject-Oriented Internet Research Guides. Use your Web browser to access this site at

   http://www.lib.umich.edu/chouse/chome.html

The guides written by D. Kovacs focus specifically on mailing lists, while many others include other resources.

   Another very good reference is the list of educational listservs and e-journals at

   http://k12.cnidr.org:90/lists.html

[Handwritten margin note: Message: Subscribe name of list first last name. Pay att'n to lower + upper case.]

Crea-cps   A discussion group on creative problem solving. Subscribe to:
   listserv@nic.surfnet.nl

Curricul   Interesting discussions on curriculum and instruction. Subscribe to:
   listserv@saturn.rowan.edu

Edtech   A discussion group for use of technology in education. An excellent place to begin appreciating the potential of technology. Subscribe to:
   listserv@ohstvma.bitnet

Ednet   A discussion group for educational networking. Subscribe to:
   listserv@nic.umanss.edu

Edres-I   Educational resources on the Internet. Subscribe to:
   listserv@unbvm1.csd.unb.ca

Edpolyan   Education Policy Analysis Forum. Subscribe to:
   listserv@asuvm.inre.asu.edu

FieldTrips-L   A forum for exchanging field trip ideas and information. Subscribe to:
   majordomo@acme.fred.org

InClass   A very good source for educational discussion. Topics focus on subjects of interest to middle- and high school teachers. Subscribe to:
   listproc@schoolnet.carleton.ca

IECC (International E-mail Classroom Connections)   A key resource for finding classroom keypals and e-mail projects. Subscribe to:
   iecc-request@stolaf.edu

Internet Teacher   A free publication for classroom teachers in public, private, and home school programs. Subscribe to:
   yam@regulus.com

K12admin   A discussion group for those interested in school administration. Subscribe to:
   listserv@suvm.syr.edu

K12artsed   Issues and discussion pertaining to arts education. Subscribe to:
   listserv@kennedy-center.org

K12small   A forum for education in small or rural schools. Subscribe to:
   listserv@uafsysb.uark.edu

Note from Kidlink:
"Kidlink is a grassroots project aimed at getting as many children in the age group 10–15 as possible involved in global dialog. Since the beginning in 1990, over 42,000 kids from 72 countries on all continents have participated in Kidlink activities. The primary means of communication is e-mail, but it may also be ordinary mail, fax, video-conferencing, ham radio, or whatever." To find out more, visit Kidlink's Web site **(http://www.kidlink.org /general.html)** or gopher to: **global.kidlink.org**

Using a search engine like alto Vista you can look for archived message or web page to see what looks like

Kidlink   The KIDLINK listserv distributes official information about the Kidlink project. Subscribe to:
   listserv@vm1.nodak.edu

Kidlit-L   A forum for the discussion of children's literature. Subscribe to:
   listserv@bingvmb.cc.binghamton.edu

Kidsphere   Extremely popular list for elementary and secondary school teachers. Discussions range from queries about marking software, to great Internet project ideas, to instructions on how to make bubbles. The volume of mail on this list tends to be high, but it is a stimulating place to begin using the Internet as a professional tool. Subscribe to:
   kidsphere-request@vms.cis.pitt.edu

LD-list   Discussions about learning disabilities. Subscribe to:
   listserv@listserv.net

LM_Net   Busy list focusing on school library media interests. Subscribe to:
   listserv@suvm.syr.edu

Media-L   A forum for media in education. Subscribe to:
   listserv@bingvmb.cc.binghamton.edu

Middle-L (Middle School)   A discussion group for teachers involved with the middle grades. Subscribe to:
   listserv@suvm.syr.edu

Novae Group   This is a newsletter rather than a discussion group. Subscribers receive regular updates and new ideas for using the Internet in the classroom. Subscribe to:
   majordomo@uidaho.edu

SchoolNet   General educational focus. One of a number of SchoolNet lists. Subscribe to:
   listproc@schoolnet.carleton.ca

SNEtalk-L   General discussion in the area of special needs education. Subscribe to:
   listproc@schoolnet.carleton.ca

Spedtalk   Special education list. Teachers, clinicians, and researchers discuss current issues on policies and new developments in this area. Subscribe to:
   majordomo@virginia.edu

Superk12   Discussion about school networking and telecommunications issues. Subscribe to:
   listserv@suvm.syr.edu

Tag-L   Talented and gifted education. Subscribe to:
listserv@vm1.nodak.edu

Teacher's Edition Online   A free newsletter with great ideas for teachers. You'll need to use your Web browser:
http:www2.southwind.net/~Ishiney
(The site provides the opportunity to subscribe.)

WWWedu   World Wide Web in education. Subscribe to:
listserv@k12.cnidr.org

"I joined the listserv Kidsphere, and that has opened many projects on various networks to me. Choosing listservs, group conferences, and newsgroups establishes relationships with others who have similar objectives and focus."

Stephanie Stevens, Teacher, San Francisco, CA, USA

Some e-mail lists for kids

If your students have their own electronic mail accounts, here are some mailing lists they can subscribe to.

K12Pals   For elementary and secondary students seeking keypals. Subscribe to:
listserv@suvm.syr.edu

Kidscafe   A world-wide discussion group for kids aged ten to fifteen. Subscribe to:
listserv@vm1.nodak.edu
(Find out more about Kidscafe discussion groups at the Web site http://www.kidlink.org)

Talkback   Discussion group for children. Subscribe to:
listserv@listserv.net

HINT If you do not have a precise address for a listserver, try subscribing through listserv@listserv.net

Youthnet Discussion group for youth. Subscribe to:
listserv@listserv.net

BR_Cafe A list for students to exchange book reviews. Subscribe to:
listproc@micronet.wcu.edu

Finding e-mail discussion lists

In addition to subscribing to some general education lists, such as Edtech or Kidsphere, you'll probably also want to locate some lists for specific subject areas, such as biology or geography. You can use the following techniques to find out about many more mailing lists. Some techniques may be unfamiliar to you, since we have not yet covered all the Internet tools you will be using. For now you can note this page for reference and refer back to it after you have learned about the World Wide Web, Gophers, FTP, and newsreaders.

• **E-mail access.** To locate many more lists with an educational focus, as well as lists for other topics, send the following message to
listserv@listserv.net
LIST GLOBAL/topic

Sending just the message <list global> without the qualifier (/topic) will retrieve an extensive list of lists.

• **World Wide Web.** Search for lists from Liszt's database of over 24,000 lists. Use your Web browser to access the database at:
http://www.liszt.com/

• **Gopher access.** A number of Gopher sites make available a resource called the List-of-Lists. One such list is at:
gopher://liberty.uc.wlu.edu
Path: /NetlinkServer/Bitnet mailing lists, etc.

• **FTP access.** Use anonymous FTP directly or through your World Wide Web client software to access the List-of-Lists, part1 and part2:
rtfm.mit.edu
Directory: /pub/usenet/news.answers/mail/mailing-lists

• **Newsreader access.** The List-of-Lists is regularly posted to these groups:
news.lists
news.announce.newusers
news.answers

HINT Post a list of educational discussion groups in the school library or staff lounge. The list entitled "Online Discussion Groups and Electronic Journals" is available from

http://k12.cnidr.org:90/lists.html

A list of Australian educational discussion lists is available from Ozlists:

http://www.gu.edu.au/gint/ozlists/ozlists_home.html

Newsgroups

For some people, one of the most exciting resources on the Internet are newsgroups. Through newsgroups (or Usenet), you can gain access to over 13,000 discussion groups on subjects ranging from fine arts to outer space. 〉25 to 30,000

Unfortunately, newsgroups are not an ideal classroom application. Some deal with adult, frivolous, or unsavory subjects, and most groups are unmoderated, so that no one screens messages before they are posted.

This is not to discourage teachers from allowing students to access Usenet newsgroups. However, you should be aware of potential problems and have a good idea in advance about how you want students to use these groups. Newsgroup science discussions or discourse around political issues can stimulate ideas and sharpen students' critical thinking skills.

You will undoubtedly want to access some of these groups in pursuing your own professional and personal interests. Newsgroups for teachers can be a valuable source of ideas. Also, they are less cumbersome than listservs, since messages are posted centrally rather than to your personal mailbox.

There are some newsgroups that are also available as listserv mailing lists, but many people prefer to access these discussions as newsgroups to avoid having to deal with excess e-mail. You might want to subscribe to listservs for one or two discussion groups that you are keenly interested in and opt for newsgroups for everything else. (Not all listservs are available as newsgroups. Also, there are many newsgroups that won't be available as listserv mailing lists.)

You can access newsgroups by using a newsreader (such as *tin, rn, nn or Trumpet*) on your system. The specific commands vary from system to system, but all of them will let you select for easy viewing those groups that you are most interested in. The newsreader will allow you to view, save, and respond to messages. In a nongraphical environment, an excellent way to view newsgroups is to use your Pine mail reader. Ask your access provider for the address of your newsserver. Then simply use the **Setup** and **Configure** menu choices within Pine to provide the option to access network news from within the mail reader. Using Pine, you can also selectively redirect Usenet discussions to students.

Tech Talk

If you don't have access to newsgroups at all, you can use Gopher or Lynx to get to sites that provide public access to newsgroups. These can be found by gophering to:
liberty.uc.wlu.edu
Path:
/NetlinkServer/Bitnet mailing lists, etc.

PERSONAL FAVORITES

Use this page to make notes on your own favorite listservs.

Listname: _____

Description: _____

Subscribe to: _____

Listname: _____

Description: _____

Subscribe to: _____

Listname: _____

Description: _____

Subscribe to: _____

Listname: _____

Description: _____

Subscribe to: _____

Listname: _____

Description: _____

Subscribe to: _____

Listname: _____

Description: _____

Subscribe to: _____

Listname: _____

Description: _____

Subscribe to: _____

Here are some groups of interest to teachers.

K12.ed.comp.literacy (Computer literacy and applications in the classroom)

K12.ed.tag (For teachers of talented and gifted students)

K12.ed.math

K12ed.soc-studies

K12.ed.art

K12.ed.health-pe (For teachers of health and physical education)

K12 ed.music

K12 ed.business

K12.ed.health-pe

K12.ed.life-skills

K12.ed.music

K12.ed.science

K12.ed.soc-studies

K12.ed.special (For teachers of special needs students)

K12.chat.elementary (General bulletin board for youngsters, including keypal listings)

K12.chat.teacher

Trumpet

A Windows or Macintosh environment makes it easier to access newsgroups. Here are some basic instructions for using the Trumpet newsreader.

Reading news

1. Decide which groups to look at. (Subscribed groups are listed in the upper-left corner of the screen.)
2. Double-click on the name of your selected group. Trumpet will respond by scanning the group for new messages.
3. A list of article titles for the current group will appear at the bottom of the screen. The **View/List** button will allow you to toggle between the list of messages and the message text. Note that related messages have been grouped. Related messages are called *threads*.
4. Use the arrow keys [→, ←, ↓, and ↑] to move between messages. Use the **View/List** toggle to return to the index.

Tech Talk

Newsgroups can be searched using your Web browser. With the latest versions of Netscape, you can even respond to messages this way. You will need to include a pointer to your systems newsserver or to a public newsserver. Your browser's **Preferences** menu offers an option for configuring **Mail** and **News**. The Internet server address for your newsserver should be inserted in the News [NNTP] Server.

Newsgroup categories

Certain abbreviations in the name of a newsgroup will tell you something of its focus or content.

alt	Alternative
biz	Business
comp	Computers
K12	Elementary and secondary education groups
news	General news and topical items
rec	Recreational (hobbies and arts)
sci	Scientific
soc	Social
talk	Debate on issues
misc	Miscellaneous

Tech Talk

If your provider does not offer access to newsgroups, you can configure a Windows-based newsreader to access one of the public newsservers. Follow these steps:

1. Use your Web browser to download the Free Agent (Windows) newsreader from **ftp://ftp.forteinc.com/pub/free_agent/fagent10.zip**

2. Find a public (free) newsserver near you. There are many all over the world. Find them at **http://dana.ucc.nau.edu/~jwa/open-sites.html**

3. Configure the Free Agent software with one of the public newsserver addresses. Be sure to select a server with a substantial number of active newsgroups.

HINT There are a number of services that will let you "search the news." These are useful for picking up general comments about a topic or finding a resource. It is also possible to use the news search services to locate e-mail addresses of news participants. Use your Web browser to try these news search resources:

Alta Vista: **http://altavista.digital.com/**
Deja News: **http://www.dejanews.com/**
Stanford Netnews **Filtering Service: http://woodstock.stanford.edu:2000/**

5. The following options under **Group** will help you to manage newsgroup articles.

Read All	Mark all articles in group as read
Skip All	Mark all articles in group as read and go to the next group
Unread All	Mark all articles in group as not read
Unread 20	Mark the last 20 articles as not read
Unread 10	Mark the last 10 articles as not read
Catch Up	Mark all articles in group as read (faster than Read All)
Catch Up All	Mark all articles in all groups as read

6. Save a local copy of an article by clicking on **Archive**. View these saved messages by clicking on **Window/Mail**. A list of local folders will be displayed.

Posting

1. **Post** allows you to send a new message to a group.
2. **Follow** allows you to post a message to the group with a follow-up to the current message.
3. **Reply** allows you to send a message to the author of the current message.

Subscribing/unsubscribing

1. To subscribe to a newsgroup, click on **Group/Subscribe**. A small window listing group categories (*alt, comp,* etc.) will be displayed. Select a category. Scroll through the list of group names and click on the names of groups to which you wish to subscribe.
2. To unsubscribe, select the group from your list of subscribed groups. Then, select **Group/Unsubscribe** from the scroll-down menu. The highlighted group will be dropped from your group listing.

Finding out more about Usenet news

The best way to find out about Usenet news is to access a newsgroup called **news.announce.newusers**. Use your local newsreader to access this group, and read the available periodic postings to find out more about what's available on Usenet and how to interact with the Usenet community.

Netiquette: Internet etiquette for students using e-mail)

DON'T type your e-mail in all capital letters. This is considered the electronic equivalent of YELLING AT SOMEONE!

DO use meaningful subject lines on your messages. This helps the recipient to sort through messages quickly or delete those that might not be of interest.

DO try to keep your message to only one subject. This allows readers to decide quickly whether they need to read the message in full. Secondary subjects are easy to miss if the first topic being discussed is not of interest.

DO sign your message with your name, institution, and e-mail address. Not all mail systems allow the reader to see the address in the header of the message. Many e-mail packages will let you set up a signature file which can easily (or automatically) be attached to outgoing mail.

DON'T send short, unnecessary messages to groups (e.g., "I, agree!"). This increases traffic on the Internet and clutters mailboxes.

DON'T reply to a whole group when only an individual reply is warranted. Be sure to check to see where a message has been sent from before activating the "reply" function. Some embarrassing personal messages have inadvertently been posted to several hundred people.

DO respect the character of individual newsgroups. After joining a group, follow the messages for a week or two before jumping in with your own comments—particularly if you intend to take issue with the comments some one else has made.

DO use emoticons, or smileys :-). Smileys are used to convey the tone of voice that is absent in e-mail.

DO consult the Netiquette Home Page: **http://www.fau.edu/rinaldi/net/index.htm**

You can also obtain more information about newsgroups by sending the following message to **mail-serv@rtfm.mit.edu**:

    send usenet/news.answers/news-newusers-intro

To get a listing of Usenet newsgroups, add these commands to your note:

    send usenet/news.answers/active-newsgroups/part1
    send usenet/news.answers/active-newsgroups/part2
    send usenet/news.answers/alt-hierarchies/part1
    send usenet/news.answers/alt-hierarchies/part2

Be prepared to get some hefty files returned in the mail.

Usenet groups for newcomers

news.announce.newusers
A good place to learn about Usenet

news.answers
Subscribe to this group to access frequently asked questions (FAQs)

alt.internet.services
FAQs plus lots of good information about Internet services

FAQs

FAQs (frequently asked questions) are a great way to get the "facts" about a wide range of topics, including how to use the Internet.

To get the FAQ file(s) for a given newsgroup, send to **mail-server@rtfm.mit.edu** (substitute dots for dashes if they appear in the newsgroup name) a command such as this:
index usenet/<news-groupname>
If any FAQ files are available, they will be listed in the returned info, and you can request them with a command such as:
send usenet/<news-groupname>/<faqfile-name>
FAQs are also available from the FTP site:
ftp://rtfm.mit.edu

GETTING STARTED

... with an E-mail Class Project

Guidelines for teachers

Classroom projects built around electronic mail are one of the principal ways that the Internet is being used in schools. These projects can range from a simple exchange of personal messages to sophisticated research and data collection.

The following guidelines can form the basis for many types of e-mail projects. Think of these steps as a framework around which to build your specific project.

Step 1: **Establish the scope of the project.** Here are some key questions to consider:

• Will each student have a keypal, or will the class as a group compose messages for transmitting to another class?
• If each student is to have a keypal, will the students all be in the same class, or from different locations? (Note: Collaborating with another class as a group is probably the easiest way to manage student communications.)
• Will your students' keypals be located in another state, province, or country?
• When will the project begin?
• Do you want to establish connectivity based on a particular project or theme (such as global ecology)?
• Do you want the correspondence between students to include specific learning objectives, such as research or data collection?

Step 2: **Establish time frames.** Be specific about project phases and deadlines.

Step 3: **Advertise your project on one or more listservs,** such as IECC (International Electronic E-mail Connections), Kidsphere, SchoolNet, or InClass. You can also post on a more targeted list, such as Middle-L, or a math teachers' discussion group for a project with a math component. Post at least eight weeks in advance. You may need to be post more than once.

Step 4: **Communicate formally with the other teachers involved,** thanking them for their participation and stating exactly what you hope will be accomplished with the exchange of letters. Be sure to explain any specific instructions you would like followed. This is particularly important if the e-mail exchanges are to be integrated with a data collection project.

Step 5: Ensure that your own students are familiar with the procedures for sending electronic mail. Posting specific instructions near the computer will help students learn the steps involved. Have them practice sending messages to one another, and walk them through any specific skills they will need, such as saving word processed files as text or uploading files. Don't forget to cover netiquette, acceptable use, and safety on the Net.

Step 6: Discuss the project with your students. Encourage them to contribute ideas on how to make it a success. Remind them in advance that they won't all receive responses at the same rate, and explain some of the reasons why messages can be delayed, such as limited access to a computer or occasional network problems.

Step 7: As participants are identified, prepare a reference sheet on who is communicating with whom, along with relevant e-mail addresses. This will be a great help if messages are returned because of incorrect addressing or if a student loses a keypal's address.

Ten tips for success with e-mail projects

1. Post a list of safety and netiquette do's and don'ts.
2. Have students practice sending messages to one another.
3. Aim for short, frequent messages.
4. Use a classroom map to track where messages are being received from.
5. Seek out new keypals for any students who are not getting responses after sending two or three messages.
6. Establish time limits for composing student messages, especially if computer time is limited.
7. For more complex projects, consider having students work with partners or in small groups.
8. Use helpers, such as parent volunteers or older students.
9. Respond right away to those who offer to participate in your project, whether or not you are able to include them. Teachers may wish to seek other projects if participation in yours is limited.
10. Review educator Ron Corio's FAQ, "Regarding E-mail Projects" (use your Web browser to access **http://www.nyu.edu/pages/hess/ docs/ronfaq.html**).

SMILEYS... make the Internet a friendlier place :-)

Emoticons, or smileys, can give sparkle to electronic mail. They also help to communicate the writer's intention whenever a comment might otherwise be misinterpreted. Students enjoy smileys. As an interesting exercise, invite them to invent their own. Here are a few samples.

:-)   A smile: "I'm just kidding, joking, having fun." This is one you'll see used a lot—sometimes without the nose, as in :).

:-("I'm sad." Often used to express displeasure with something that's just been written.

;-)   Wink (a variation on "just kidding")

;->   A winking, mischievous smile

:-o   Surprise

:-O   Shock

:-&   Tongue-tied

:'(Crying

A few less useful ones... but still fun:

(-:   "I'm kidding, joking, or having fun—and left-handed."

[ ]   Hugs

: *   Kisses

*<:-) Santa Claus

%-)   I've been sitting at the computer too long.

Also watch for acronyms:

BTW   By the way

FYI   For your information

IMHO   In my humble opinion

IMNSHO In my not so humble opinion

LOL   Laughing out loud

TTFN   Ta Ta for now

Project Ideas

Student Keypals

Learning outcomes
• Students will exchange electronic messages with other students around the globe.

Grade level: Can be adapted for all

Getting started
• Send your requests for keypals to IECC (International Electronic E-mail Connections), Kidsphere, SchoolNet, or Inclass. Or, access and register your project at the IECC World Wide Web site at **http://www.stolaf.edu/network/iecc/** .
• Specify the focus, such as French language exchange or messaging related to a particular project.
• Individual students can find keypals using the K12Pals list at **listserv@suvm.syr.edu** .

Extending: Snail-mail exchange
Using "snail-mail" can add texture and excitement to an electronic mail exchange, especially if you lack the equipment necessary to scan and upload photos and artwork. A normal postal exchange can work just as well.

Here are some ideas for a snail-mail exchange:

• Have students exchange class pictures, brochures, school newspapers, or travel brochures.
• Students can create drawings of their homes or neighborhoods and exchange these. Use the pictures as the basis for classroom discussion about cultural differences.
• Have students create and exchange pictures around a theme, such as holidays, Earth Day, world peace, or helping the poor. Use these pictures as a starter for class discussion of the chosen topic. The same topic can be used as the basis for the students' electronic messaging or reports.
• Students can select and exchange stories from their local newspapers. Deciding which stories best reflect the students' community can be an interesting class exercise.

Project Ideas

Introducing Friends

This is an easy and interesting project for those new to electronic mail. Students interview a friend and submit their interviews via e-mail to a listserver that posts introductions from students around the world.

Learning outcomes
- Students will gain skill in interviewing, writing, and presenting information.
- Students will learn to send e-mail messages.
- Students will learn about cultural differences.

Grade level: 3–8

Getting started
- Subscribe to the account at the Kidintro Mailing List at listserv@sjuvm.stjohns.edu
- Allow class time for students to read mail being posted to the list.
- As a class, brainstorm a simple interview format that students might use with their interview partners. Typical questions might include likes and dislikes, unusual interests or talents, or humorous anecdotes.

Developing
- Allow class time for student pairs to take turns interviewing each other.
- Assist students to use their word processors to write introductions to their keypals. Here is one possible format for students to use in developing their messages.

  Paragraph 1: Describe what your friend looks like, and a bit about what he or she likes and dislikes.
  Paragraph 2: Tell about your friend's interests and opinions.
  Paragraph 3: Write an amusing story about your friend.
  Paragraph 4: Describe your friend's strengths and talents.

- Have students submit their introductions to the Kidintro list, being sure to include the name of their school, town, state or province, and country in the subject line of the message.

Extending

- Have students regularly read introductions posted to the listserver.
- Have the class discuss some of the things they have learned about other cultures from reading messages posted to the list.

For more information on the Introducing Friends project, use your Web browser to access

http://pen.k12.va.us/~ãpembert/kidintro/kidmail.html

Following interviews with their friends, these students are ready to introduce their classmates to students in other parts of the world.

Project Ideas

E-mail Surveys and Questionnaires

In this project, students develop a questionnaire based on the topic of personal "favorites."

Learning outcomes
- Students will develop and exchange electronic questionnaires.
- Students will incorporate an existing file into an e-mail message and/or forward a message.

Grade level: 4–8

Getting started
- Have your students discuss and list possible "favorites" for discussion, for example:
  - favorite season
  - favorite color
  - favorite subject in school
  - favorite TV show
  - favorite book
  - favorite place to visit
  - favorite music group
  - favorite food
  - favorite movie
  - favorite sport.

Developing
- Develop a questionnaire listing the selected questions. You can provide an electronic copy of the list to each of your own students; they, in turn, may send the file to each of their keypals. Students will enjoy comparing the responses they receive.

Variation
- Older students may wish to develop a questionnaire focusing on a research topic, such as a survey of students' leisure-time activities, their attitudes about violence on television, or their recycling habits. Suitable topics will flow from curriculum areas.

Extending
- Use the data collected in this project to build a database of responses. Plan in advance how to formulate the questions to simplify data input. Short-answer and multiple-choice responses will be easier to tally than open-ended responses.
- Using database software, collate and analyze the results of the surveys in a math or science lesson.

Project Ideas

Exchanging Research Projects

Learning outcomes
- Students will research a country in the library and on the Internet.
- Students will conduct an online interview (using e-mail) with a student from the country they have chosen to research.
- Students will prepare written reports on their own country and submit these to their keypals for comments.

Grade level: 4–12

Getting started
- Determine which country will be the focus for this project. Use the IECC listserv or Web site at **http://www.stolaf.edu/network/iecc** to advertise for participants.
- Have the class develop a list of topics to investigate as they learn about the country they intend to research. The list should include standard geographical information such as climate and location, but also include topics of particular interest to students, such as favorite sports in a country, or subjects that are studied in school.

Developing
- If students are able to use Internet tools such as the World Wide Web, they can explore the Internet for information on the country they have chosen.
- Alternatively (or in addition), they can use magazines and books from a local library to conduct their research.
- Once the students have completed their preliminary research, they should develop a list of questions to address to a keypal in the country they are researching. These questions will form the basis of an electronic mail interview.

Extending
- Once students have completed their interviews and written their reports, they should send what they have written to their keypal interviewees for feedback.

Variations

- Students enjoy exchanging their stories and reports with other classes. These can be a report that they have completed for a unit of study or a creative writing endeavor.
- Have students put together a "travel guide" on their own country, state, province, or community and exchange these with other classes. This project is most exciting if more than one remote classroom is involved, so that each of the participating classes receives reports from more than one country, province, or state. If your students have access to Gopher or Web resources, they can use these to research their reports.
- Have students research a current issue or event and create a "newswire" service. First, explain what a newswire service is, and clip some examples from a local newspaper. Then, have students research and prepare their reports. Students from another classroom can look at the reports and select their favorites for a simulated online news broadcast. Learning is enhanced when students have the opportunity to share their thoughts on world issues. Follow up this project with a discussion about the advantages and disadvantages of getting the news from a wire service.

Students can conduct research or perform experiments and compare results with students in other schools or countries.

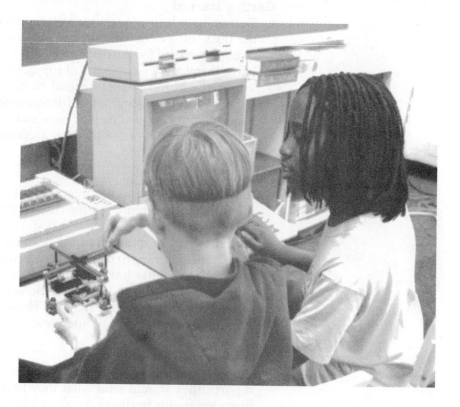

Publish
kids book
reviews
electronically
list

A mailing list
to share info.

Project Ideas

Sharing Book Reviews

BR_Cafe is a listserv where kids can discuss their favorite books. A requirement for participating in Cafe discussions is to submit a review of a favorite book. Students are thrilled by the idea of having others read their work. Here's how your students can contribute.

Learning outcomes
* Students will access, over the Internet, book reviews written by other students.
* Students will create their own book reviews and submit them for posting on the Internet.

Grade level: 4–8

Getting started
* Subscribe to BR_Cafe so that you and your students can receive a few sample of book reviews. To subscribe, send the following message to:
listproc@micronet.wcu.edu
Subject: <none>
Message: subscribe BR_Review <firstname lastname> (replace the names with your name or school name)

Developing
* To send your book reviews to the list, use the following format.

To: br_review@micronet.wcu.edu
Subject: Book Title/Book Author(s)
Message (include as much of the following information as you can):
Genre (e.g., mystery, science fiction, romance, general fiction, poetry, short story, non-fiction, humor, reference, other):
Title:
Author:
Year published:
Publisher:
ISBN:
Intended audience:
Your age:

Your gender:
Your name:
Your location:
Your e-mail address:
Narrative review:

You can obtain more information about BR-Review and BR_Cafe by sending a message as follows to:
listproc@micronet.wcu.edu
Subject: <none>
Message: info br_review
info br_cafe

Extending
- Have students share their reviews by reading them aloud, or by sending them as an e-mail message to other members of the class.

Variations
- Students can publish their own stories on the World Wide Web by sending them to KidPub@en-garde.com . Stories should be sent as individual mail messages and should include brief information about your school and class. For more information, use your Web browser to access
http://escrime.en-garde.com/kidpub/how to.html

(in the U.K., information is available from
http://www.ehche.ac.uk/%7Ewiredue/kidpub)

Figure 4-3

A sample book review

```
Title: MacDonald Hall Goes Hollywood
Author: Gordon Korman
Published: 1991
Publisher: Scholastic
ISBN: 0-590-43941-3
Ages: 8 and up
Name: Darren Romijn
Age: 12 (grade 7)
Acadia Jr. High School
175 Killarney Ave.
Winnipeg Manitoba
R3T 3B3
e-mail: vnielson@minet.gov.mb.ca

   Review: This book is about a movie star
that comes to Macdonald Hall (a private
school) to make a film. Bruno tries to get
into the movie but the headmaster bans the
students from the movie set. Bruno won't
stop until he gets to be in the movie.
This book was really funny! If you like
funny books you'll definitely like this
one!
```

Summing up

While electronic mail is only one of the ways in which the Internet can be introduced into the classroom, it is potentially one of the most versatile. With a little creativity, teachers can use e-mail as an effective tool to achieve learning outcomes in basic skills such as computer literacy and communications, as well as in more specific subjects such as science, geography, or language studies. Through electronic mail projects, students can learn about teamwork and global cooperation.

Advanced users may want to experiment with using e-mail to transfer software, or to exchange graphics, sound, or even multimedia files. But for newcomers, even basic electronic messaging can be wonderfully rewarding. A simple exchange of text messages can dissolve the walls of the traditional classroom and open a door to exploring the world.

The next chapter will look at how the World Wide Web can expand the traditional boundaries of the classroom by opening up a world of information and allowing students to share their own learning experiences.

Exploring the World Wide Web

Chapter 5

❝A Language Arts teacher asked me to teach her ninth and eleventh grade students how to make a Web page. Several of my student assistants volunteered to teach these kids enough to put a writing project or two online. These projects are not perfect nor very sophisticated, but they do function. It is also our first experiment in electronic portfolios as a means of alternative assessment.❞

— CURRIE MORRISON, TECHNOLOGY COORDINATOR, NATHAN HALE HIGH SCHOOL, SEATTLE, WA, USA

The World Wide Web inspires learning. Students and teachers are quickly excited by the vastness of this resource and the discovery of how easy it is to navigate. On the World Wide Web, students can learn about current news events and contemporary science. They can travel to the past and read correspondence from the Civil War, or visit a museum that provides a glimpse of an earlier time.

This chapter examines the World Wide Web and introduces two popular tools for navigating it. It includes suggestions for how teachers can get started using the Web, and concludes with ideas for lessons that will help you to integrate the Web into classroom learning.

Chapter goals

- To provide an overview of the World Wide Web and its role in the classroom
- To introduce the concept of client/server computing
- To introduce key concepts related to Web technology
- To provide basic instructions for using Netscape and the non-graphical browser, Lynx
- To describe how to search for information on the World Wide Web
- To suggest a selection of Web resources for teachers and students
- To provide ideas for introducing the Web into the classroom
- To give basic instructions for publishing Web pages

The Web as a tool for learning

The World Wide Web is an important complement to traditional learning materials, both print and audio-visual. School librarians are constantly challenged to meet broad curriculum needs on limited budgets. Having access to the Web is an excellent way to supplement the school media collection. Ideally, students need to know beforehand how to use both print and Internet resources for their research, and how to assess the value of each for any given project.

In the classroom, the World Wide Web can also be used as a publishing tool, and as such it can be relevant to a broad spectrum of classroom learning activities. An exciting venture for students is to develop their own Web pages. These can profile their school or their community. Students can also develop Web pages around units of study. A student report can be a Web page, complete with graphics and pointers to useful information resources on the Net.

For many students, the possibility of having their work published on the Internet is a powerful motivator. In addition, materials that students have put together can be a helpful learning resource for other students. It's not often that students take time to read through traditional reports done by other students, but publishing a Web page on a specific topic is an ideal way to share learning.

> "Last year I discovered the WWW as a publishing tool and research medium with my Grade 3/4 class. Although I'm on deferred leave this year, I continually find new Web sites and projects that I'm filing for next fall, planning to integrate the World Wide Web into my classroom."
>
> *Nancy Barkhouse, Teacher, Atlantic View Elementary School,*
> *Lawrencetown, NS, Canada*

Understanding the basics of the World Wide Web is the first step to using it effectively in the classroom. Chapter 1 briefly introduced the World Wide Web. This chapter will examine how it works, and then explore the possibilities for using the World Wide Web in the classroom.

World Wide Web: overview

The World Wide Web project was developed to provide easy access over the Internet to a variety of media. Unlike Gophers, which are menu based, the World Wide Web is based on a display of pages that can integrate text, pictures, sound, and video (Chapter 6 is all about Gophers.) Web pages display paragraphs about a topic, and also provide links to further information, using a computer technology called *hypertext*.

Hypertext links lead you to more information whenever you choose to follow them (Fig. 5–1, page 106). A simple example of a hypertext link would be a situation in which you are reading a document onscreen and are given an opportunity to click on a word to find its definition. Or, you might be viewing a document about health and nutrition, and discover a link to another document that provides in-depth information about vitamins.

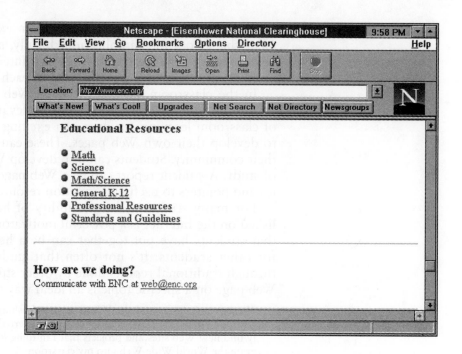

Figure 5-1
Clicking on highlighted hyperlinks will bring up a new page (below).

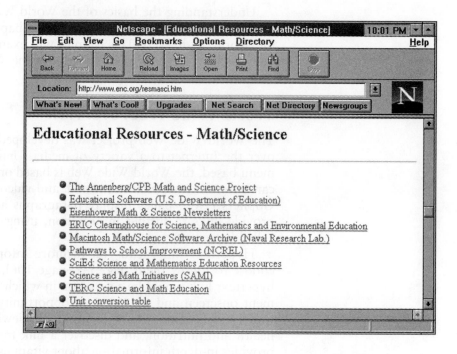

Hypermedia is another term you will encounter on the Web. Hypermedia is similar to hypertext in that both denote the ability to access further information from a document. But hypermedia makes it possible to access other kinds of information, such as pictures or sound files, in addition to text. As you might guess, hypermedia is the basis for many multimedia applications. As Web pages become more complex in design, incorporating more sound and video files, the World Wide Web can be described as a way of delivering multimedia over the Internet.

Client/server technology

A number of Internet applications, including the World Wide Web, are built upon client/server technology. Client/server is a key concept in the world of the Internet. Simply put, in a client/server environment, two pieces of software work together as a team.

The client is responsible for
- the user interface (what the software looks like to you on your desktop)
- initiating the communications process
- displaying information sent from the server.

The server
- retains information (such as Web pages and related files)
- analyzes requests coming from the client
- responds to requests by sending information back to the client.

In a nutshell, the client is the program that you use locally, and the remote server does what the client says.

Figure 5-2
Client/server computing

A key advantage to client/server computing is that it allows you to use your desktop computing power (the client) while taking full advantage of remote mainframes (the server) to store the massive resources available through the Internet. Another advantage is that it allows information to be passed back and forth over the Internet without the connections between computers having to remain open. The connection on a remote server stays open only long enough to respond to your immediate request for a menu or a file. You, in turn, read the item only after it has been passed to your client computer.

Web browsers

The client software used to access the World Wide Web is called a *browser*. New and improved Web browsers are always on the horizon; one of the most popular to date has been Netscape. Versions of Netscape exist for both the Windows and Macintosh environments. Your access provider may have supplied you with a browser, or at least can tell you where to obtain the latest versions of popular Web browsers.

> **HINT** The latest version of Netscape includes a newsreader and mail function. Clicking on a URL in a message connects you to the Web page. The integrated package can greatly simplify training. You can obtain the latest version at **http://home.home.netscape.com/home/**, or by using FTP at **ftp://ftpl.netscape.com**

In addition to allowing you to access Web pages, Netscape, Lynx and other browsers offer a convenient way to access other types of resources on the Internet—notably, Gophers and FTP (file transfer) sites (see Chapters 6 and 7). Here is a list of some of the different kinds of Internet functions that are accessible with a Web browser.

- Web pages (hypertext and multimedia resources)
- Gopher information
- files from FTP sites
- Web searches
- Archie searches (for finding software on the Internet)
- Veronica searches (for searching Gopher menus)
- listserver archives
- Usenet news
- telnet (for logging on to other computers)
- MOOs (for online discussions in real time)
- Hytelnet (a hyperlinked gateway to many library and bulletin board services)
- Internet fax services.

URLs

Although at first you'll probably navigate the Web simply by highlighting and clicking on the links that are incorporated into your Web browser or presented on a Web page, you can navigate more efficiently by using URLs (*Uniform Resource Locators*). In effect, URLs are "addresses" that specify the location on the Internet of computers having different types of information. The first part of the URL (before the colon) indicates the access method or the type of resource you want to retrieve. The part of the URL that follows the double slash (//) specifies a machine name or site. Here are some examples.

http://www.clark.net/pub/robert/home.html This is a Web site (http stands for *h*yper*t*ext *t*ransfer *p*rotocol).

gopher://unix5.nysed.gov This is a Gopher site.

file://wuarchive.wustl.edu/mirrors/msdos/graphics/gifkit.zip A URL that starts with file:// is used to access a specific file on the Internet. A slightly different format is used to access a file on your own hard drive. Here is an example of a URL that might be used to retrieve a file from your computer's C drive: file:///c|\netscape\bookmark.htm

ftp://www.xerox.com/pub/file.txt With the FTP type of URL, you can access and transfer files.

telnet://dra.com The telnet URL will access a login screen for a remote computer.

news:alt.hypertext If your browser has been configured to point to your newsserver, an address like this gives you access to newsgroups using your Web browser.

In the following sections and in the next chapter, we'll show you how you can use a Web browser to access specific locations on the Internet.

HINT Remember that Web sites are constantly changing. In particular, directory names and filenames may quickly go out of date. If a URL does not seem to work, check each character to be sure that you have entered it accurately. Then, try deleting the final filename and/or directories. Once you've accessed a specific location, you can often find the exact information you're searching for just by following the links. If you still are not successful, try finding the item using a search engine such as Alta Vista.

Using Netscape

Basic navigation

When you first start your Web browser, it will connect to a Web server and display an initial home page (often that of the Netscape

Corporation). From here, you can link to other documents by clicking on the words that are displayed in bright blue. Notice that the blue links turn purple once you've accessed them. The blue or purple (and sometimes underlined) words are *hyperlinks*. Hyperlinks can point to other references in the same document or to completely separate files on the Internet. Many educational Web pages or pages developed by individual schools include links to similar sites.

In Netscape, you can also navigate using the Directory Buttons. Click on **What's New!**, **What's Cool!**, or **Net Directory** to begin navigating. Netscape also provides a toolbar for quick navigation. The toolbar enables you to move back and forth between pages that you have viewed in the current session. You can also load images, search for text in a currently displayed document, and stop the access/transfer process.

> **HINT** Although hyperlinks are traditionally blue, other colors are possible. You may see black pages with bright yellow links and other imaginative color combinations. When searching for links, look for obvious visual highlights.

Using bookmarks

Once you start navigating, you will quickly identify sites that you'll want to return to again and again. Luckily, it's not necessary to type in the complete URL each time you want to return to a location. Once you access a site that interests you, you can add it to your list of bookmarks by selecting **Bookmark/Add** on the Netscape menu. (Click on your right mouse button for a pop-up menu.) In a subsequent session, when you want to return to that location, you can select **Bookmark/View** and double-click on the entry. When you return to the main Netscape screen, the requested Web page should appear.

The Netscape Bookmarks screen also gives you the opportunity to search for, copy, edit, and provide a brief description for your bookmarks. Experiment with the menu options to familiarize yourself with the possibilities for managing your bookmarks.

If you're just getting started with Netscape, you can ask another teacher to provide you with a copy of his or her bookmarks, and you can use these as an initial set of pointers.

> **HiNT** If either of these bars is not visible, pull down the Options menu and ensure that the Toolbar and Directory selections are checked. You can toggle these features on and off by clicking on the name of the item in the Options menu list.

Figure 5-3
The Netscape button bar

Figure 5-4
The Netscape toolbar

Quick summary: Netscape toolbar functions

Back
Brings you back to the pages that you've previously viewed. As it accesses locations, Netscape retains information on where you've been (via a history list) and will quickly redisplay pages according to the most recently viewed page when you click on the Back button.

Forward
Brings up the next page in the history list.

Home
Brings up the home page. This is the page that automatically loads when you call up Netscape.

Reload
Re-accesses the document you have just viewed and redisplays it on your screen.

Images
Reloads images into the current document.

Find
Searches the text of the current document for a specified character or word.

Stop
Interrupts the data as they come in from the network.

Open
Produces a dialog box that allows you specify the URL location you wish to access.

Figure 5-5
Netscape bookmarks screen

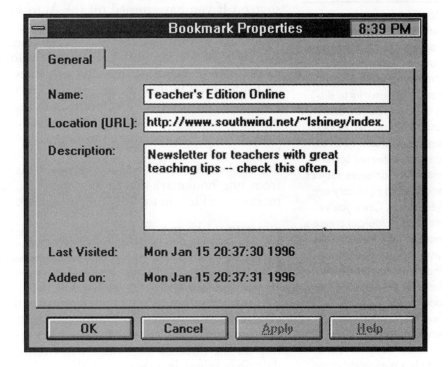

HINT Selecting **File/View in Browser** on the Bookmarks screen menu will let you view your bookmarks as a Web page.

Netscape options

The Netscape **Options** menu lists features that you can turn on or off to change certain parts of your screen display. While you will probably want to leave most of these options turned on, such as the **Toolbar**, the one possible exception is the **Auto Load Images** option. When this is turned on, all the images incorporated into a Web page will be automatically downloaded and displayed. If you are dialing in to the Internet, waiting for images to download can sometimes be painfully slow, and if the image is simply decorative, it may not be worth waiting for. With a dial-up connection, it is sometimes more desirable to turn off the **Auto Load Images** switch. To do this, just click once on the option so that the check mark disappears. If you click again it will reappear. (This on/off feature is known as a *toggle switch*.) If you have turned off the **Auto Load Images** feature, Web pages will display more quickly. Whenever you decide that you would like to view the images, you can toggle the **Auto Load Images** switch back to on, and click on the **Reload** button. For a quick reload with images, just click on the **Images** button in the toolbar.

Under the **Options** menu you will also see **Preferences** listed. If you click on this, the **Preferences** dialog box will appear. The options are given at the top of this screen. You can click on a selection to view the specific choices available in any given category. Under **Applications and Directories** you can alter a specific file with the **Bookmarks/Add or View** options. This is where you can change from one bookmark file to another (e.g., your professional bookmarks vs. a file you use for student access).

Another selection under Preferences will tell Netscape where on your computer your telnet application can be found. Your access provider may have supplied you with a specific program for telnetting on the Internet (e.g., the EWAN terminal emulator). Chapter 7 describes telnet in greater detail, but for now you might want to note that you must specify where the application is located on your computer by using the **Applications and Directories** window (**Options/Preferences** menu) for Netscape to find it. You can use the

Bookmarks can be a great help for organizing classroom projects. Because you can easily change them, you can develop one set of bookmarks to distribute to your students and have another working set for yourself. You can develop different bookmarks for different subject areas, such as history or geography. Once you've done this, you can create a master set of bookmarks with links to each of the individual bookmark files. Just add the URL for the bookmark (e.g., **file:///c|\netscape\science.htm**) as a new bookmark, and supply a meaningful name using the fields for editing bookmark information.

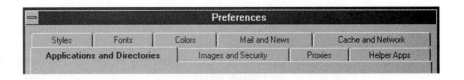

Figure 5-6
Netscape Preferences dialog box and bookmark file (below)

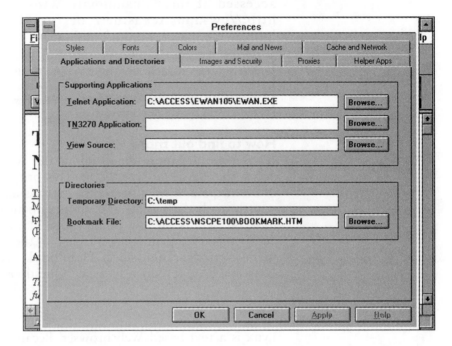

Browse feature to select the file to avoid having to type the full file-name.

Viewers and helper applications

Sound files, large graphic files, video files, and other special files require that viewers or helper applications be installed on your system before you can access these files automatically through Netscape. Under the **Preferences/Helper Applications** menu, a form is provided that allows you fill in the names of your helper applications. For example, for JPEG image files, you may choose to use a viewer called LView. To set up access to this program from within Netscape, you would need to modify the form by replacing the **Ask User** with the filename for Lview. Use the **Browse** button to automatically insert the directory location for LView in the window.

Multimedia helper applications for any given software are found in many places on the Internet. One way to locate these is to clear the **Location** window and type in the URL **http://home.netscape.com/assist/helper_apps/index.html** . This document will explain more about using helper applications. It will also link you to sites that provide some of the helper application programs you might need. Be sure to review the link called *short helper document*, which provides examples on how to configure helper applications in various platforms. Viewers and helper applications can also be accessed at the Consummate Winsock App List located at **http://cwsapps.texas.net/** or for Macintosh computers at **http://www.macatawa.org/~mthomas/** .

> **HINT** An increasingly popular technique is to send a document in Adobe's PDF format, which requires an Acrobat reader. The PDF format will allow the original font and layout for a document to be preserved. You can obtain the free Acrobat reader at **http://www.adobe.com/** . Use the viewer to sample the *New York Times* fax services at **http://nytimesfax.com**

How to find out more

As you require more detail about the World Wide Web, you can access the *Netscape Handbook*. This provides a complete overview of Netscape and how to use it. There is an online tutorial to walk you through the basics, and an alphabetical index where you can look up details on any point you'd like to learn more about. To access this document, click on **Help** at the far right of the Netscape menu options. Then select **Handbook**. You can also access the Netscape FAQ (Frequently Asked Questions) using the Help menu.

Lynx

Lynx is a text-based Web browser. Because it does not capture the multimedia dimension of the Web, it is less ideal, but for schools with limited access to the Internet it may be the only option. On the plus side, because Lynx does not display images, it can sometimes be a faster way of navigating the Web. It has other practical features as well, such as its ability to automatically mail a document that is displayed. While it is possible to use the Internet tool called telnet (described in Chapter 7) to get to a public Lynx client, in order to use semi-automated features (such as listing favorite Web sites in a bookmark file), Lynx must be available on your access provider's machine.

Lynx help

Lynx has an excellent **Help** function. Typing **h** for help will give you the opportunity to access several general information guides, an explanation of the various keystroke commands, and the *Lynx User's Guide*. There are a number of powerful features within Lynx, such as being able to search for a particular term within a document. You can find out about Lynx features by accessing the *Lynx User's Guide*.

Yahoo

The easiest way to search the Internet is to click on the **NetSearch** button on the Netscape button bar and type a search term (or keyword) in the designated field. One of the best places to begin searching the World Wide Web is Yahoo. Here you'll find subject information broken down by broad categories such as Art, Science, or Social Sciences, with more specific subject headings under each of these links. To access this site using Netscape, clear the location field and type the URL **http://www.yahoo.com** . (Another way is to click on the **Net Directory** button, scroll down the resulting screen to Yahoo, and click on the link.)

Begin by browsing the directory in any subject category. Click on the links that interest you, and use the Netscape toolbar to return to previous screens. You can click on Go and View History to review places you have visited. While browsing, don't forget that you can set bookmarks for locations that you might wish to revisit.

> **HINT** You can set up Yahoo as your default home page. Many people find it convenient to have their browsers start up with a subject index, such as Yahoo, displayed immediately. Yahoo provides instructions on doing this within Netscape. At the search screen, click on **Options**. Next, click on **Yahoo Easy Access**.

GETTING STARTED

... with Netscape

Exercise for Teachers: A Visit to Yahoo

This exercise introduces several useful resources for searching the Internet.

Getting started

Step 1. Visit the Yahoo home page, either by using the button bar or by typing the URL **http://www.yahoo.com** in the location field. At Yahoo, scroll to the top of any page you'd like to visit to access a search window.

Step 2. Click on the search window and type in a topic that interests you. For best results, choose a fairly specific term (e.g., *earthquakes* rather than *natural disasters*). Next, click on the **Search** button. The resulting screen itemizes the matches found for the search term used.

The Yahoo search results are limited to only those Web resources that are listed at Yahoo. But Yahoo offers another feature that allows you to move quickly to other search engines on the Internet.

Figure 5-7

Type a search term in the field and click on the Search button for results (right).

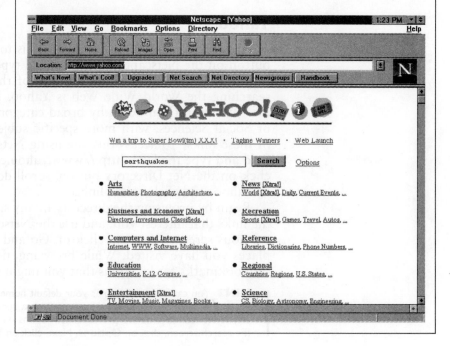

The Teacher's Complete & Easy Guide to the Internet

HINT Looking for beginners' guides? Try a Yahoo search using *beginners guides* as your search term.

Step 3. Scroll to the bottom of the search results screen to the heading **Other Search Engines**. Here you will find links to other search options. Click on one of the search engines listed and wait for a results screen to display. Once you have searched a term within the Yahoo database, Yahoo will automatically input your keyword as you direct your search to other search engines. How many "hits" (successful matches) do you get on Open Text, Alta Vista (Fig. 5–8, page 118), and WebCrawler?

Step 4. To complete the learning exercise, scroll to the bottom of the Yahoo search screen where the search engines are listed and click on **More**. Scroll down the page to get an overview of the tools that you can use to search the Internet. Eventually, you will want to set up bookmarks for your favorites.

Variation
Try this same exercise using Lynx. Use your cursor keys to navigate and type search terms in the designated fields. Typing **g** will bring up the prompt for typing in the URL for Yahoo.

Figure 5-7A

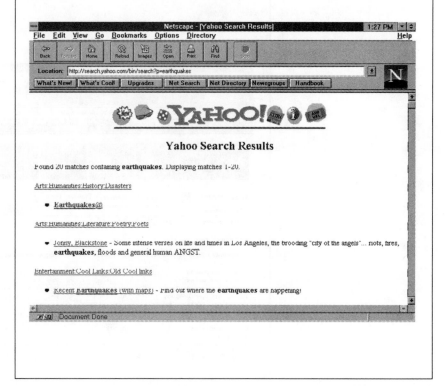

Figure 5-8

In searching Alta Vista, you can quickly change from searching for Web pages (above) to searching for Usenet newsgroups (below) by clicking the down arrow in the Search toggle window.

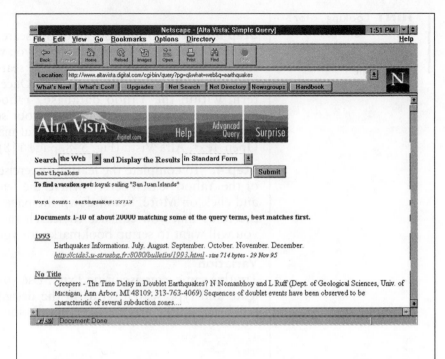

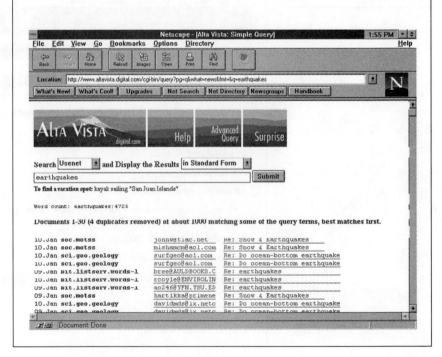

The Teacher's Complete & Easy Guide to the Internet

Hints for searching the Internet

Finding exactly the information you are looking for on the Internet requires knowledge and persistence, but knowing how to search will give you confidence in having your class use this resource as a learning tool. Here are some points to be aware of.

• **Yahoo is just one of a number of search engines.**   Other possibilities include WebCrawler, Lycos, Veronica (see Chapter 6), and Open Text. Note that Yahoo provides you with a gateway to a number of alternative search engines. Each of these will yield slightly different results, based on the focus and comprehensiveness of the search tool. Some provide full-text searches of Web pages, and some search for keywords in links that have been set up. Other search tools let you focus on specific types of Internet material, such as newsgroup archives or FTP software sites. If you don't find what you are looking for using one search engine, try another. Eventually, you will find one or two favorites, and you can set up bookmarks for them.

• **If your search term is too specific, you may need to broaden it in order to find the information you seek.**   For example, if you were looking for travel information on Montreal, and used only the keyword *Montreal,* you would find a few files, and possibly what

HINT Looking for a particular reference on a very long page of information? Don't forget the search tool on your Web browser. In Lynx, you can search for a term using a slash /. Once you've typed your term, press **enter**, then search for the next occurrence of your term using the letter **n**.

you are looking for. If, however, you also searched using the keyword *travel*, you would come across an archive for the rec.travel discussion group, which posts in-depth travel guides. Several detailed files on Montreal are included here that a too-specific search might miss.

HINT Try these search engines:
OpenText Search Index: **http://www.opentext.com**

InfoSeek: **http://www2.infoseek.com**

Alta Vista: **http://altavista.digital.com**

Excite: **http://www.excite.com**

• **Be aware of the different ways in which information can be posted on the Internet.** There are search tools for different Internet resources: Yahoo searches Web pages, Veronica searches Gopher menus, and Archie searches a database of filenames from FTP sites. There is also a fairly sophisticated resource called WAIS (*Wide Area Information Server*). Sometimes the information you are searching for might be available as a WAIS database. Sometimes information might be hidden in a database that was set up at a particular location within a Web site. For example, Penn Pages from Pennsylvania State University offers a database of their research in such areas as nutrition and agriculture.

• **Be aware of resources that can help you find your way around the Internet.** These include the Clearinghouse for Subject-Oriented Resource Guides; Internic, which makes available a database of Internet databases; and special lists, such as Yanoff's List (*Special Internet Resources*) or John December's Guide to Computer-Managed Communications. Pointers to these and other sources can be found at Yahoo or either of these sites:

Beginner's Luck (also known as the Internet Pearls Index)
    http://www.execpc.com/~wmhogg/beginner.html

Awesome List
    http://www.clark.net/pub/journalism.html
    (Check both Awesome and Truly Awesome.)

• **Although there is abundant information on the Internet, not everything is readily or freely available.** It helps to have a sense of Internet resources: universities, government and research institutions, schools, museums, community groups, and, increasingly, commercial organizations provide information over the Internet. However, where information has been painstakingly gathered, or when it falls under the realm of traditional publishing, only sample files will likely be available, or the material will be available for a cost. The *Encyclopedia Britannica* is on the Internet, but you must

HINT To sample the ways you can search the Internet, access the All-In-One Search Page at **http://www.albany.net/all inone** . This page compiles various Internet search tools, including Web pages and software archives.

pay to access it. Spending time cruising the Net and exploring resources such as Yahoo will help you become familiar with what is and what is not available on the Internet.

• Remember that one of the very best resources on the Internet is other people. If you're searching for a specific piece of information, sometimes participants on a listserver or in a newsgroup can be a great help. The FAQs (Frequently Asked Questions) from some of the discussion groups can be useful as well. You can find pointers to these at Yahoo.

 ## GETTING STARTED

... with the Word Wide Web

Exercise for Teachers: A Visit to EdWeb

Since the World Wide Web is so vast, here is an exercise to help you get a feel for how you might use the Web in the classroom. You can also take this activity as a starting point if you are planning a teachers' workshop.

EdWeb is a Web site with a mandate to provide a focus for ideas on how the Internet can be used in education.

Step 1. Use your Web browser to access EdWeb at **http://K12. cnidr.org** . This site is CNIDR (Center for Networked Information Discovery and Retrieval), the home for a number of good educational resources. Click on EdWeb. Scroll down the page and click on the EdWeb Home Room.

Step 2. One of the best ways to see how teachers and students are using the Internet is to sample Web pages that have been developed by schools. You can access lots of school pages from EdWeb. Scroll down the page to the link titled *Web66 Registry of K12 Schools* on the Web. Click on this link. Now, select an area you'd like to explore. You can choose links for a given country or global listings for K–12 schools. Use the Netscape **Back** button on the toolbar to return to previous pages.

Step 3. Use your Web client software to move back to the EdWeb home page (in Netscape, you can use the **Go** and **View History** selections to return quickly to a site that you've accessed earlier in a session), and then look into other links that appeal to you. The *Role of the WWW in Education* provides such interesting topics as the *History of the Web*, the *Importance of Hypertext*, and the *Web as an Educational Tool.*

(continued)

You might want to sample the *Web's Future in the Classroom*. How do some of these ideas mesh with your own thoughts about how the Web will be used in the classroom of the future?

Step 4. Return to the EdWeb Home Room page. This time, **page down** and select the *Educational Resource Guide*. The Guide offers some excellent pointers to additional Internet resources. Be sure to use the **Bookmark** feature of your browser to save items that you'll want to return to. Click on and check out the list of other useful educational resources on the Web. One of the best features on this list is the pointers to state-sponsored educational sites. Be sure to bookmark your favorites as you explore this site.

A sampling of educational Web sites

The number of Web Sites on the Internet is growing at an astonishing rate. In addition to the great number of sites that are of professional interest to educators, more and more schools are developing their own sites on the World Wide Web. The Web has metamorphosed teachers and students alike into successful cyberjournalists. Appendix B contains many curriculum resources on the Internet, and listed below are some particularly noteworthy Web sites that you might want to sample as a way of familiarizing yourself with the wealth of educational resources on the Internet.

Academy One   Not to be missed, this is an international online resource that includes a Curriculum Database and Index to Online Projects as well as announcements about dozens of Internet projects happening throughout the school year.
  http://nptn.org/cyber.serv/APneP

An Education-Oriented Guide to the Web   Don't miss this site— it is intelligently designed, with a well thought out structure that helps teachers discover how the Web can be used as a learning tool.
  http://www.cs.uidaho.edu/~connie/interests.html

Armadillo   This directory of WWW educational resources has been developed for K–12 school teachers and students. It lists resource materials that teachers can quickly access for lesson plans or as supplementary educational resources for students.
  http://www.rice.edu/armadillo/Rice/Resources/reshome.html

Artsedge   An outstanding resource for arts information, with many links to learning resources.
  http://artsedge.kennedy-center.org

HINT Whenever you do not have the correct address for a resource, try searching for it by name using the Open Text or Alta Vista search engines.

AskERIC Virtual Library Here you'll find lesson plans, satellite images, and links to many other educational resources.
http://ericir.syr.edu

Berit's Best Sites for Children This site points to some excellent resources for K–12 school students aged five to fourteen. The site is organized by general topics that are easy to relate to curriculum areas, including Animals, Astronomy, Dinosaurs, Environment, etc., as well as pointers to elementary schools on the Web.
http://www.cochran.com/theosite/KSites.html

Busy Teachers' Web Site This site was developed with two goals in mind: to offer teachers direct-source materials, lesson plans, and classroom activities; and also to provide an enjoyable and rewarding experience for the teacher who is learning to use the Internet.
http://www.gatech.edu/lcc/idt/Students/Cole/Proj/
K-12/TOC.html

Carrie's Site for Educators This site offers another useful set of links developed with the educator in mind. Check out in particular the *Internet in the Classroom*.
http://www.mtjeff.com/~bodenst/page5.html

Cisco Educational Archive Links to the NASA SpaceLink, Frog Dissection, and more. This site has a *Virtual Schoolhouse* with a meta-library of K–12 school Internet links. The *Classroom* area at

Figure 5-9
Busy Teachers' Web Site

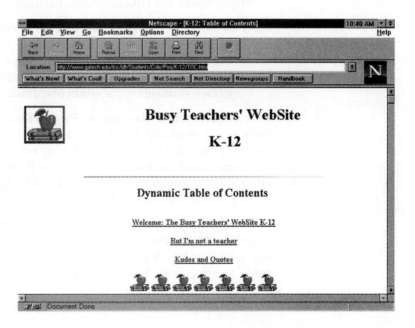

this site offers educational links by subject. The *What's New* feature at the archive is a useful way to track current resources, and *Schoolhouse NOC* provides information on school networking.

http://sunsite.unc.edu/cisco/edu-arch.html

Classroom Connect Education   Links from Wentworth Worldwide Media in Lancaster, PA. An exceptionally good resource for teachers looking for helpful information on the Web, including a FAQ for an Internet acceptable use policy. This site offers a searchable index of educational links as well as a jumpstation to online resources. Wentworth also publishes a wonderful newsletter for teachers, *Classroom Connect*.

http://www.classroom.net/

CyberDewey   If you long for the Internet to be as carefully organized as your local public library, try a visit to this site. The traditional Dewey Decimal library classification system has been used to structure the links.

http://ivory.lm.com/~mundie/DDHC/CyberDewey.html

Cyberspace Middle School   An alphabetical index of interesting interactive multimedia topics and activities on the Web. Each contains a short description of what you will find there. Since this home page began as part of a science program for middle school science teachers, the emphasis is on science. You can help broaden that focus by contacting the address below. Topics include Astronomy, Geology, Mathematics, and more.

http://www.scri.fsu.edu/~dennisl/topics/topics.html

D.K. Brown's Children's Literature Web Site   An excellent resource for elementary school teachers. The focus here is on children's literature. One teacher states, "This may be the single most useful site for elementary teachers that I have found to date."

http://www.ucalgary.ca/~dkbrown/index.html

Doc's Education Resource Pages/Don Cram's List of Links
Very good resource for accessing some basic curriculum-related resources for K–12 students. These education-related Web pages were collected by Don Cram, a mathematics teacher at Kahuku High and Intermediate School, Oahu, HI, USA.

http://www.nmia.com/~cram/

Educational Hotlists from the Science Learning Network's Franklin Museum   You'll find many valuable resources at the Franklin Institute Science Museum. The hotlists identify Web sits of value to educators. Items are added to the hotlist every day, so you may want to consult them often.

http://sln.fi.edu/tfi/hotlists/hotlists.html

Eisenhower Clearinghouse for Math and Science   A repository for K–12 mathematics and science instructional materials funded by the U.S. Department of Education.
　　http://www.enc.org

Exploratorium   From the Palace of Fine Arts in San Francisco, this site includes hundreds of interactive exhibits in broad subject areas such as color, sound, music, emotion, etc. Elementary through secondary students will find this a fascinating site to explore. Includes a monthly selection of the best science and art sites.
　　http://www.exploratorium.edu/

Global Show-n-Tell   An exhibit of children's work on the Web.
　　http://emma.manymedia.com/show-n-tell/sites/sites.html

History Database and Meta Page   Comprehensive resource for history studies.
　　http://www.directnet.com/history

InfoList   Rick Lakin publishes the InfoList newsletter to help keep teachers up to date about new curriculum resources on the Internet. At this Web site, you'll find back issues posted, complete with links, so that you can easily gateway through to sites that interest you. Also check out Rick's personal bookmarks.
　　http://www.electriciti.com/~rlakin

Jan's Favorite K-12 Resources & Projects   An excellent set of links organized by Jan Wee, a middle school media resource specialist. These are organized by topic and curriculum focus. (Whatever this book may have missed in compiling resource lists can be found at Jan's site!)
　　http://badger.state.wi.us/agencies/dpi/www/jans_bkm.html

Janice's K-12 Outpost   A regular newsletter featuring some of the best sites for educators; highlights new resources. This online publication began in 1993 and has been a favorite with teachers. Be sure to sample back issues.
　　http://k12.cnidr.org/janice_k12/

Jumbo   This site calls itself the "official Web shareware site," and it's an excellent resource for newcomers interested in obtaining shareware and freeware. Just find the shareware you want, and click on the program name to download. The site also offers a Getting Started Kit with instructions on how to install and run programs.
　　http://www.jumbo.com/

K-12 Learning Resource Server   Developed by the College of Education at the University of Illinois, this is a particularly well-organized Gopher site that includes curriculum resources and a range of practical information. You can access it using your Web browser.
　　gopher://gopher.ed.uiuc.edu

Kathy Schrock's Guide for Educators A classified list of Internet sites. The links are useful for developing and enhancing curriculum and for teachers' professional development.
http://www.capecod.net/Wixon/Wixon.htm

Kids on Campus Hands-On WWW Demonstration The Cornell Theory Center sponsors Kids On Campus, a computer day for area elementary school students, as part of the University's celebration of the National Science Foundation's National Science and Technology Week. Originally designed as part of the computer event, this site pulls together great resources for kids. Look for the Hands-On WWW demonstration at
http://www.tc.cornell.edu/Kids.on.Campus/

KidsWeb Links to great "kid stuff," broken down by broad subject area. Topics include Animals, Books, Dinosaur Stuff, Geology and Archeology, Magazines for Kids, Movies, Museums and Galleries, Outer Space, Other Pages with Links for Kids, and more.
http://www.npac.syr.edu/textbook/kidsweb/

Mac Educators Page (Macintosh Educators Page Supporting Each Other in a DOS World) A key resource for educators using Macintosh computers, this site includes pointers to many Mac resources. It also includes science and general education links, and many others.
http://www.infonet.net/showcase/macintosh/

Magpie This resource from the University of Wales, Aberystwyth, is intended for educators who wish to explore the educational resources of the Internet. Particularly good for identifying key contacts and resources in Europe and the U.K.
http://www.dcs.aber.ac.uk/~jjw0/index_ht.html

MegaMath An exciting collection of math resources.
http://www.c3.lanl.gov/mega-math/welcome.html

Mini Grants, Information and Freebies This site specializes in practical, useful information for teachers. Worth taking time to sample.
http://www.c3.lanl.gov/~jspeck/mini-grants.shtml

Mustang An offshoot of Web66 (see below), this resource helps teachers learn about publishing on the WWW. It shows how teachers are using the Web, and includes pointers to the best examples and resources for various educational specialties, such as K-6 Educators or Science Educators.
http://web66.coled.umn.edu/

NASA Spacelink Very good resource for science information and projects.
http://spaceliink.msfc.nasa.gov/

NetTeach News   This publication is available as a subscription and has been one of the earliest publications about teaching and telecommunications. Back issues are available on the Web.
http://www.chaos.com/learn/index.html

Network Nuggets   A listserver as well as a Web site for educational resources. Contains a well-developed set of links from the British Columbia Ministry of Education. Highly recommended.
http://www.etc.bc.ca/~/coop/index.html

Online Educator Weekly Hot List   This site is related to a publication called the *Online Educator*. The site gives capsule summaries of new and interesting resources for classrooms and links to the sites so that you can sample the ones that may be of interest. Set up a bookmark to this resource so that you can sample the offerings on a weekly basis.
http://www.cris.com/~felixg/OE/index.shtml

Physics Lecture Demonstrations   A must if you are interested in physics. From astronomy to magnetism to waves, this site covers it all.
http://www.mip.berkeley.edu/physics/physics.html

Pitsco's Launch to Educational Resources   The Resources for Educators Link at this site provides a comprehensive set of links to a wide range of sources that will interest educators, including funding, projects, technology plans, and special-education links.
http://www.pitsco.com

Quest: NASA K-12 Internet Initiative   One of a number of NASA educational resources on the Web, this site is intended to help K–12 teachers fully utilize the Internet as a basic tool for learning. A good resource for information about classroom projects, grants and international projects such as MayaQuest. Select Overview to access a schematic of what's available at this site.
http://quest.arc.nasa.gov/

Sandra's Clip Art Server   For student publishing projects, this is a great resource. You can click to more than two dozen clip art sites, including such specialized collections as Orthodox Christian Clip Art, Golf Clip Art, and Jewish Clip Art. *Caution: Check this site out before you let students go rummaging around.* Some graphics accessible from here might be unsuitable for classroom use. Remember that you can use bookmarks to preselect the resources you want your students to access.
http://www.cs.yale.edu/homes/sjl/clipart.html

Scholastic Gopher   This is a good resource for classroom lessons, and covers many subjects from computer technology to the change

of seasons. There is a very useful Middle School Science Library.
http://www.scholastic.com/public/Learning-Libraries.html

SchoolNet   Canadian-based educational resource with a wealth of useful content.
http://schoolnet2.carleton.ca

Science   This is a "must-visit" for Grades 3 to 6 (ages eight to twelve).
http://www.nbn.com/youcan/

Teacher Talk   A public forum for K–12 school teachers, this site allows users an extremely easy way to share ideas, engage in debate, or simply get to know colleagues around the world.
http://www.mightymedia.com/talk/working.htm

Teacher Topics   The goal of this site is "to make life a little easier for K–12 classroom teachers and students." It provides quick access to K–12 curriculum-based resources. It is organized around common units of classroom study, such as insects, plants, rainforests, and the human body, and includes a hotlist of pointers to additional curriculum resources. You'll be able to identify resources that you can use immediately in units of study.
http://www.asd.k12.ak.us/Andrews/TeacherTopics.html

Teacher's Edition Online   This site features a Teaching Tip of the Day and Lesson Plan of the Day, as well as instructions for subscribing to the online newsletter. The Web version includes links to resources as well as *Class-to-Class*, a resource for linking classes through e-mail.
http://www.southwind.net/~Ishiney/teach.html

Sample *Teacher's Edition Online*, an online magazine for elementary teachers. Published by Lajean Shiney (a fourth grade teacher at Lawrence Elementary School in Wichita, Kansas), it contains classroom tips, curriculum ideas, and teacher-to-teacher and "Ask Dr. Brainstorm" features. An excellent example of an online magazine.

http://www.southwind.net/~Ishiney/index.html

Technology Based Learning Network   Canadian resource for using technology for education. The site includes some useful pointers to resources for elementary through secondary students.
http://www.humanities.mcmaster.ca/~misc2/tblca1.htm

The Education Center   Another comprehensive set of links, this site strives to be "an educational resource dedicated to providing educators with dynamic curricula, projects, and connections to education experts and peers.
http://gnn.com/gnn/meta/edu/index.html

UCI Science Education Programs Office   An excellent collection of science and math resources on the Web.
http://www-sci.lib.uci.edu

Uncle Bob's Kids' Page   An extensive listing of kid-related sites, some educational and some just fun. A popular resource for elementary school.
http://gagme.wwa.com/~boba/kidslinks.html

WebEd k12 Curriculum Links   This page has been under construction since 1993. It is the work of a librarian in search of networked information that will support the curriculum of a local school district. The owner of this site welcomes comments and contributions, and aims to make the page the "most valuable list of evaluated K–12 sites in the Universe."

http://badger.state.wi.us/agencies/dpi/www/WebEd.html

Web66   Find out how to set up your own Internet server and how to link to other educators and students. An extensive listing of useful information for teachers. Includes the *Classroom Internet Server Cookbook* with step-by-step instructions on how to set up a Web site.

http://web66.coled.umn.edu/Web 66

World Lecture Hall   This set of links provides pointers to distance learning courses on the World Wide Web. Here you will find a wealth of resources of particular value to secondary school teachers: essays, commentaries, tutorials, course outlines, sample exams, and a good selection of full courses.

http://www.utexas.edu/world/instruction/index.html

We've left space on the next page for you to list your own favorite Web sites. Happy hunting!

PERSONAL FAVORITES

Use this page to make notes on your own favorite Web sites.

Site: _____

http:// _____

Notes: _____

Site: _____

http:// _____

Notes: _____

Site: _____

http:// _____

Notes: _____

Site: _____

http:// _____

Notes: _____

Site: _____

http:// _____

Notes: _____

Site: _____

http:// _____

Notes: _____

Figure 5-10
**Using the Internet to
research class projects**

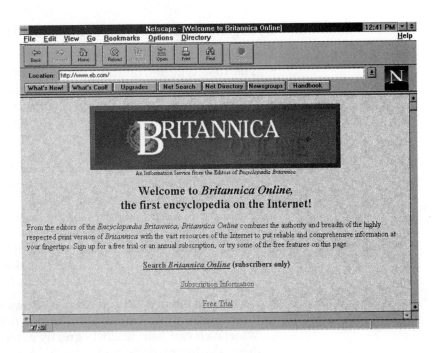

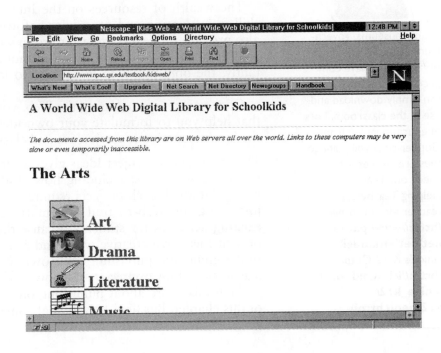

Bringing the World Wide Web into the classroom

The Project Ideas in this chapter are of three general types.

- The first type introduces your students to a Web browser and shows them how to find things on the Internet. It is essential that students know how to find the information they need. This is similar to learning how to use a card catalog in a library. Students will need to know how to use a Web browser, how to access a site using a URL, and how to search the Net using Yahoo or some other search engine. The Project Ideas that follow contain lessons to help students master these skills.

    Learning how to navigate the Web can be spread over several lessons. Use your judgment about how much time to spend on navigating activities and which features of the browser will be the most useful to your students. For example, a basic skill would be knowing how to move in and out of a document, but saving a file or viewing source information are skills that can be learned later.

- A second category of Project Ideas shows students how to use the Internet to complement print-based information. The World Wide Web can help teachers greatly extend the research that students do for projects and reports. A study of earthquakes, for example, can extend beyond the culling of print materials in the library to accessing online weather research stations, news reports, and even special sites set up for reporting on earthquakes.

    The wealth of resources on the Internet helps students gain skill in evaluating and organizing information. These resources also provide an ideal context for group work. One goal in such a project might be to learn about earthquakes, but more importantly, the objective is to learn how to locate, sift through and organize information.

    Once you get started using the Web, you'll soon find resources that help you to formulate your own ideas on how to integrate the Internet into your curriculum and class projects.

- The third type of Project Ideas gives a sense of the range of curriculum possibilities, including how students can develop Web pages. Although such projects require a higher level of skill than just using the Web to find information, they are particularly exciting activities for students because they give them a way to present their own creative work and research findings to others. In designing and publishing their own Web pages, students and teachers can fully appreciate the power of the Internet.

    We'll talk more about publishing on the Web toward the end of this chapter. But first, let's look at some Project Ideas that will get students started using the Web.

Many museums, government agencies, and news organizations have compiled resources that you can simply download and use in the classroom. Lots of educational Web and Gopher sites will point to these resources. Also, check out Teachers Helping Teachers, a teacher idea exchange (**http://www.pacific-net.net/~mandel**) and Janice's K-12 Outpost (**http://k12.cnidr.org/janice_k12/k12menu.html**).

Project Ideas

Learning to Navigate the World Wide Web

Learning outcomes
- Students will learn to use a Web browser and become familiar with the kinds of information they can find on the World Wide Web.

Grade level: 4–8

Getting started
- Identify the default home page that should appear when your students first log on to the World Wide Web. It is simplest to use the default home page that comes with your browser, but if you have been using the Net for awhile yourself, you may want to have them go to a different home page or even to a customized home page on the local system that you've set up yourself. (For more information on how to do this, check the section at the end of this chapter on developing Web pages.)
- Take time to allow students to become familiar with their Web client software. Explain and have them explore the various menu options and buttons for navigation. Explain the concept of links, and have them sample various links. Point out how the information in the URL window changes as they access different sites.

Developing
- Explain the concept of a URL to your students. Be sure to explain how the Internet can be used to access different kinds of resources (e.g., Web sites as well as Gopher sites). List some examples of URLs on the board. Be sure to include URLs for local files (e.g., *file:///C\/internet/randy.htm* in which the file *randy.htm* is located in the *internet* subdirectory on the local C drive).
- Review some of the reasons why a URL might not work, reminding students that a server might be down or excessively busy, or that a file might be removed. Be sure to suggest that they try the technique of omitting the filename at the end of the URL if they have trouble accessing a site the first time.

Extending

- Now your students are ready to apply what they have learned. Following is a sample scavenger hunt (which may be photocopied or otherwise reproduced for classroom use). In this exercise, students are given a series of specific URLs, and will be asked to provide one or more pieces of information from each site. In some cases, they may have to explore to find the required information.
- Finally, students will have an opportunity to search the Net using WebCrawler. Be sure to give them ample time to complete the assignment. Accessing each site and having a chance to explore will likely require more than one class session. Instruct them to complete the sheet in a more or less random fashion, so that they are not all trying to access the same site at the same time. Tell them that if they have difficulty accessing one site, they should move on to another and try again later.

Students will need time to explore the Web browser on their own before using it in a class project

INTERNET LEARNING HUNT

Directions: Complete as many of the items below as you can. In each case, begin by typing the designated URL. Once you access a site, hunt for the information you are asked to provide. If a site you are trying to reach to seems to be taking too much time, cancel the connection and return to it later.

1. **http://volcano.und.nodak.edu/**
   Name a place where a volcano has recently erupted.

   When did this eruption take place? _____

   _____

2. **http://sln.fi.edu/tfi/virtual/vir-summ.html**
   Benjamin Franklin was an expert in many different fields. You can find out about Benjamin Franklin at the Benjamin Franklin Museum. Name two fields in which Benjamin Franklin excelled.

   _____

   _____

3. **http://www.fws.gov/**
   The U.S. Fish and Wildlife Service is one place to find out about animals. Try this link. Look for Wildlife Species Information, and name two species of animals that you can learn about here.

   _____

   _____

4. **http://www.bev.net/education/SeaWorld/homepage.html**
   Next, visit Sea World. The blue whale is the largest animal on earth. What is the record size of a blue whale?

   _____feet   _____pounds

5. **http://www.c3.lanl.gov/~cjhamil/SolarSystem/homepage.html**
   Find out about our solar system at Views of the Solar System. This information resource tells us that Jupiter has sixteen satellites. Can you name one? _____

6. **http://www.sas.upenn.edu/African_Studies/**
   K-12/menu_EduKNTR.html
   This URL is for African Studies WWW Country-Specific Information. Select a country from those listed. Now look for the World Fact Book information.

   What country did you select? _____
   What is the population for your country? _____
   What is the population growth rate? _____
   What is the life expectancy? _____

7. **gopher://wiretap.spies.com**
   On the Internet, you can get whole books to download and read. This Gopher site is one place to obtain books. Access this site. Click on Electronic Books at Wiretap. Name one work by Charles Dickens that you can find at this site. _____

   _____

8. **http://www.cco.caltech.edu/~salmon/world.heritage.html**
   Here you will find the UNESCO World Heritage list.

   What heritage site is shared by the U.S. and Canada? _____

   _____

   Name another heritage site in either the U.S. or Canada. _____

   _____

9. **http://ipl.sils.umich.edu/index.text.html**
   Visit the Internet Public Library. Visit the Ready Reference area, where you'll find a section for News/Current Events. Name an item featured under Issues in the News.

   Issue: _____
   Look at some of the information provided about this issue. Would you find these materials helpful if you were writing a

   class report on this topic? _____

10. **http://www.woodwind.com:80/cyberkids/CyberKidsIssues.html**
    You can also find magazines on the Internet. *Cyberkids* is a kids' publication on the Internet. Have a look at a recent issue, and identify a feature article that interests you. Write the title here: _____

11. Use the **back arrow** button on your browser to return to the *Cyberkids* home page. Now check out the Cyberkids Launchpad link. Navigate to a site that interests you. Write down the URL and a brief description of the site you've found.

    URL: _____
    What this site is about: _____

12. **http://webcrawler.com/**
    The WebCrawler lets you search for information on a topic of your choosing. Access the site, then put in the name of your state or province. Click on the word **Search**. Wait for the system to search your topic. List two resources that you found that could be helpful if you were doing a school report on your state

    or province. _____

    _____

Project Ideas

HINT You might want to invite the school librarian to participate in this exercise or suggest ways to expand it.

Searching for Information Online

Learning outcomes
- Students will develop thinking skills related to searching for information electronically.

Grade level: 6–10

Getting started
- Discuss with students some of the ways in which the Internet is the same as, or different from, a library. Here are some points to consider.

LIBRARY	INTERNET
Clear organization by subjects	No clear organization
Subject headings assigned to information	Finding things requires a keyword search
Librarian available to help	No Internet experts; people have to find things for themselves
Librarian selects materials to suit users	Organizations post their own materials; some subjects might be neglected
Resources limited by physical space	Resources almost unlimited (just add new servers)
Information can be out of date	Can include very latest information
Printed format not easily captured	Electronic format easily captured
Sometime closed when you need it	Sometimes too busy; information may have moved to another site

Developing
- Ask students to think about some of the things they might need to consider when searching for material online. Have them work out the following questions with paper and pencil and share their answers:
  1. List the following topics (or alternatives) across the top of your page:
     animals   weather   politics
  2. Under each word, give examples of some more specific terms you could use to search for information on the topic. (e.g., animals: *dogs, livestock,* or *wildlife*)

3. Pick one of the more specific terms and think of some alternative terms you might use to search for information on these (e.g., dogs: *canines; livestock: farm animals*).
4. Take one of your more specific terms and try to think of a term that you could combine it with to make it even more specific (e.g., *dogs* and *training; wildlife* and *habitat*).

- Introduce the concept of truncation (shortening a word to produce more "hits"). Ask students to write down how they would change the word *farming* to make sure they also find references to *farmers* and *farms* (e.g., farm*).

- Pose this question to your class: *How might you go about finding a resource that would tell you the name of the grouping of stars that looks like a bear?* Ask students to think of some other examples where the computer might be confused about what you're looking for if you enter only one term. Here are some samples to get them thinking: *Indian* (for information on North American Aboriginal peoples), *football* (for information about soccer), *courts* (for information on the legal system).

Figure 5-11

Boolean logic

Using Boolean logic ensures an appropriate focus for your search.

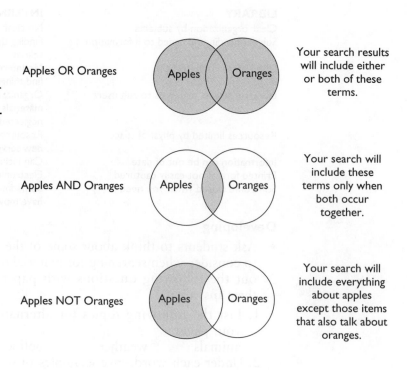

Apples OR Oranges — Your search results will include either or both of these terms.

Apples AND Oranges — Your search will include these terms only when both occur together.

Apples NOT Oranges — Your search will include everything about apples except those items that also talk about oranges.

At **http://www.went-worth.com/classroom/search.htm** you will find pointers to several popular World Wide Web search engines. This site includes a description of various search tools. Print out a copy of the page to use in discussing the different search engines with your class. Ask them to speculate on why there might be so many different ways to search the Web.

Extending
- Draw a diagram on chart paper to illustrate the concept of Boolean searching—that is, using *and*, *or*, and *not* in a search (see Fig. 5–11). Explain that most search engines on the Internet assume that when you include two words in your search you want those words to occur together (e.g., dog training)

- Have students name all the reasons they can think of to explain why they might not be able to find the information they are seeking on the Internet. (Reasons could include a faulty search strategy; spelling mistakes; information may not be there at all; information may be available only in a specialized database that needs to be searched separately, such as a database that stores full-text magazine articles.)

Analyzing their search strategies helps students to sharpen their reasoning and organizational skills.

Project Ideas

Searching for Information on the World Wide Web

Learning outcomes
- Students will develop skill in locating information on the World Wide Web using Yahoo, WebCrawler, and Lycos.

Grade level: 5–9

Getting started
- Ideally, this exercise should be done in conjunction with an actual research project. Alternatively, each student could select a suitable topic for online searching. Be sure to approve student topics in advance to ensure that searching is appropriate and well focused. Sample topics include: tundra, rainforests, deserts, lakes, oceans, stars, forests, taiga, grassland, earthquakes, volcanoes, nutrition, wasps, place names, animal species, current events.

Variations

- (Grades 5–10) Have teams of three or four students each select a different search engine to search for information on the same topic. Ask one student in each group to browse for resources by using the Yahoo subject breakdown, The Whole Internet Catalog at **http://www.gnn.com/wic/newrescat.toc.html** , or by visiting the Internet Public Library at **http://ipl.sils.umich.edu/** . Have all students prepare a list of any useful resources they have found, and discuss together which search technique was most useful. Then have them report back to the class.

- (Grades 5–10) You will find a number of places on the Net that offer a range of searching tools from a single site. A particularly comprehensive one is the All-in-One Search Page. This search page includes a selection of tools for searching the World Wide Web and a range of more specialized tools, such as one for

(continued on page 142)

WORLD WIDE WEB SEARCH

1. Access Yahoo at **http://yahoo.com** .
   Input your search term(s) in the search window and then click on **Search**.

   How many items did your search return? _____
   List two items that could be helpful for researching your topic.

   _____

   _____

   Be sure to set up a bookmark or write down the URL for any resources that you want to return to later.

2. Now try the search again using WebCrawler. Access WebCrawler at **http://webcrawler.com**. Input your search term(s) and click on **Search**.

   How many items did your search return? _____
   List two items that could be helpful for researching your topic. _____

   _____

3. This time search Lycos, which is at OpenText (**http://lycos.cs.cmu.edu**). At this site, check out **Search Options** to see the ways you can customize your search.

   How many items did this list return? _____
   List two items that could be helpful for researching your topic:

   _____

   _____

searching newsgroups. As an exercise, have students access this site
at **http://www.albany.net/~wcross/all1srch.html** . Choose a topic
that might interest your class, such as nutrition or beluga whales.
Assign *one* Web search engine to each student or pair of students.
Have them report their findings to the class. What useful references
did they find? Was the search tool easy to use? Was there anything
they didn't like about this particular searching tool? Students will
want to make note of this page for future projects.

- (Grades 1–4) Develop a list of animals and assign an animal to
  each student for research. Have students access the WebCrawler
  search engine at **http://webcrawler.com** . This search engine has
  a user-friendly interface that younger students will be able to use
  easily. Explain how they can type in the name of their animal to
  retrieve information about it. Have them sample one or two
  items and write down something they have discovered about
  their animal. Have them access any of the following sites to
  obtain more information.

NetVet: **http://netvet.wustl.edu**

Electronic Zoo: **http://netvet.wustl.edu/e-zoo.htm**

SeaWorld Animal Database: **http://www.bev.net/education
/SeaWorld/animal_bytes/animal_bytes.html**

Animal Links Page: **http://www.halcyon.com/kellogg/kelani.html**

There are also a number of online learning tutorials about animals.
Have students try these pages.

All About Bats (from Bat Conservation International):
http://www.batcon.org

California Gray Whales:
http://www.slocs.k12.ca.us/whale/whale0.html

Guidelines for using the World Wide Web in the classroom

- A good rule of thumb is to avoid pursuing as Web projects activities that would work just as well without the Web. For example, don't search for poetry resources online if your school library already has several excellent poetry anthologies. Do, however, think about using the Web if you are in search of in-depth, up-to-the minute weather information or an interactive learning resource.

- One of the best ways to organize classroom use of the Web is to set up a series of bookmarks related to your research project that students can use as a starting point. Ask the school librarian for help with this. If your librarian knows how to use the Net, he or she may be able to identify quickly some of the best resources for your project. If necessary, a preconfigured bookmark file can be copied to individual student machines.

- A valuable technique for enhancing learning is to create opportunities for students to share what they have learned.

One way to share would be to have students create a Web page with pointers accompanied by short personal accounts. These can be stored on a local hard drive. Alternatively, you could have students cut and paste information from a Web site, print it, and collect it in a binder that other students can then page through.

- Although it is generally preferable to have students use the Web only for specific projects, there are a number of sites that can be used as a resource for gifted students or as an enjoyable learning activity for students who finish classroom work early. You could set up your own page with pointers to safe sites (see Chapter 3), selected kids' sites (such as Theodore Tugboat, Uncle Bob's Page, or KidsWeb), favorite museum sites, or a "site of the week."

- When assigning students Web page projects, warn them that URLs can change. If you are having them investigate particular sites (such as museums on

the Net), be sure to have addresses for some back-up sites that students can explore if the original sites don't work out.

- Remember that your aim is not to explore everything that's on the Web, but to work with students in uncovering resources that are particularly relevant to your classroom. If Net access is available in the classroom or school library, try featuring a different subject area each month—geography, wildlife, astronomy, government.

- Probably the most important point to keep in mind is that you don't have to know everything about the Internet or the World Wide Web to introduce a Web project to your students. In fact, an ideal way of using this resource is to involve your students in researching sites and then have them share their discoveries with one another. The teacher's role is not to have all the answers, but to delight in and also learn from students' discoveries.

Project Ideas

Museum Reports

This is similar to a book report but with a Web twist. The exercise is designed to help students explore the World Wide Web in a meaningful fashion. The information they collect can become a helpful resource for other students.

Learning outcomes
- Students will explore Internet sites that have a learning focus.
- Students will gain skill in evaluating Web resources and communicating information to others.

Grade level: 4–8

Getting started
- Museums and science centers offer a wealth of interesting opportunities for learning on the World Wide Web. Any of these might prove to be relevant for a particular unit of study. To find out what is available, have your students prepare museum "reports." One site that you can use to visit a number of science centers around the world is **http://www.cs.cmu.edu/~mwm/sci.html** . Access the site.
- Have students each select a science center they would like to visit. Then have them fill in the information sheet that follows and report back to the class.
- Instruct them to design an eye-catching header for their museum report in which they include the name of the museum and a small picture reprinting its theme. If you have a graphics program and a color printer, students might want to actually download sample graphics from the site to use for their headers.
- File their reports in a binder and make this available as reference for other students to use in exploring the Web.
- Consider this "class report" strategy for collecting references to other types of sites on the Web, such as a selection of sites with environmental information or some favorite kids' sites. Develop a bookmark or Web page (**museums.htm**) to help other students easily access sites that have been reviewed favorably.

Link to the Virtual Library Museums Page:
http://www.comlab.ox.ac.uk/archive/other/museums.html

MUSEUM REPORT

What is the name of the museum that you visited? ———

What is the URL? _____

_____

What is the focus of this museum? (e.g., art, sea animals, history of computers, insects) _____

_____

_____

Describe a special exhibit or feature at this museum that your classmates might find interesting to explore.

_____

_____

_____

Did you find any other resources at this museum that might be helpful if you or one of your classmates were researching a project? _____

What did you like best about this site? _____

_____

_____

_____

Overall, how would you rate this site? (Circle one)

Great   Pretty good   OK

Could be better   Could be a lot better

Figure 5-12
Museums on the Internet

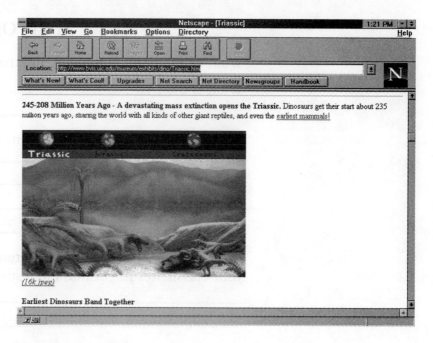

Netscape - [Triassic]   1:21 PM

File   Edit   View   Go   Bookmarks   Options   Directory   Help

Location: http://www.bvis.uic.edu/museum/exhibits/dino/Triassic.html

What's New!   What's Cool!   Upgrades   Net Search   Net Directory   Newsgroups   Handbook

245-208 Million Years Ago - A devastating mass extinction opens the Triassic. Dinosaurs get their start about 235 million years ago, sharing the world with all kinds of other giant reptiles, and even the earliest mammals!

(16k jpeg)

Earliest Dinosaurs Band Together

Variation

- (Grades 1–4)   In this activity, students will create a classroom "scrapbook" of a visit to a museum exhibit. Have each student draw a picture of something in the exhibit and write one or two sentences about what they discovered.

> **HINT** To find exhibits that your students might like, visit the Hotlist at the Science Learning Network's Franklin Institute (**http://sln.fi.edu/tfi/jump.html**), or consult the Elementary School links at the Busy Teacher's WebSite:
> (**http://www.gatech.edu/lcc/idt/Students/Cole/Proj/K-12/TOC.html**).
> You can also check the Hands-On Children's Museum at
> **http://www.wln.com/~de/tapac/hocm.html**

> **HINT** If a classroom helper is available, you can have students download pictures by clicking on the right mouse button from within Netscape and selecting the **Save Image** option. Save the images with a .gif extension. Then print the pictures using a paint package or the L-View viewer available from **http://cwsapps.texas.nct** . If the pictures have been downloaded, have students create color highlights or attractive borders for them.

Using online newspapers and magazines

One of the major ways in which the Internet can have an impact on the classroom is in terms of students' access to news. With the Internet, students can have access to up-to-the-minute news sources, such as news discussion groups or Web pages set up to follow current events. This provides an excellent opportunity for students to

Ask enthusiastic student "surfers" from an upper grade to help you develop a bookmark file or Web page resource of good activities for younger students. A good place to start searching is Berit's Best Sites for Children: **http://www.cochran. com/theosite/KSites.html**

Figure 5-12

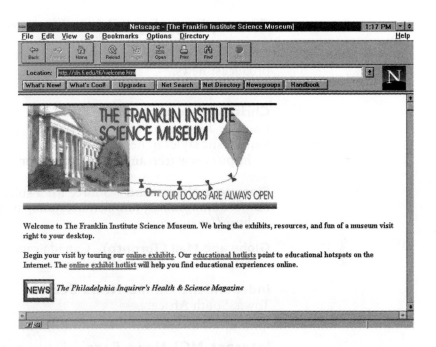

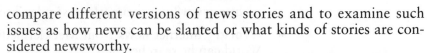

compare different versions of news stories and to examine such issues as how news can be slanted or what kinds of stories are considered newsworthy.

News resources on the Internet can easily be used to track coverage of a story over a period of weeks. For example, students might look at how an election is reported in two different newspapers. Such an activity might be enhanced by accessing discussions within newsgroups dedicated to political issues. Some newspapers and magazines provide archived stories. These can be used to study the events that led up to a story in the light of its outcome.

At the Electronic Newsstand (**http://enews.com**), you will get a list of the current contents for some popular magazines along with one or two sample articles. You can also get selected articles from back issues of magazines. While this resource is intended to entice visitors into subscribing to magazines, it is a good resource for teachers. By browsing sources such as the Electronic Newsstand, you'll discover ways to use online news and magazine stories in the classroom. One magazine recently featured the reflections on life of a ninety-three-year-old woman, while another offered a full-text article on animal poaching in the Amazon rainforest. Such topics could easily be tied to the curriculum.

Because the magazines at this site are intended for adults, this is not a good location for students to roam freely in, but it is a valuable resource for teachers.

Use news broadcast transcripts available from CNN to have students compare the presentation of the news in print and in broadcast. The transcripts could also be used as templates for students to develop their own news interviews and reports.

A sampling of good Internet news sources

CNN   Source for current news, including complete transcripts of broadcast news.
   http://www.cnn.com

Christian Science Monitor   Full-text version available. Excellent resource for comparison with popular press to illustrate different journalistic styles in news coverage.
   http://www.freerange.com/csmonitor

Electronic Newsstand   Source for a substantial selection of articles from magazines, newsletters, newspapers, and more.
   http://enews.com

Globe and Mail (Toronto)   Canada's national newspaper.
   http://www.GlobeAndMail.ca

Independent Online News Service   Cape Times from Cape Town, South Africa.
   http://www.independent.co.sa/news/

Internet MCI News Page   Daily news feeds from Reuters NewsMedia.
   http:www2.pcy.mci.net/news/index.html

iWorld   Internet news from Mecklermedia. Back issues of Internet World can be searched here.
   http://www.mecklerweb.com/

Journalism and Communication Education and Research
International links to academic and educational journalism resources.
   http://www.algonet.se/~nikos/journ/jschools.html

My Virtual Newspaper   This site offers up-to-date links to newspapers around the world.
   http://www.refdesk.com/paper.html

Nando Times   Popular newspaper from Raleigh, North Carolina.
   http://www.nando.net

New York Times   An eight-page version of the *New York Times*. This site requires an Adobe Acrobat viewer, which can be downloaded from the site.
   http://nytimesfax.com

NewsLink   This source claims to be the most comprehensive news resource on the World Wide Web, and it probably is. It includes pointers to newspapers, broadcast sources and magazines, and an excellent selection of special links.
   http://www.newslink.org/

PBS   Online NewsHour and a number of exciting learning projects, including electronic field trips.
http://www.pbs.org

The Media Info Source   This site lists newspaper publishers with online services (including those under development), as well as resources of interest to the news media community. Information is updated regularly.
http://www.mediainfo.com/edpub/e-papers.home.page.html

The Media Literacy Project   Provides information and pointers to Internet resources of value to educators interested in issues related to electronic media.
http://interact.uoregon.edu/MediaLit/HomePage

TechWeb   Links to high-tech publications with full-text information.
http://techweb.cmp.com/techweb/

The Irish Times   Daily news and a comprehensive selection of articles from the *Irish Times*.
http://www.irish-times.com

Time-Warner's Pathfinder   This resource includes full-text information from Time and other magazines, as well as interactive conferencing with regular featured guests.
http://www.pathfinder.com

Times Newspapers Ltd.   British news source that includes the *Sunday Times* and many excellent news features.
http://www.sunday-times.co.uk

USA Today   Regularly updated news and a number of useful archives for student research, such as archives of stories on health issues.
http://www.usatoday.com

Yahoo   News sources on the Internet are increasing at a breathtaking rate. Today, more than 800 supplemental online services are operated or are under development by newspapers worldwide. A good way to find new additions, local sources, and topic-related sources is to check Yahoo. It even lists a selection of student newspapers.
http://www.yahoo.com/News/

The next Project Ideas is intended to help students discover biases in news reporting and to develop analytical thinking skills as they consider what news reports suggest about Russian society and how it differs from their own.

Project Ideas

News from Russia

Learning outcomes
- Students will use news reports to learn about a foreign culture.
- Students will consider how well news reporting reflects a community.
- Students will develop writing skills as they translate their findings into a letter to a friend.

Grade level: 7–8

Getting started
- Have students locate St. Petersburg, Russia, on a map.
- Give students some background on Russia's political history, and take time to discuss what students might already know about life in Russia.

Developing
- Have students access the St. Petersburg Press (**http://www.spb.su/sppress/**), a weekly English-language newspaper from St. Petersburg. While its intended audience is English-speaking people living in Russia, it is nevertheless a good way to give students a glimpse of day-to-day news events in Russia.
- Have all students look at one or two current issues of the newspaper, and have a class discussion in which students are asked to consider how life in Russia is reflected in the news stories. Have them compare the news stories with stories appearing in their own local paper. Discuss in particular how well newspaper reports reflect their communities. This is a particularly interesting exercise, because a look at a foreign newspaper calls into high relief the tendency of all newspapers to focus on "bad news" rather than "good news."
- Next, have students delve into the newspaper's archives. Assign a different issue to each student. Issues should include feature stories, breaking news, business, commentary, classifieds, and culture. Allow sufficient time for students to examine their assigned issues carefully. If time allows, some students may want to look at more than one issue.

Figure 5-13
Media on the Internet

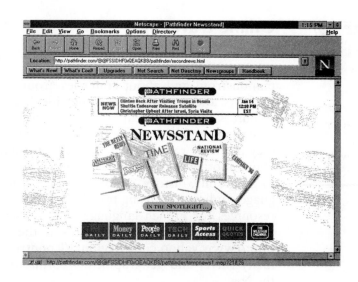

HINT Students can extend their research by accessing this link to all things Russian: **http://www.bucknell.edu/departments/russian/**

Extending

• As a last step, have students write about their discoveries. Ask them to imagine that they are student visitors in Russia. They are writing a letter home and will be using the incidents that they read about to communicate to someone who has never been to Russia just what Russia is really like. Emphasize that in their letters students should communicate both the things that are different about Russian issues and those that are similar to news at home.

Use travel sources to explore a country along with a class project involving students who exchange e-mail with key-pals from other countries.

Online traveling

Part of the value of the Internet is the fact that through it we can reach more than 160 different countries. Tapping into online information from and about countries around the globe will captivate students and stimulate learning. Ideally, students will use online resources to supplement printed material that is available in their classroom or library. The advantage with online resources is that they are wide ranging and can be kept totally up to date. Learning about another country and compiling a report on it can be relevant to geography, history, and other social studies areas, as well as language studies (e.g., using travel information about France as project resources for French language studies). You can link to resources for countries around the globe using the Yahoo Regional index at **http://www.yahoo.com/Regional/Countries/** . You can also use the many travel and geographical information resources available on the Net.

A sampling of Internet travel guides

CIA World Factbook   Published annually in July by the Central Intelligence Agency for the use of U.S. Government officials, this is a great resource for factual information about countries around the world. The Factbook can also be found at many places on the Internet, such as

> **http://www.odci.gov/cia/publications/95fact/index.html**

City.Net   Comprehensive guide to cities around the world.
> **http://www.city.net/**

Country Maps for Europe
> **http://www.tue.nl/europe/**

GNN Travel Centre   Have students take an imaginary trip and report on sights from around the world. The WIC Travel icon points to travel information for specific countries.
> **http://nearnet.gnn.com/gnn/meta/travel/index.html**

Galaxy   A substantial collection of travel and country information, this resource includes links to many guides, directories, travel publications, and FAQs for specific countries. This is another meta-index, like Yahoo.

> **http://galaxy.einet.net**

> **http://galaxy.einet.net/galaxy/**
>   **Leisure-and-Recreation/Travel.html**

> **http://galaxy.einet.net/GJ/countries.html**

Some good travel writing can be found at the GNN Travel Centre. Use this resource to generate ideas for student writing projects or to enhance a geography lesson.

National Atlas Information System (NAIS) Canadian resource with an interactive mapping tool, a community atlas, a geographical factbook, a place name search, a geography quiz, and more.
http://www-nais.ccm.emr.ca/ schoolnet/

Tiger Mapping Service Census and geographic information for the United States. Students will enjoy looking up place names and being able to zoom in on them on a map.
http://tiger.census.gov/

Travel Weekly This site is one of the very best Internet sources for information about other countries. The focus is on travel news, but pointers to U.S. and world destinations are very good. The site also has useful pointers to government travel information, map resources on the Web, and more.
http://www.traveler.net/

W3 A central agency for development of the World Wide Web, providing pointers to servers around the world. This listing can be overwhelming, but its regional organizational structure will ensure that students are able to locate information on the Internet for virtually every country.
http://www.w3.org/hypertext/DataSources/WWW/Servers.html

World Flags Pictures of flags from around the world, with links to the CIA World Factbook (see above). Students will be intrigued by an index that identifies world flags by their design elements, such as the presence of stars or the inclusion of a natural land feature as part of the design.
http://www.adfa.oz.au/CS/flg/col/Index.html

World Wide Web Virtual Library—Geography A comprehensive set of pointers to information resources for individual countries, this site has links to other sites such as the Guide to Australia and Information on India.
http://www.icomos.org/WWW_VL_Geography.html

Figure 5-14
**Using the Internet to
learn about our own and
other countries**

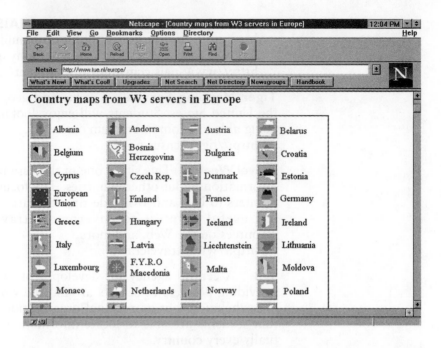

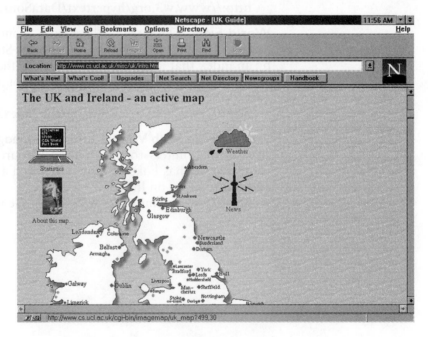

The following Project Ideas is designed to have students explore the Internet as a way of refining and developing their understanding of Africa and its peoples.

Project Ideas

Exploring Africa Online

Learning outcomes
- Students will use the World Wide Web to learn about Africa.
- Students will learn to question their assumptions, synthesize their ideas, and gain practice expressing their ideas in writing.
- Students will gain practice in finding information on the Internet and in working as part of a team.

Grade level: 5–8

Getting started
- Have students access an Internet news resource, print news source, or print encyclopedia to obtain basic information about Africa.
- Post a map of Africa in your classroom. Have a brainstorming session in which students discuss what they already know about Africa. When information relates to a specific country, pinpoint that country on the map.

Developing
- Before attempting further research, have students respond to the true/false questions listed on the next page. Compare answers and discuss. (The online version of this questionnaire is available from

  gopher://gopher.adp.wisc.edu:70/00/.browse/.METAASPCM/.ASPCM02/.00000049)

- Use the questionnaire as a springboard for Internet research about Africa. Have the class identify the broad areas of knowledge reflected in the various questions (e.g., geography, people, history, politics, religion, languages, culture).

Curriculum resources about Africa on the Internet are particularly rich. Pointers to educational resources about Africa are available from

http://www.sas.upenn.edu /African_Studies/K-12/menu_EduBBS.html

This site offers lesson plans, handouts, and full-text articles for studies in African history, geography, politics, languages, religions, social studies, and culture.

QUESTIONNAIRE: PERCEPTIONS OF AFRICA

True or False?

1. Much of Africa consists of rainforest.
2. Most African economies are based upon agriculture.
3. Few modern/technological cities exist in Africa.
4. All Africans are Black.
5. Most African nations are governed by White regimes.
6. Africa has an abundance of mineral wealth.
7. Traditional African religions are prominent in Africa.
8. Africa is a country with Nelson Mandela as president.
9. Africa changed little until its contact with the West.
10. Most African nations received their independence in the 1960s.
11. Africa is the same size as the continental United States.
12. One can see snow in Africa.
13. Most African men tend to marry more than one wife.
14. Africa is a place of great physical danger from wild animals, which roam freely through the countryside.
15. Most African art forms, such as carved masks, would never be used for decoration in an African's home.
16. Divination is a popular form of traditional religion.
17. Drums are the primary form of communication used in Africa.
18. Swahili is a major language spoken in Africa.
19. Most Africans speak several languages.
20. African political and economic affairs have little interest to the rest of the world.

- Divide the class into pairs or groups of three, and assign a different African country to each group. Each student should take responsibility for researching on the Internet two or more of the topics identified in the previous step. Their task will be to prepare one or two paragraphs on their area of research. Students may want to begin their research by accessing the Country-Specific Pages available at the University of Pennsylvania African Studies Web Page (**http://www. sas.upenn.edu/African_Studies/AS.html**). They should also conduct Web searches using one or more of the search tools that can be found at the All-In-One Search Page (**http://www. albany.net/~wcross/all1srch.html**). Invite them to share with their teammates any particularly good resources they locate.

Extending
- As a follow-up, have the class exchange African discoveries. Ask each student to tell the group what he or she has learned about Africa that they didn't know before or found particularly surprising.
- Have the class return to the Perceptions of Africa questionnaire and see if any assumptions have changed.

Variations
- (Grades 5–8) Assign student groups to investigate the broad topics identified above for other countries and develop similar reports. For more in-depth reports, select a single country and assign different topic areas for students to investigate.
- (Grades 3–5) Assign each student an African country. Locate the countries on a classroom map. Have students access the African Country-Specific pages and identify just a few key pieces of information for their country: climate, population, capital city, language spoken, etc. Have students record their findings on a chart. When they have finished assembling their data, have them discuss similarities and differences they have discovered among the countries.

Project Ideas

A Potpourri of Web Projects

The goal for many teachers is to get enough of an idea of what's available on the Web to be able to pick up on relevant resources that complement existing curriculum and classroom activities. These project ideas provide some examples of what is available and how make use of it in the classroom. You will discover more ideas for projects as you explore the sites listed in Appendix B.

- **Book Reports** (Grades 4–8). Have students sample the book reports posted at the Book Nook. There are some great lists of good children's books waiting to be reviewed by kids. Students can select one of these or another of their choosing, write and submit a review to the Book Nook.
  http://i-site.on.ca/Isite/Education/Bk_report/

- **Local Heroes** (Grades 4–8). Stony Mountain School in Manitoba, Canada has developed a Web page based on the idea of local heroes. Discuss the concept of a hero with your class and have them suggest ideas about who might qualify as a hero in their own community. Then have students access the Local Hero home page from Stony Mountain School and compare their ideas with those included at the site. Have each student write a story about a local hero and submit the class favorites to Bonnie McMurran, a teacher at Stony Mountain (mcmurren@ minet.gov.mb.ca). The URL for this site is
  http://www.mbnet.mb.ca/~stonymtn/localhero.html

- **Learning about Planets** (Grades 4–8). Visit the Planet Earth home page Solar System Information. This is a terrific place for students to use as a starting point for studying the Solar System. Have younger students search for the names of the planets and their relative sizes, and record this information on their own handmade charts. Older students can prepare in-depth reports, following relevant links and searching for other information on the Web.
  http://www.nosc.mil/planet_earth/planets.html

- **Flags of the World** (Grades 4–8). Have students download images of flags from around the world and incorporate these into geography reports. This site provides images of flags from a great many countries with links to additional information about the county.
http://www.adfa.oz.au/CS/flg/col/Index.html

- **Solving Math Puzzles** (Grades K–12). MathMagic is a stimulating Web site for kids who like solving mathematical puzzles. Current and past puzzles are posted for different grade levels. Visit the site yourself, or select a student to visit this site and come back with a puzzler to present to the class for solution.
http://forum.swarthmore.edu/mathmagic/

- **Online Scrap Books** (Grades 4–10). Have students make an electronic scrapbook. First, check out Amy's Amazing Adventure. This site is a creative account of Amy's experience at summer camp. Amy has also identified resources on the Net where a visitor to her Web page can learn more about a topic. The site will generate other ideas for similar classroom projects. The exercise will help develop student skills in writing and Web-based research.
http://sln.fi.edu/camp/camp.html

- **Developing Language Skills through Fables** (Grades 1–4). Students can use the Fluency through Fables site to help develop language skills Lessons include vocabulary development and comprehension exercises. Have students access the site and read the current or an assigned fable. Have them complete the exercises online. Then use the discussion questions for an actual in-class discussion or written exercise. Have them compose a group response to the discussion and select a volunteer to submit your class response for posting at this site.
http://www.comenius.com/fable/

- **Learning about Science** (Grades 7–12). John Sechrest has developed a distance learning science Web site for students. Through this site, students develop reading, writing, critical thinking, and problem-solving skills. The site provides examples of topics and related Internet resources that can be researched. It also includes links to a range of sites. Have students work through the learning units on hypothetical reasoning and then have them use the Student as Scientist model to develop their own projects. Once research has been completed, the model can become a format for student Web pages. Access this site to determine other ways that the material could be used for learning about science.
http://www.k14.peak.org

- **Creating a Personalized Newspaper** (Grades 4–12). Crayon is an online resource that allows students to create their own version of an online newspaper. The site draws its news items from actual current Web sites, then mixes and matches them according to your specifications. Allow students to access the site and develop their own customized versions of a newspaper. The newspaper templates that the students create can be saved as HTML files. These then can be accessed and read periodically or daily as a way for students to learn about current events. Take a few minutes each day to have students share with the class items from their online newspapers.
http://sun.bucknell.edu/~boulter/crayon/

- **Women's History** (Grades 7–12). Students can learn the contributions women have made by visiting the Encyclopedia of Women's History. The entries included in the Encyclopedia are all from students. After your students have had a chance to look at this resource, have them share what they've learned with the class. Encourage them to research and submit their own reports to support this project.
http://www.teleport.com/ ~megaines/women.html

- **Learning about Tornadoes** (Grades 4–8). Have students research tornadoes and prepare oral reports for the class. They can find out such things as how tornadoes are formed, where they form, how they are rated, how they die, and what to do if a tornado hits. For comprehensive information on this topic, they can visit the Tornado Web Page:
http://cc.usu.edu/~kforsyth/Tornado.html
Other weather-related resources are available from WeatherNet (**http://cirrus.sprl.umich.edu/wxnet/**) and from Explores, a weather resource for K–12 classrooms (**http://thunder.met.fsu.edu/explores/explores.html**).

- **Learning about Hurricanes** (Grades 5–8). The five-part series Storm Science is a resource developed with the elementary student and teacher in mind. You can supplement this resource with recent online news reports on hurricanes or other storms.
http://www.miamisci.org/hurricane/hurricane0.html

- **Geography Studies** (Grades 5–12). Have students develop their own maps based on selected geographical features. The site also offers a Canadian Geographical Names server and a quiz.
http://www-nais.ccm.emr.ca/schoolnet/
Also check out the wonderful set of map resources available from
http://rowan.lib.utexas.edu/Libs/PCL/
   Map_Collection/map_sites.html

- **Learning about Maps** (Grades 5–10). Use this resource as an introduction to a map-study unit. Have students access the site to learn about different types of maps and to view examples of each. You can also print parts of this page and use it as a handout for a map-study unit.
  http://loki.ur.utk.edu/ut2kids/maps/map.html

- **Midlink Magazine** (Grades 4–8). This is an electronic magazine for students in the middle grades. Issued bi-monthly, Midlink offers an exciting range of learning activities. It includes written contributions from kids, reports on student Internet projects, and pointers to resources that students will enjoy. Each month features a special theme. Some issues contain examples of student portfolios that have been prepared using largely electronic resources. The magazine is an appealing way for middle grade students to get involved in online activities, and you can use this resource to generate your own ideas.
  http://longwood.cs.ucf.edu/~MidLink/

  Cyberkids is a similar resource, with stories and artwork by kids:
  http://www.woodwind.com/mtlake/CyberKids/CyberKids.html

- **Currency Conversion** (Grades 4–9). This excellent Australian resource for learning about currency exchange walks students through the activity step by step. Students can check on currency exchange rates for many different countries dating back to January 1, 1990. They are asked to contribute and compare information on food costs, including the cost of a meal from McDonald's in different countries.
  http://www.pegasus.oz.au/~gorokep12/curcomp1.html

- **Viewing the Earth** (Grades 5–9). This resource gives students a different perspective on the Earth. They can specify longitude and latitude and view locations from the perspective of the Sun or Moon, and they can see the division between night and day in different time zones. This site also points to some public domain software for downloading.
  http://www.fourmilab.ch/earthview/vplanet.html

- **Parts of Speech** (Grades 4–6). Wacky Web Tales is a fun resource that tests students' skill at identifying parts of speech. Students select a story, then fill in parts of speech in the designated fields. They submit their completed forms, and a "wacky" story is returned. (Some teachers may remember this activity as "Madlibs" in pre-computer days. There are Madlibs elsewhere on the Internet, but this source has an exceptionally clear focus.)
  http://www.hmco.com:80/hmco/school/tales/

- **Math Puzzlers** (Grades 3–10). A new set of puzzles is offered every week at this resource. Select a puzzle for your class to solve. Then check for the answers each Thursday when new puzzles and answers to the previous week's puzzles are posted. Puzzles are available for Grades 3/4, 5/6 and 7+. Strong math students may enjoy exploring the math puzzle archives, where previous puzzles are posted along with their solutions.
  http://gnn.com/gnn/meta/edu/curr/math/brain/index.html

- **Learning about Earthquakes** (Grades 7+). The Internet provides many excellent resources for learning about climate and geological phenomena. This site has been designed to instruct about earthquakes by asking questions, and then pointing students to locations where they can find answers.
  http://www.ligature.com

- **Writing** (Grades 5–8). Have your students contribute something to the *Kidopedia*, an encyclopedia written by children. Schools across the world are making their own Kidopedias, and the best articles from each are collected here (at the *Best of Kidopedia*). This resource will generate some ideas for starting your own local Kidopedia.
  http://rdz.stjohns.edu/kidopedia/

"The Kidopedia site is a natural area for teachers and students to contribute. Individual and group work are greatly enhanced. Students can easily become part of a much larger project, while appreciating the uniqueness of their own area. When my class began work on our school Web page, we used it as an extension to the social studies program."

Nancy Barkhouse, Teacher, Atlantic View Elementary School, Lawrencetown, NS, Canada

- **Resume Writing** (Grades 9–12). Have students access and review the *Résumé Writing Guide for Beginners*, available from Pitt State, and the tips on résumés and cover letters at the Career Center. Students may discuss and compare findings before developing their own résumés, either for imaginary or part-time or summer work.

Pitt State: **http://www.placement.pitt.edu/PTSO/Resguide.html**
Career Center: **http://www.kaplan.com/career/**

HINT For more ideas on classroom project ideas, be sure to check these resources:

Using the Net in School includes a NASA-developed Internet search tool designed specifically to locate educational resources (**http://quest.arc.nasa.gov/net-learning.html**).

Collaborative Projects Registry: How to Find Projects on the Internet (**http://gsn.org/gsn/gsn.projects.registry.html**).

Figure 5-15
Midlink magazine

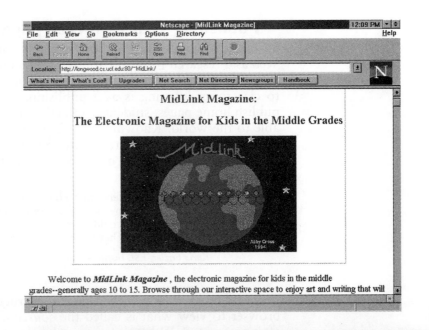

Publishing your own Web pages

So far, we have looked at how students can use the World Wide Web as a research tool, and at how some of its resources can be useful teaching tools. Yet perhaps the Web's most powerful application to classroom learning is as a publishing tool. With the ability to publish home pages, students can make the work that they do available to the world. Knowing how to program in HTML (Hypertext Markup Language) and to create learning resources that can be shared with others is the most exciting part of the Web for many students.

> "What the Web offers students that books, magazines, or videos don't is the opportunity to publish their work for a worldwide audience, which motivates them to write. I wish you could have seen my students last spring creating a Web page for their school. They were so proud!"
>
> *Karla Frizler, ESL Instructor and Founder, Frizzy University Network (FUN), San Francisco, CA, USA*

You can see how a Web page is constructed by using your Web browser to view what is called the *source document*. In Netscape, after accessing a Web page, you can click on **View** and **Source**. The cryptic-looking page that is revealed is in fact the Web page you

Figure 5-16
A secondary school Web page

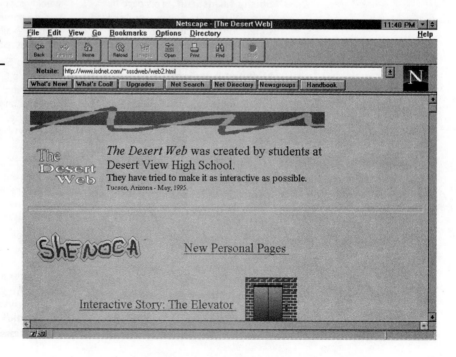

The Teacher's Complete & Easy Guide to the Internet

have accessed, and displays the specific codes that must be interpreted by your Web browser. While a first look at a Web source page can be intimidating, if you take a closer look you'll see that it's not much more than a text document with a series of codes enclosed in brackets. If you take a close look at the sample below, you can discern a combination of the text that appears in the normal viewing of a Web page and a series of tags (which appear in

```
<HTML><HEAD><TITLE>Online Educator
 Samples</TITLE></HEAD>
<BODY bgcolor="#fffff0">
<A HREF="SAFETY.html">[Safety]</A>
<A HREF="OWL.html">[Writing]</A>
<A HREF="NASA.html">[Space]</A>
<A HREF="CUREVEN.html">[Events]</A>
<A HREF="CYBERJ.html">[Cyberjournalists]</A>
<A HREF="QUAKE.html">[Quake]</A>
<A HREF="GEOG.html">[Geography]</A>
<A HREF="EMAIL.html">[E-Mail]</A>
<A HREF="MUSEUM.html">[Museums]</A><br>
<A HREF="../OEWELCOME.html"><IMG WIDTH=220 BORDER=0
    VSPACE=4
SRC="../OEFOLIO.GIF"></A><br> <ADDRESS>A sample article
from our monthly publication
    </ADDRESS>  <hr NOSHADE  SIZE=3>  <STRONG>January
1995</STRONG>
    <hr>
<H1>Caution and good sense keep Net safe</H1>
<P>Taking your students online will open up a whole
world of educational possibilities. It also will present
them and you with the opportunity to come in contact with
questionable material and subjects.
    <P>The Internet can deliver pictures from Jupiter and
Mars into your classroom, and it can also bring nudes and
other inappropriate photos. You can download great works
of literature and documents such as the Declaration of
Independence into your classroom computer, and you can
just as easily get instructions on how to build pipe
bombs or mix chemical explosives.
```

bold type in this example). These tags are just a set of commands that tell your system's viewer

- where specific images should be placed:
  <IMG WIDTH=220 BORDER=0 VSPACE=4 SRC="../OEFO LIO.GIF">
- where to display a link to another file:
  <A HREF="MUSEUM.html">[Museums]</A>
- which text to display in a larger font:
  <H1>Caution and good sense keep Net safe</H1>
- which text to display in bold letters:
  <STRONG>January 1995</STRONG>
- where to place a hard return (which in Netscape appears as a line across the page):
  <hr>

While it is beyond the scope of this book to explain the details of HTML, there are many useful online resources to help you learn about it. Once you have grasped the basics, you will be able to create simple Web pages. These can be used as an online resource, or they can remain on your hard drive for local viewing.

HTML pages can also be printed. You can create a template for students to use in completing projects, and with a laser or bubble-jet printer, HTML pages (minus the images) can look like professional-quality documents.

To get an idea of the kinds of things that students are publishing on the World Wide Web, check out Web 66 (**http://web66.coled.umn.edu/**). The name plays on that of the old highway, Route 66, which at one time was the key east–west link between states. The purpose of this site is to help schools link with one another through their Web sites. The primary goals of Web66 are

- To help K–12 educators learn how to set up their own Internet servers.
- To link K1–2 WWW servers and the educators and students at those schools.
- To help K–12 educators find and use appropriate resources on the WWW.

At Web66, you can link to pages that have been developed by schools and access a substantial amount of material for learning about developing Web pages and setting up your own Web server. Providing Web pages to the world will involve two key elements: (1) Web page development and (2) software that can "serve up" these pages to other people's browsers upon request. For the Macintosh environment, this site offers the *Web66 Classroom Internet Cookbook Server*, or you can link to resources that provide

Figure 5-17
**Web66 helps schools link
with one another
through their Web sits.**

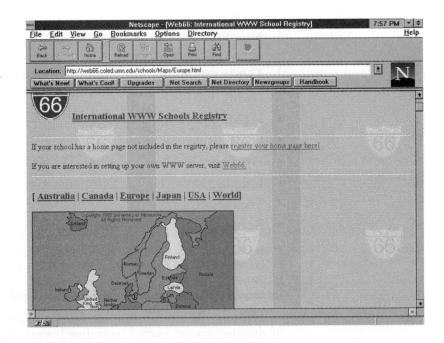

basic instructions and software for a Microsoft Windows server, Unix server, and others.

There are also links to HTML style guides, tutorials, and information. The link *WWW Information*, then *Complete HTML Information*, provides access to the following list of guides as well as a number of references for more advanced applications. Any of the guides listed below can help you master the basics of HTML tagging. In particular, Ian Graham's guide is thorough and well organized; the Crash Course offers a "quick and dirty" overview; *Guides to Writing HTML* Documents provides many useful pointers, including examples of bad Web page design.

- A Beginner's Guide to HTML by the National Center for Supercomputing
- A Beginner's Guide to URLs
- HTML Documentation by Ian S. Graham's (igraham@utirc.utoronto.ca)
- HTML Quick Reference by Michael Grobe (grobe@kuhub.cc.ukans.edu)
- Crash Course on Writing Documents for the Web
- An Information Provider's Guide To HTML
- Documents Related to HTML
- Guides to Writing HTML Documents

HINT Check the Scout Toolkit regularly for information and links to effective network tools:

http://rs.internic.net/ scout/toolkit

HINT Try EdWeb's HTML Crash Course for Educators:
http://k12.cnidr.org:90/htmlguide.html

or Creating Your Own Web Pages:
http://www.cs.uidaho.edu/~connie/interests.html

- HTML FAQ
- HTML Quick Reference
- HTML Tutorial
- Hypertext Markup Language (HTML)
- Introduction to HTML Documentation
- The HTML Language
- Revised HTML Documentation

HINT At GNN, you'll find the Home Page Construction Kit, which gives basic instructions for setting up a Web page as well as a pre-coded HTML template that you can download.
http://gnn.com/gnn/netizens/construction.html

Happily, Web publishing no longer requires you to type in a lot of detailed codes: some streamlined ways have been developed for producing Web-coded pages. A number of word processing applications, such as Word for Windows and WordPerfect, allow you to develop documents in HTML format with great ease. Below are some specialized products for Web page development. Most are freeware or are relatively inexpensive as shareware.

- HTML Assistant
- HotDog Professional
- Web Wizard
- HTML Wirter
- Microsoft Internet Assistant for Word for Windows
- BBEdit Extensions
- HTML Editor for the Macintosh
- Web Weaver

You can link to these applications and to many other resources for Web page development through the World Wide Web server (**http:the//the-inter.net/www/future21/html.html**). You will also find a good selection of applications at The Consummate Winsock Apps List (**http://cwsapps.texas.net/**).

HINT WebLint is a good resource for checking HTML codes. You can cut and paste pieces of code to have it checked, or simply submit the URL for the page you would like to have checked and—voilà!
http://www.unipress.com/web-lint

Once again, the challenge is not so much figuring out the technology, but rather using it in a meaningful way in a classroom setting.

The Web66 WWW Schools Registry (**http://web66.coled.umn.edu/ schools.html**) provides links to hundreds of schools around the world, broken down by geographic location. Accessing this site and using your Web browser is an ideal way to sample the range of school-produced Web pages. In addition to providing basic information about the school and sample class newspapers, many schools also include links to some their favorite sites on the Web.

> "My students are excited and eager both to publish their own work and to see what other kids have done. They think of the Web as some kind of huge 'Just Grandma and Me,' except that they can make the click-places themselves. They love getting e-mail from people who mention seeing their work, and they love sending e-mail to others whose work they like."
>
> *Clare Macdonald, Computer Teacher, Bernadotte School,*
> *Copenhagen, Denmark*

School Web pages have themselves become a way of contributing ideas to the rest of the world. One class collected Halloween stories from other schools (via e-mail) and developed a Web page based on them. Another class was given the task of identifying useful curriculum-based resources and establishing links that either their own classmates and teachers or anyone else accessing their site could use. Students can also use the Web to display their own research reports, creative writing or artwork, or they can profile local community services or events.

But publishing Web pages is not just a way to broadcast the existence of your school to the world. Web publishing is also a significant classroom learning tool. Central to what students will need to master is how to gather, organize, and present information. Working through an activity that involves organizing a set of links or interrelated pieces of information is directly related to developing analytical thinking skills. Gathering information from community groups or another class and develop a Web page offers the opportunity to build and refine verbal and written communication skills. Web pages can be the focus for a cultural exchange in which a school in one country teams up with one or more schools in another country to design a collective site on a topic of common interest, or as a way of highlighting each nation's history, culture, and diversity.

Class projects in Web page publishing can be wide ranging. At Monta Vista High School in Cupertino California (**http:// www.mvhs.edu**), students developed an Internet resources database of useful curriculum materials. Many of the resources they identified were incorporated into Web pages that, in turn, could be used to introduce other students to the Internet. Students involved in the project were expected to locate, evaluate, and describe resources, and to create Internet tutorials and actual lessons, including learning

HINT Check out Ten Tips for Webmasters at **http://www.smartpages. com/worldlink/master. html/**

goals, objectives, procedures, and worksheets that a class might use in a computer lab.

While Monta Vista's project may seem to be particularly sophisticated, Web publishing is not just for students in the upper grades. Atlantic View Elementary School posts a Web page developed by a Grade 3/4 class. Topics from these student's Web pages include:

- food allergies in children
- winter surfing in the North Atlantic
- Lesley Choyce—local author, musician, publisher, surfer
- Gordon Stobbe, our best-known local fiddler
- Rose Porter and Marshland Studio
- in-school performance by Razzmatazz for Kids
- our multicultural folk dance program
- the participation of some of our students in the Nova Scotia International Tattoo
- autobiographies of the students in our class (Grade 3/4B)
- work in progress: the piping plover, an endangered species that nests in our community.

> **HINT** For additional ideas on the development of Web pages in schools, visit the Desert View High School Home Page:
> **http://wacky.ccit.arizona.edu/~susd/dvhome.html**
> And don't miss the Cotton Fields pages, developed by seven-year-olds:
> **http://www.hipark.austin.isd.tenet.edu/home/projects/first/cotton/cotton.html**

One good place to sample school Web sites is at the Classroom Web (**http://www.wentworth.com/classweb/**). Here you can look at school Web pages from many different countries, including Australia, Canada, Denmark, Germany, Japan, Mexico, New Zealand, and Sweden, as well as the fifty states. The pages include school projects, student papers, poetry, drawings, class and school information, information about the students' own countries, and often, links to favorite educational sites.

Posting Web pages

While student Web pages can always be accessed as individual files on a local computer, eventually you will want to post your pages for the world to see. If you are not running a server in your own school, it may be possible to post your Web pages on an existing Internet server for little or no cost. You may wish to contact a local university or Internet service provider about hosting your page. You could also use one of several Internet sites that offer posting for schools, including Classroom Web (**http://www.wentworth.com/classweb/**) and Canada's SchoolNet (**http://schoolnet2.carleton.ca**). In Australia, the SchoolsNET site will post home pages for schools (**http://www.schnet.au**).

HINT Use your Web browser to link to the archives site for the WWWedu mailing list: **http://k12.cnidr.org:90/wwwedu.html**

Figure 5-18

The Cotton Fields pro-
ject was developed by
seven-year-olds at
Highland Park
Elementary School,
Austin, TX.

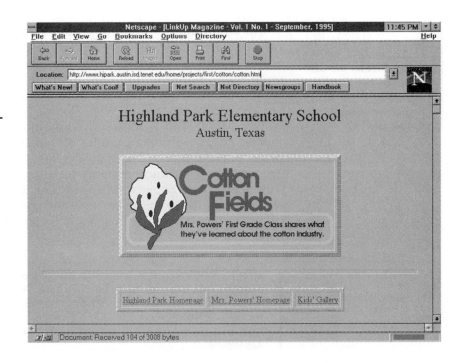

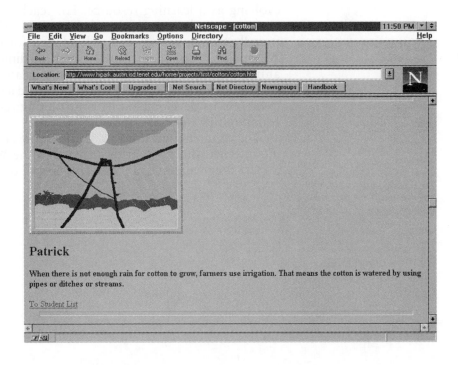

HINT Gleason Sackman maintains the HotList of K–12 Internet School Sites for the USA. You can sample these sites state by state at **http://www.sendit. nodak.edu/k12/**

An important resource for teachers looking at ways to incorporate the Web page development into classroom learning is the School Web Exploration Project (**http://k12.cnidr.org:90/ swep.html**). SchoolWeb is an international coalition of individuals, universities, and other organizations that have as their goal expanding the use of the World Wide Web in K–12 education. The idea behind SchoolWeb is to link schools interested in developing and posting pages with organizations and institutions that are willing to provide server access. The sponsors agree to donate disk space, user accounts, and technical support to help schools develop their site. The SchoolWeb project site maintains a listserv to allow people interested in the program to communicate with one another. It also offers a starter kit to help schools get started on the World Wide Web.

HINT WWWedu is a listserv discussion group dedicated to the use of the World Wide Web in education. To join WWWedu, send a message to **listproc@kudzu.cnidr.org** . The body of the message should read: subscribe wwwedu <your name> .

Also, be sure to check out the additional links to HTML resources listed in Appendix B.

Summing up

The World Wide Web is central to the way in which the Internet is evolving as a learning resource. For teachers, the Web will become an increasingly valuable tool. This is partly because more user-friendly techniques are being developed for designing sophisticated Web pages, with such features as three-dimensional rendering and animation. But the Web derives its greatest value as a learning resource from the fact that students and teachers are actively participating in its development by contributing resources from their own communities and classrooms.

The chapters that follow describe some additional tools for using the Internet. But none of these matches the Web with respect to the impact they will have in the classrooms of today—and tomorrow.

6

Gophers

"I discovered Gopher about two months ago and cannot believe how much information is out there. I have found the Veronica option very helpful as it allows me to build a directory of items that are specific to my interest. ... I am legally blind, and have always said that the most difficult aspect of blindness is the lack of readily available information. Gopher has the ability to change all that. For the first time, I feel like I can easily and independently access important campus and worldwide information. ... I use a speech synthesizer and a PC-compatible computer to access the Gopher system.**"**

— Anonymous user at Michigan State University, quoted in R. Wiggins (1993), "Gopher: A tool for accessing network-based electronic information." The Public-Access Computer Systems Review, 4(2)2, 4–60

Although much of the excitement about the Internet focuses on the World Wide Web, an earlier tool, Gopher, is still one of the easiest ways to access information. Using Gopher, you can fetch satellite weather images from the University of Illinois weather machine, a lesson plan for teaching Macbeth, a capsule profile of Bahrain from a recent edition of the *CIA World Factbook,* or information on Komodo dragon lizards.

Gopher's great strengths lie in the simplicity with which information is presented and in its universality. Although sleek, graphical versions of Gopher are available for Windows- or Macintosh-based systems, Gopher is just as easy to use in a text-only environment— where a lot of us still live. You may have sampled some Gopher sites while exploring the World Wide Web, as many Web sites point to Gopher sites as sources of additional information. Gopher sites are easy to recognize, as they present options in a straightforward, numbered list.

This chapter takes a look at the kinds of resources you'll find on Gophers.

Chapter goals

- ■ **To provide an overview of Gophers**
- ■ **To explain key features of Gopher software**
- ■ **To introduce some useful Gopher resources, including Gopher-Jewels and Veronica**
- ■ **To identify a selection of Gopher sites of particular interest to teachers**

Gopher: Overview

This very useful Internet tool was developed in 1991 at the University of Minnesota. The name is derived from the Gopher mascot for the University's Golden Gophers athletic team. Happily (and not coincidentally), the name also describes exactly what Gophers do—they "go fer," or retrieve, information from the vast resources on the Internet. For many types of information, Gopher's way of presenting information—that is, in hierarchical lists—is admirably efficient.

Gophers were initially designed to provide access to local campus information at the University of Minnesota. However, Internet technology made it easy to adapt the Minnesota Gopher to point to and retrieve information resources from other locations, virtually anywhere in the world. Today, Gophers streamline access to the Internet by presenting information through an easy-to-use, menu-based interface.

The menu in Figure 6-1 is from the Reference Desk at NyserNet in New York State (**gopher://nysernet.org:70/11/Reference%20Desk**). The categories here are similar to those in a library. If you are using a Web browser or graphical Gopher client software, you can double-click to access any of these categories. In a non-graphical environment, you would need to type in the number for the item of your choice. In addition to providing a general subject breakdown for Gopher resources, NyserNet provides pointers to other important Gophers, such as Gopher-Jewels and the Rice University Subject Tree.

Figure 6-1
Using Netscape to access the Internet Reference Desk, a typical Gopher menu.

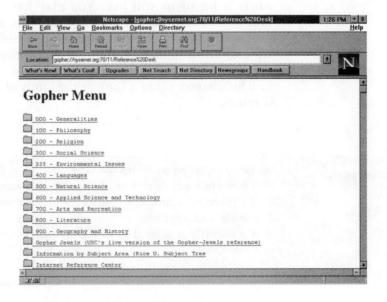

Tech Talk

For complete information about Gopher, access Information About the Gopher Program at **gopher://mudhoney.micro.umn.edu/00/Gopher.FAQ**

While basic navigation of the Internet using a Gopher menu is fairly easy, there is a lot more to know if you want to get the full benefit of using a Gopher. One of the first things to be aware of is that Gopher, like the Web, is based on client/server technology (see Chapter 5).

With a Gopher client, you can access dozens of servers in different parts of the world in just a few minutes simply by selecting Gopher menu options which are set up to point to specific pieces of information on remote Internet servers. Gopher technology has been developed to the point of allowing you to access Web pages, but you will still require a Web browser to view them.

Using Gopher

The first step in entering the Gopher information universe ("GopherSpace") is to access Gopher client software. This is available for just about every computing platform. If you are dialing in to a university or Internet access provider, chances are they will be running a Gopher client on their system. In a non-graphical environment, you can access Gopher simply by dialing in to your Internet node and typing **gopher [return]** at the system prompt. In a Windows or Mac environment, you can call up the Gopher client by double-clicking on the Gopher icon, once you've logged on. Most often, your Internet access provider will give you a range of Internet software, and a Gopher client, such as WSGopher (Windows) or TurboGopher (Macintosh) may be included. If a specific Gopher client is not included in your software package, it may be because you've been provided with an integrated software package. Increasingly, Web browsers are being used in place of special-purpose software, such as Gopher client software.

> **HINT** If your vendor has not provided you with a software client, or if you want to sample other possible clients, you can use FTP (described in Chapter 7) to access Gopher software at: **boombox.micro.umn.edu:/pub/Gopher**

The first menu that appears when you access Gopher is known as the *home Gopher system*. The home Gopher is a starting point in your own environment. Some service providers will point to the original University of Minnesota Gopher as the place to begin navigation. With most graphical clients, you can reset the home Gopher to suit yourself once you have the address of a Gopher you'd like to use as a starting point. If you find a particularly helpful Gopher location, you may be able to bring up that site automatically each time you call up your Gopher.

Regardless of where you start from, Gopher clients are designed to connect to and access information from any Gopher server on the Internet.

> **HINT** With graphical access to the Internet, you will probably prefer to use your World Wide Web browser (e.g., Netscape) to gain access to Internet Gophers.

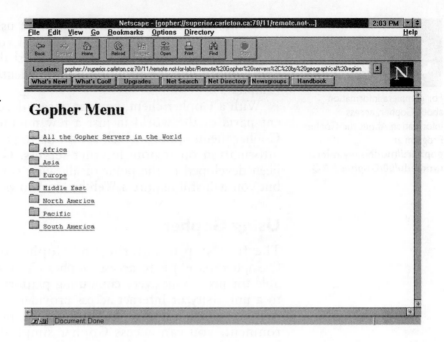

Cruising the Internet using a Gopher client is great fun for awhile, but you will soon want to find specific resources for using the Internet as a learning tool. You'll want to know how to access resources quickly, how to print or save files, and where in GopherSpace some of the best educational resources are located.

Gopher clients incorporate a range of useful functions, and mastering Gopher commands will help you and your students use Gophers more efficiently. Figure 6-3 lists the commands that can be used from a Unix-based Gopher client to move through Gopher menus. (You can access this list of commands online by keying a **?**.)

Similar functions are available from a Windows or Macintosh client, where they can be accessed through a combination of pull-down menus and button icons. Figure 6-4 shows some sample icons used by WSGopher. These buttons allow you to perform various functions, such as fetching a list item that is highlighted in a menu, searching a file that is displayed on a screen, and saving or printing a document. (You can learn more about Windows- and Macintosh-based clients by using the **Help** menus.)

Using bookmarks

One Gopher feature that will help you streamline its use, regardless of your computing environment, is the ability to set bookmarks. Gopher bookmarks are similar to bookmarks in Netscape or Lynx. The bookmark feature lets you build a personal menu of Gopher

Figure 6-3
Sample Gopher commands in a non-graphical environment

NAVIGATING GOPHERSPACE

Press Return	To view a document
Use the Arrow Keys or vi/emacs equivalent	To move around
Up	Move to previous line
Down	Move to next line
Right Return	Enter/Display current item
Left, u	Exit current item/Go up a level
>, +, Pgdwn, space	View next page
<, -, Pgup, b	View previous page
0-9	Go to a specific line
m	Go back to the main menu

Bookmarks
a   Add current item to the bookmark list
A   Add current directory/search to bookmark list
v   View bookmark list
d   Delete a bookmark/directory entry

Other commands
s   Save current item to a file
D   Download a file
q   Quit with prompt
Q   Quit unconditionally
=   Display technical information about current item
o   Open a new Gopher server
/   Search for an item in the menu
n   Find next search item

Figure 6-4
Gopher button icons

resources. If you have begun using bookmarks within your Web client, you know how convenient they are for keeping track of useful sites that you encounter while surfing the Net. When you create a Gopher bookmark, you save the pointer information to specific Gopher resources. Figure 6-5 (page 178) shows an example of information that is retained in a Gopher pointer.

This pointer is all that your Gopher client needs in order to retrieve a piece of information over the Internet. The line **Type 1** indicates that this is a pointer to a directory. What will be retrieved when this menu item is selected is the Subject Tree from Rice University. When you set up a bookmark, your Gopher client will automatically save the path, host, and port information that it will need to retrieve the item. (Port 70 is the default port used by most Gopher servers.)

Figure 6-5
Gopher pointer information in a non-graphical environment

```
Type=1
Name=Subject Tree from
     Rice University
Path=1/Subject
Host=riceinfo.rice.edu
Port=70
URL:
Gopher://riceinfo.rice.edu:
     70/11/Subject
```

In a Unix environment, you can add a bookmark to your personal bookmark menu by typing **a**, or you can add a reference to a directory by typing an upper-case **A**. In order to access or view bookmarks that you have set up previously, type **v** for **View**. Bookmarks will be remembered for subsequent sessions. You can get to your bookmarks at any time from within Gopher. Unix client bookmark commands are itemized in the listing of Sample Gopher Commands (Figure 6-3).

The ability to set up bookmarks for future reference is also available with the graphical Gopher clients. Figure 6-6 shows an example of a bookmark that has been saved in WSGopher.

Downloading files

Another way to keep track of the information you locate using Gophers is to save it—either on your server's remote system, or on your local microcomputer.

From within a Unix-based client, you can save a file on the remote system by typing **s**, and responding to the window prompt for a filename by pressing **enter**. Unfortunately, this results in the file being located on the remote system. With dial-in access to the Internet, in order to transfer the file from the remote system to your local computer you would have to perform a separate download using one of the protocols available on your communications software (such as Xmodem, Zmodem, or Kermit). This option is most useful when your own local network is *directly* connected to the Internet—in other words, it is not a dial-in connection.

A better way to save a file when you want to have it available on your local system is to use an upper-case **D** (Unix client) to download Gopher information to your microcomputer immediately. With the download option, you can download full-text documents, binary files, and pictures.

Figure 6-6
Sample Gopher book-mark menu

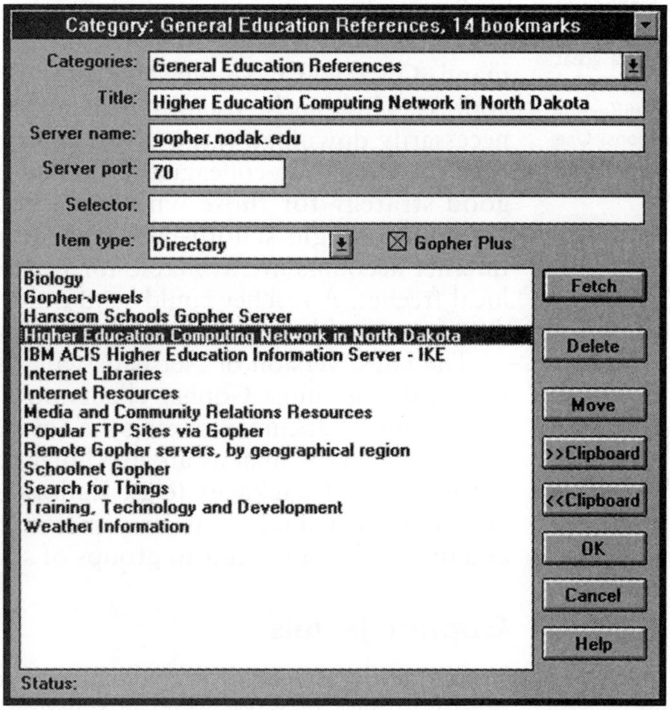

Here are the basic steps for downloading from a Unix-based Gopher client:

1. Point the arrow at the menu item you want
2. Type capital **D**
3. Look at the list of protocols that are displayed in the box (Zmodem, Xmodem, Kermit, etc.)
4. Select the protocol.

The best option is Zmodem (if it is available), followed by Xmodem or Ymodem, and then by Kermit. You may need to consult the manual for your communications software in order to determine which protocol to use, though Zmodem will work in most cases. Your communications manual will also provide you with more information about downloading protocols.

It's even easier to download files using a Windows- or Macintosh-based client. In a graphical environment, you can use the **Save** option from the pull-down menu. TurboGopher (Macintosh) will normally save items as MacWrite documents, but you can choose to save them as text (ASCII) documents for another word processor by using the appropriate **Set** button in the **Options** dialog box.

HINT If you are using your Web browser to access Gophers, downloading from a Gopher site is identical to downloading from a Web site.

HINT The Gopher at the University of California at Irvine offers a great collection of resources for learning about different Internet applications. Use your Gopher client to access **peg.cwis.uci.edu**

Path:
/Accessing the Internet/ PEG, a peripatetic, eclectic Gopher/ Internet Assistance

From a Unix client, you can also save a document by forwarding it as an e-mail message. To mail a document, use the **m** (**Mail**) command. Once you have typed m, you'll be prompted for an e-mail address. This can be useful if you want to read a file later but not necessarily download it, or if you want to send a piece of information to a friend or colleague. E-mailing Gopher files can also be a good strategy for those who are accessing Gopher information through a single school-based account, and where alternative Internet accounts are available for teachers and students through a local freenet. A teacher could send a document to one or more student freenet addresses, or to his or her own personal e-mail address.

The latest version of Netscape will also allow you to mail documents, though most Gopher clients do not. However, you can simply download documents using the **Save** menu option and then send them through the mail as an attachment to a message. Because most graphical mail packages (e.g., Eudora) will let you create group mailboxes, it would be an easy matter to save a file from Gopher and then redistribute this to groups of students, for example.

Gopher-Jewels

Undoubtedly, the biggest challenge in using the Internet generally (and Gophers in particular) is figuring out the location of those pockets of information that you would find most useful. Teachers will be particularly interested in Gopher sites that offer information that is relevant to the curriculum. This could include anything from language studies to biology. Fortunately, a number of Gopher sites (such as Rice University) provide access by subject. In Figure 6-5, we looked at the pointer for the Rice University subject tree. Subject trees are also available from other university Gophers and from the Library of Congress at the Gopher address **marvel.loc.gov** .

Another useful subject resource is Gopher-Jewels, which attempts to group subject resources in a meaningful fashion. Gopher-Jewels provides the ability to search its own list of subject resources with the option:

15. Search Gopher Jewels Menus by Key Word(s) <?>

Figure 6-7 shows a sample root menu for Gopher-Jewels.

HINT In addition to using Gopher-Jewels, you can use other Gopher subject trees to find information in partcular subject areas. Two especially good subject breakdowns are the Washington and Lee University Gopher at **liberty.uc.wlu.edu** and RiceInfo at **riceinfo.rice.edu** .

The Education menu option includes access to K–12 educational Gophers and resources. Figure 6-8 shows some of the educational resources accessible through Gopher-Jewels.

Figure 6-7
Sample root menu for Gopher-Jewels

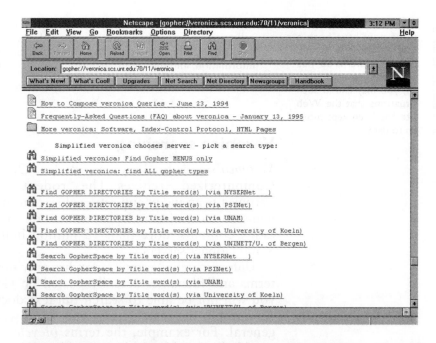

Figure 6-8
Educational resources accessible through Gopher-Jewels

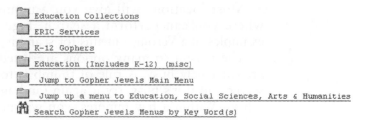

Gopher-Jewels is accessible from many locations on the Internet. Your service provider may include a pointer to Gopher-Jewels under Other Gopher and Information Resources. You can also locate Gopher-Jewels by accessing

gopher://cwis.usc.edu:70/11/Other_Gophers_and_Information_Resources/Gopher-Jewels/academic/education/education .

HINT Many organizations now have both a Gopher and a Web site. Because the Web has acquired greater popularity, you may find in such situations that the Web site has been kept more up to date.

"The Internet Gopher program is not actually a computer program at all, but a collection of magical incantations handed down from Dark Age conjurers. It works by sending magical 'demons' through the air, which scour the world for information, and then return to cast illusions containing the answer."

"Gopher-faq." gopher://mudhoney.micro.umn.edu//00/Gopher.FAQ
(January 16, 1996)

Veronica searching

Veronica stands for *Very Easy Rodent-Oriented Net-wide Index to Computerized Archives.* The "rodent" in this case is Gopher. Veronica is an index and retrieval system that can be used to locate items on most of the Gopher servers on the Internet. The Veronica index contains more than 15 million items from approximately 5,500 Gopher servers.

Unfortunately, Veronica searches only through an index of menu terms and filenames actually posted on Gopher. This means that you will not be able to search full-text documents using Veronica. As a result, the search terms you select will need to be somewhat general. For example, the terms *bicycles, crime,* and *vegetarian* would all probably yield reasonable results, but a very specific topic (such as *Chinese porcelain*) would likely yield nothing more than a notice for a course on Chinese porcelain at a community college located halfway across the country. A too-specific search might yield nothing at all.

You will find Veronica listed as a menu choice at many different Gopher locations. Veronica searching is also available through Gopher-Jewels and at **gopher.tc.umn.edu** under *Other Gopher and Information Servers/Veronica.*

Most locations will give you a number of choices of servers where you can perform a search. Figures 6–9 and 6–10 show examples of a Veronica menus for searching.

The reason so many options are listed is that Veronica servers are extremely busy. A rule of thumb is to try to access a Veronica server and if it's busy, try it again (and again). Then try one of the others. Within a few minutes, you will undoubtedly gain access to at least one of the servers.

In a Veronica search, you will need to determine whether or not you want to search only Gopher directories, or would also like to include actual files. In the latter case, you would choose the option

Search GopherSpace by keywords in Titles

This search will find *all types* of items containing your specified search words. The resources may be ASCII documents, Gopher directories, image files, binary files, and directories.

Figure 6-9

Veronica search menu in GopherSpace

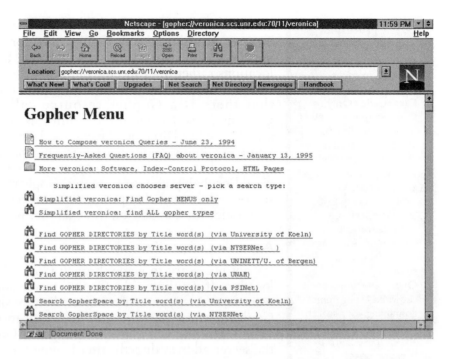

Figure 6-10

A simplified Veronica search enables you to select Gopher directories only, or to include keywords in titles.

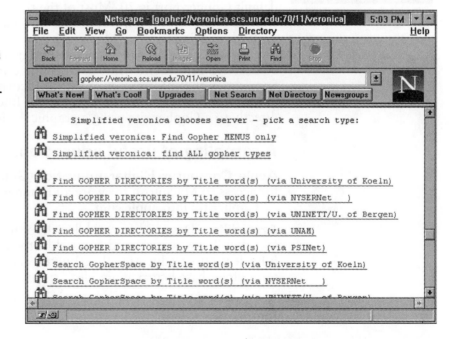

Basic process for searching Veronica

1. Access one of the search locations from the Gopher menu (choose **Directories Only** or **GopherSpace** at any of the locations listed).
2. When prompted for a search term, type in your keyword(s) and press **enter**.
3. Wait for a response from the server.
4. If the server is busy, input your search again to the same or another server.
5. Once a menu has been returned listing items containing your search term, you can access any of these items by pressing **enter**. You can also set up a bookmark for any given menu item.

Search GOPHER DIRECTORIES ONLY for keywords in Titles

This search will find only Gopher directories for item titles containing the specified words. This search will be more useful in finding locations rather than specific files.

For example, if you need information on dyslexia and you recall that there is a Gopher resource called something like the Clearinghouse for Disabilities Information, you might choose to search Gopher Directories using the keyword *Clearinghouse*. But if you don't know about the Clearinghouse and are just hoping that someone has posted something on a Gopher about this topic, you would probably choose to search GopherSpace. However, in doing so you would probably pick up a number of useless references, such as a notice for a course on dyslexia that is given in another city.

Accessing a specific Gopher site

It's not necessary to wade through GopherSpace to get to a specific location. If you know the Gopher server address for a location you want to access, you can get there directly simply by providing your Gopher client with the specific server location.

In Unix, you can gopher directly to a Gopher location by typing the server address directly after issuing the Gopher command at the system prompt.

system prompt > **gopher gopher.schoolnet.carleton.ca**

If you are already in Gopher, use the o command to access a window that will prompt you for a server address. Remember that the default Gopher port is 70. Most of the time, this is the port you will want in order to access a Gopher server on a remote system.

With a Windows- or Macintosh-based client, you can also go directly to a site (Fig. 6–11). Sometimes this option is available under the **File** menu (in WSGopher, click on **New Gopher**). Sometimes the information must be incorporated into the bookmark edit screen. Use your **Help** menu to find out exactly how to go directly to a Gopher site using a graphical client.

A sampling of useful educational Gopher sites

Apple Computer Higher Education Gopher Server   Go here for access to Macintosh freeware and shareware.
Gopher to: **info.apple.com**

Armadillo   Designed for middle school teachers with a particular focus on Texas natural and cultural history, this site presents a useful selection of educational resources and is great for generating technology-based curriculum ideas.

Gopher address: **riceinfo.rice.edu** (Under: *Other Gopher and Information Resources/Armadillo*)

Hints for searching Veronica

- Veronica supports Boolean operators (*and, not,* and *or*). Stringing worlds together in a search yields the same result as using *and* (e.g., *acid rain* will find *acid* references together with those for *rain*). Use *or* sparingly, as the results will likely be hit and miss.
- An asterisk (*) can be used as a wild card, but only at the end of a word. A *wild card* is a key-stroke that you can substitute for actual letters in a filename or keyword. For example, if you or your students were looking for information on farming, you might search for *farm** to make sure that you also picked up ref-erences to *farmers* and *farms*.

- Multiword searches can yield more precise results (search *women voters*, for example, rather than just *women*).
- Using a *-t* flag will limit a search to a certain type of document. For example, if you were looking for a .gif file of van Gogh's *Sunflowers*, you could search the term *sunflowers* along with a *-tg* flag to retrieve a .gif file as the file type. (The type-flag can appear either before or after the search term: i.e., *-tg sunflowers* is the same as *sunflowers -tg*.)
- A Veronica search can yield a number of identical items. Don't be disappointed if an apparent 150 hits turns out to be into only five or six unique items because

the same items were posted on a number of different servers.
- Check out the Veronica FAQ (Frequently Asked Questions), which is often available on the same menu as the Veronica servers.
- If you find yourself frustrated by seemingly endless busy signals, plan to access Veronica during non-peak periods, such as Sunday morning before 9:00.

Some locations also offer a *Jughead search*. Generally, Jughead will locate main items on only one or a select-ed few servers. While this may seem somewhat limited, Jughead is generally a quick way to find infor-mation at an unfamiliar location.

Figure 6-11
Going directly to a Gopher location

Fetch this Gopher Item		3:32 PM
Title:	AskERIC	Paste
Server name:	ericir.syr.edu	Ok
Server port:	70	
Selector:		Cancel
Item type:	Directory ☐ Gopher Plus	Help
URL:		

HINT When using a Web browser, preface your Gopher addresses with the URL designation **gopher://** . However, Gopher clients do not require this prefix—just the Gopher address you want to go to.

AskERIC Virtual Library   A Gopher/FTP site of selected resources for education and general interest. Contents include lesson plans, ERIC digests, references tools, access to library catalogs, and archives of education-related discussion groups.

Gopher to: **ericir.syr.edu**

CiCNet K-12   Selected Internet resources of interest to K–12 school educators, administrators, and students. You'll find two kinds of information here: text descriptions of various online resources, and direct pointers (or links) to online resources. Includes classroom activities and projects.

Gopher to: **gopher.cic.net** (Under: *Other CICNet Projects and Gopher Servers/K-12*)

Consortium for School Networking (CoSN)   Key source for up-to-date information on how to get quick, easy, and cost-effective access to the Internet and online resources. The Consortium describes itself as "the national voice for advocating access to the emerging National Information Infrastructure in schools." Good resource for technology planning.

   Gopher to: **digital.cosn.org**

EdCen Information and Resource   Good selection of educational resources. Check out The Classroom, telecomputing information and software resources.

   Gopher to: **edcen.ehhs.cmich.edu**

Empire Internet Schoolhouse   This site provides a selection of elementary and secondary educational resources, projects, and discussion groups from every corner of the Internet community. Designed with new Internet users in mind.

   Gopher to: **nysernet.org**

IBM Kiosk for Education (IKE)   A Gopher-based server offering IBM information for users in the higher education community. An excellent general resource for information on technology in education. Check out the IKE-BBS Archives.

   Gopher to: **ike.engr.washington.edu**

KidLink Gopher   The focus of the information here is the KidLink series of projects, all of which are intended to involve youth aged ten to fifteen in global dialog through e-mail and other telecommunications exchanges.

   Gopher to: **gopher.kidlink.org**

National School Network Testbed (BBN)   Lesson plans, acceptable use policies, pointers to federal agencies, and other key resources for bringing technology into elementary through secondary schools.

   Gopher to: **copernicus.bbn.com**

Ontario Institute for Studies in Education   Interesting collection of resources for less readily available topics: history, philosophy, women's studies, as well as pointers to other educational resources developed with the involvement of OISE students.

   Gopher to: **gopher.oise.on.ca**

Science Teachers' Corner   This Gopher attempts to provide "one stop shopping" for Internet sciences resources. They even offer a recipe for constructing your own Gopher. A number of other useful resources and pointers are available at this site.

   Gopher to: **gopher.oise.on.ca** (*Under: Internet Resources for Education*)

SchoolNet An excellent Canadian resource. Includes educational information, discussion areas, and learning tools, including creative projects such as the Electronic Innovators program.
Gopher to: **gopher.schoolnet.carleton.ca**

U.S. Consumer Information Center Traditionally, the Consumer Information Center has been a place for teachers to obtain brochures for class projects. Now the Center is online.
Gopher to: **gsa.gov:70+/11/staff/pa/cic**

U.S. Department of Education Gateway to volumes of educational information, including research, statistics, and educational software. (Hint: Try a Jughead search here.)
Gopher to: **gopher.ed.gov**

Washington and Lee University Comprehensive site. The Netlink server provides links to many useful resources such as Usenet news postings and Hytelnet, which can be used to reach libraries, bulletin boards, and other sites requiring an actual logon.
Gopher to: **liberty.uc.wlu.edu**

Ten tips for success with Gophers

- Gopher bookmarks can go out of date as resources get moved around on the Internet. When this happens, you will need to reset your bookmarks.
- Gophers can be very busy. If you get a message indicating that port 70 is not available, it is likely a busy signal. Try again later. Often just a few minutes' wait is necessary.
- If you've just discovered a great Gopher site, keep track of it by setting up a bookmark immediately.
- Remind students to save to a floppy disk (rather than to the hard drive) when they are saving information from a Gopher.
- On a Unix client, the = command will display pointer information for a menu item. Look for a similar display of pointer information on your graphical client.
- Learn more about Gophers by using the Gopher Tips and Help Documents available through Gopher-Jewels under Gopher-Jewels Information and Help.
- You can access a range of other subject trees from within Gopher-Jewels. Select Internet and Computer Related Resources. Then select A List of Gophers with Subject Trees.
- Don't forget to use the Gopher **Search** option (/ in Unix or the **Find** button in Netscape) to search for a specific word in a text file or a lengthy menu that is currently being displayed by Gopher.
- Check out the FAQ, "How to Compose Veronica Queries."
- When you see a Jughead search as an option—give it a try. Jughead will display the range of menu options available at a site in a single menu, rather than as multiple menus that you have to work your way through.

PERSONAL FAVORITES

Use this page to make notes on your own favorite Gopher sites.

Gopher to: _____

Path: _____

Notes: _____

Gopher to: _____

Path: _____

Notes: _____

Gopher to: _____

Path: _____

Notes: _____

Gopher to: _____

Path: _____

Notes: _____

Gopher to: _____

Path: _____

Notes: _____

Gopher to: _____

Path: _____

Notes: _____

Gopher to: _____

Path: _____

Notes: _____

Gopher to: _____

Path: _____

Notes: _____

Gopher to: _____

Path: _____

Notes: _____

What you'll find at the Virtual Reference Desk
The Virtual Reference Desk brings together frequently sought information sources and tools. Coverage includes specific tools (e.g., dictionaries) and sources for such topics as medicine or Gophers.
Gopher to: **peg.cwis.uci.edu**
Select **Library**, then look for the *Virtual Reference Desk*.
Here are just some of the resources you can find at the Virtual Reference Desk:

1. About the Virtual Reference Desk
2. Internet Mall (tm) (SHOPPING-991 stores, shops) by Taylor/
3. GOPHERS: 22 different Gopher groups/
4. INTERNET ASSISTANCE/
6. 6,000,000+ journal articles (via CARL UnCover)/
7. ACRONYMs dictionary/
8. AIDS-Related Information/
9. AskERIC (Educational Resources Information Center)/
10. CIA World Factbook (search by word) <?>
11. CIA World Factbook 1994/
12. Cancer Information for Patient and Layperson/
13. Congressional Directory 104th (search by NAME) <?>
16. Consumer Products and Services Available on the Net/

18. Dictionary American English Dictionary (searchable) <?>
19. Dictionary Webster's Dictionary/
23. Disability Information/
24. E-MAIL ADDRESSES: Internet-wide searches/
25. E-MAIL ADDRESSES: X.500 Gateway/
26. ELECTRONIC FORUMS (listservs): Educator's Guide to E-Mail Lists
28. ELECTRONIC FORUMS (listservs): Search—Educator's Guide to E-M. <?>
30. ELECTRONIC FORUMS (listservs): Search—List of Lists <?>
31. Economic Bulletin Board/
32. Electronic Journals/
33. Electronic Newsstand (tm)/
34. FOOD and DRINK/
35. FedWorld (NTIS)—100+ electronic government bulletin boards/
36. Foreign Currency Exchange Rates (current only)

38. Gardening (via Texas A&M U)/
40. Gopher-JEWELS/
43. INTERNET ASSISTANCE/
44. Information Organization—by Subject (Library of Congress)/
45. LIBRARIES/
52. Periodic Table of the Elements (Physical Properties)/
56. Roget's Thesaurus <?>
60. Stock Market Reports\; S.E.C. Filings/
79. Weather Worldwide current conditions (via Uofl)
80. Webster's Dictionary/
81. Weights & Measures (U. Oregon)
82. \PEG, a Peripatetic, Eclectic Gopher/ (Check this out!)

FYI:
More than 1,000,000 visits to the Virtual Reference Desk will occur in this year. Maybe one will be from you!

Project Ideas

Using Gophers for Environmental Research

Learning outcomes
- Students will learn how to access information on Gophers.

Grade level: 4–7

Getting started
- Ask students to name some of the things that they know are harmful to the environment (e.g., burning fossil fuels, etc.).
- Have students share their feelings about the importance of the environment and the consequences of not caring for it. Here is a poem from the EcoGopher that you can use to stimulate discussion.

> ### Poem about the Earth
> *I am the ill Earth.*
> *People have cut down the trees,*
> *which are my lungs.*
> *They have polluted the air,*
> *which is my brain.*
> *They have polluted the streams,*
> *which are my blood vessels.*
> *They have polluted the oceans,*
> *which are the chambers of my heart.*
> *My wrath has gotten gigantic.*
> *My wrath is hurricanes and tornadoes.*
> *I am the ill Earth.*
> *If people trash me,*
> *I will die and so will they.*
> > Misha Mayr, age 9, El Paso, TX

Developing
- Divide the class into teams. Challenge each team to identify and prepare a list of measures that might help preserve the environment. Each team should be able to list at least fifteen different strategies.

HINT If you are using a Gopher client rather than a Web browser, omit the **gopher://** part of the addresses listed here.

- Students will use Internet Gophers to help develop their lists. Provide them with the following Gopher addresses as starting points.

  EcoGopher Gopher://ecosys.drdr.virginia.edu
  Envirolink Gopher:// envirolink.org
  Econet Gopher://Gopher.igc.apc.org
  Environmental Education Gopher Gopher:/
  /nceet.snre.umich.edu

- Once the students have completed their research, have teams compare their findings.

Variation

- (Grades 6–12) Have students prepare research reports on a range of environmental topics. Students should include a description of their topic, examples of its impact on the environment, and some suggested strategies for dealing with a particular environmental problem or issue. Here are some possible topics that students might choose to research:

  Acid rain
  Alternative energy/Energy
  Biodiversity
  Nuclear power
  Endangered species
  Forestry renewal
  Greenhouse effect
  Hazardous waste/Pollutants
  Oil Spills
  Ozone depletion
  Pesticides
  Recycling
  Renewable energy
  Sustainable agriculture
  Water quality
  Impact of automobiles on the environment.

To help students get started, have them access the Guide to *Environmental Resources on the Internet*, available at the Clearinghouse for Subject-Oriented Internet Resource Guides (**gopher://una.hh.lib.umich.edu**) (select *inetdirs*). They can also use the Gopher addresses listed in the previous exercise as starting points.

HINT A great gopher site for helping teachers discover ways to incorporate the Internet into classroom learning is **quest.arc.nasa.gov** . Here you'll find an excellent selection of lesson plans categorized by grade level and subject, as well as two particularly useful resources: *A Teacher's Guide to Using the Internet* and *Teaching a Class about the Internet.*

HINT *A Guide to Internet Resources for K–12 School Librarians* is available from the Clearinghouse for Subject-Oriented Internet Resource Guides. To locate a copy, gopher to **una.hh.lib.umich.edu** and check in the directory *inetdirs*.

Summing up

Gophers are an important reminder that the Internet is a rapidly changing environment. Many people view Gophers as older Internet technology that is quickly being replaced by the more dynamic environment of the World Wide Web. While it's true that lots of Gopher resources are (or soon will become) available on the World Wide Web, some will not. Teachers who are aware of the range of tools that could be useful in the classroom will be the best judges of which tools will be of most value to their students. Given a choice, most students will prefer the Web to Gopher resources, but teachers will appreciate the wealth of information available on Gophers that can contribute to student learning.

This chapter has given a glimpse of the power of the Internet to transmit information using Gophers. The next chapter describes a number of other tools that can bring the Internet into the classroom.

HINT Looking for full-text resources on the Internet? Try Alex, the first directory to tie several collections of electronic texts together. It actually looks a bit like a library catalog. This project provides access to over 900 titles from Project Gutenberg, Wiretap, the On-line Book Initiative and other electronic text projects. Gopher to: **rsl.ox.ac.uk** (under the *Librarian's Corner/Alex*).

You can also find this resource on the World Wide Web: **http://www.lib.ncsu.edu/stacks/alex-index.html**

Chapter 7

Additional Internet Tools

"Physicists at MIT stood by and watched last week as scientists in California used the Internet to manipulate their fusion reactor from more than 3000 miles away. ... Stephen Wolfe, the physics operations leader for the trial, said, '... we've shown that it doesn't much matter anymore where the physicists and the machines are located, as long as you've got a fast link.'**"**

— QUOTED IN "THE INCREDIBLE SHRINKING LABORATORY," *SCIENCE,* 268 (5207; APRIL 1995), 35.

While more and more applications are being integrated into the World Wide Web, knowing about some additional tools will give teachers a better idea of how the Internet is structured, and access to further resources. The applications discussed in previous chapters—electronic mail, the World Wide Web, and Gophers—represent the areas of greatest interest for teachers using the Internet in the classroom. But FTP, telnet, MOOs, and online video-conferencing also have a distinctive role to play.

Consider, as an example, the fact that you cannot access a computer on the Internet via the World Wide Web or Gopher if that location is not actually running a Web or Gopher server. There are some interesting and useful bulletin board services (BBSs), such as Big Sky Telegraph, that have a wealth of resources for teachers, but to use these effectively, you need to use telnet. Similarly, a teacher may negotiate with a local university to have a class use a specialized piece of software. But if the server is not linked to a Gopher or the Web, gaining access to the software would require the use of telnet. Passing a piece of software or an information file from one computer to another requires the use of FTP (*File Transfer Protocol.*) And if you would like to have your students carry on a real-time dialog with another class, you might be interested in doing this through a MOO.

Chapter goals

- ◾ **To explain the basic process for obtaining files using FTP**
- ◾ **To identify some file types and explain the concept of file compression**
- ◾ **To introduce a method for finding files using a Web-based Archie search**
- ◾ **To identify some useful FTP sites**
- ◾ **To explain the basic telnet process**
- ◾ **To provide an overview of MOOs**
- ◾ **To provide a general introduction to Internet video-conferencing using CU-SeeMe**

This chapter will explain a number of more specialized Internet tools and how they can be used in the classroom.

FTP

FTP is the process used to transfer files from one computer to another, and it can be an extremely powerful and useful application. You can use FTP to obtain updated versions of some of the Internet tools you are currently using. You may use FTP to obtain new viewers for your Web browser. FTP may also be a way for you to access useful shareware or freeware (such as learning software, marking programs, or information files). If you have direct Internet access, you might even use FTP to transfer files from your local machine to another machine on the network.

Although your Internet access provider may have supplied software specifically designed for transferring files (e.g., Fetch or WinFTP), it is possible—and much easier—to transfer these files using Netscape or a similar Web browser. The procedure involves simply designating the URL for the FTP site, just as you did for accessing a Web (**http://**) site. (You may recall from Chapter 5 that a URL for an FTP site looks something like: **ftp://nic.umass.edu** .)

Some Web pages include links to FTP sites. Selecting one of these links brings up a list of files and directories at that site. In this way, you may already have been navigating FTP sites. For example, if you have explored Sandra's Clip Art Server (which was included in Chapter 5 as a favorite Web site), you may have noted that some of the links at this site point to FTP sites that contain graphics.

For many people, it may not be necessary to go beyond the FTP navigation that is available through Web pages. The information in this chapter will give you a procedure for downloading files, and an idea of some things to watch for when navigating such sites.

FTP using Netscape

Here are the steps for retrieving a file from an FTP site using Netscape.

• **Step 1.** Clear the location field and type in the URL, which in this case begins with **ftp://** . When you press **enter**, Netscape will retrieve an actual directory of files from the remote site. If the reference is to a folder, you will see an icon that looks like a folder. Filenames will include the size of the file and whether or not it is compressed. (Compressed files are those that have been "shrunk" to make them easier to transfer and store. This concept is explained in detail later in this chapter.)

• **Step 2.** Scroll through the list to find the directory or file you would like to access. Then simply click on the filename to retrieve

Figure 7-1

A file directory at an FTP site

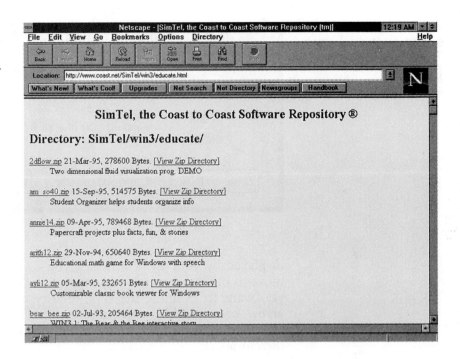

Figure 7-1: A file directory at an FTP site

it. If the file is a text file, it will be displayed on the screen just as a normal file would that might be a part of a Web page. Other types of files, such as large-image files or PostScript (special printer) files, will display only if you have preconfigured your browser with an appropriate viewer (see Chapter 5 for more information about viewers). In some cases, clicking on the file results in an **Unknown File Type** box being displayed (Fig. 7–2, page 196).

• **Step 3.**   The Unknown File Type dialog box gives you three options: **Save to Disk, Cancel Transfer,** or **Configure a Viewer.** In most instances, you'll want to Save to Disk. Simply click on this option to initiate the save.

FTP using Lynx

In a text-based computer environment, you can also use Lynx to transfer files via FTP. Here are the steps involved.

• **Step 1.**   Type **g**, and then type in the URL for the FTP site from which you want to retrieve a file. The URL will specify the Internet address of the site you want to access and may include the names of directories and subdirectories, separated by slashes—for example:
    ftp://nic.umass.edu/pub/ednet/educatrs.lst .

• **Step 2.**   Navigating an FTP directory using Lynx is essentially the same as navigating a Web page. When the initial directory is

Tech Talk

An ASCII file is a text-only file, i.e., a readable file that contains no special characters or formatting codes. The file extension for an ASCII file is **.txt** .

Binary files can be either files that perform a task (such as a software application) or they can be specially coded files, such as word-processed files or compressed files.

Figure 7-2
Should the Unknown File
Type dialog box appear,
click on one of the
options.

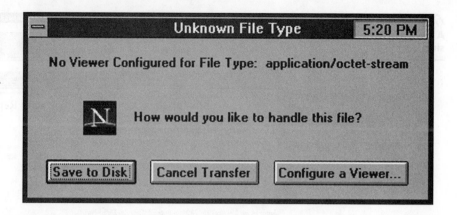

displayed by your Lynx browser, you can use your cursor keys to move to other directories you might want to access. For example, if you want to examine the subdirectory called *pub*, use the **down arrow** key to highlight this directory, then press **enter** or the **right arrow** key. Use the spacebar to move down a lengthy list of files and directories.

• **Step 3.**   Once you spot the file you want to download, highlight the filename and press **enter**. A text file will automatically be displayed on the screen. If the file is a binary file, you will be prompted to type **d** to download or **c** to cancel.

• **Step 4.**   *For text files*: Once the file is displayed on the screen, you can download it by pressing **p** (for print). The next screen will allow you to choose among
• mailing the file to your Internet mailbox and printing or downloading as you would a normal mail message.
• having the complete file scroll rapidly across the screen. This option lets you download the file as a *log file* (an option in your communications software that lets you capture data as they scroll, or appear on the screen). Your communications software manual will tell you which key to use to turn the log file on and off.
• downloading a file using a technique (also called a *protocol*) such as Kermit, Xmodem, Ymodem, or Zmodem. Your communications software manual will provide more information on these, but if you are dealing with a text file, you will be able to capture a file more quickly by saving it as a log file.

For binary files: The Lynx browser will usually immediately recognize any file that cannot be displayed on the screen. When this happens, you will be given a prompt at the bottom of the screen asking whether you want to download or cancel. If you choose to download, the next screen presents you with one or more down-

Tech Talk

Be sure to scan any down-loaded files for viruses before running them on your system. If you don't currently have antivirus software on your computer, ask a local software dealer about obtaining some. McAfee's Viruscan is a popular program that scans for viruses on a PC, while Disinfectant is available for the Macintosh. Another type of program prevents viruses before they become active (e.g., FluShot for the PC, Gatekeeper for Macintosh). To find out more about computer viruses, access the FAQ at **http://www.dmu.ac.uk/ ~rpandit/virhelp.html**

loading options that are available on your local system, such as Kermit or Zmodem. Select the downloading protocol by using your cursor keys to highlight your choice, and then press **enter**. The system will respond by displaying the name of the file that is to be downloaded. You have the opportunity to change the filename at this point if you like. When you press **enter** again, the system will automatically begin to download the requested file onto your hard drive or floppy disk.

If you are not provided with a choice of downloading protocols, but instead are given only the option to save to a file, your Lynx client software will save the file into your file space on your access provider's computer. In this case, you will need to determine what process is in place at the service provider's for downloading. (Sometimes a set of menu options is in place, and sometimes you must activate a transfer program such as Kermit.) Contact your service provider—or a knowledgeable friend or colleague—for more help with this.

These few steps are most of what you need to know to transfer files from within Netscape or Lynx.

Compressed files

While it is relatively easy to download uncompressed text files, sooner or later you will need to deal with a compressed file. These are files that have been "shrunk" using a software program in order to save disk space or to speed up the time required for transfer. There are many different programs that can be used to compress files. The key is to identify and obtain the particular type of software you need to decompress the type of file you have at hand.

Tips for transferring files

1. Always look for an Index or ReadMe file at the remote FTP site. These will help you find your way around an unfamiliar location.
2. Many locations include their share-ware and informa-tion files in a directo-ry called *pub*. The pub directory is a good first place to look on an unfamiliar system.
3. FTP sites can get very busy. If you are attempting to trans-fer a file from a pop-ular FTP site, you may find that you are not able to access it during peak hours. In this case, Netscape will display a message indicating that the connection has failed. Try again later.
4. You can set up bookmarks for your favorite FTP sites or check to see if your browser includes any "built-in" bookmarks to popular FTP resources.

One type of compressed file you will commonly see is *zipped* files. These have a .zip extension. To "unzip" these, you will need a shareware program called PKUnzip. This is available at many locations on the Internet. Sometimes you will see the file automatically included with a group of zipped files that need to be unzipped. You can locate a copy of PKUnzip by searching for it using the Archie Web browser (described below).

To decompress a file using PKUnzip, type the program name (*pkunzip*) followed by the name of the zipped file you want to decompress (e.g., *xxxxx.zip*). Note that the name for this program can vary, so don't be thrown if someone gives you a file they call *PKUnzip* yet which has a somewhat different name. PK204g.exe is a compressed version of both PKUnzip and PKZip, which is the complementary program used to "zip up," or compress, files. When run, this program unpacks itself.

> **HINT** To get a complete list of all file compression/archiving methods and the programs to decompress them on the PC, Mac, Unix, and other systems, use FTP to access the following site and retrieve the file called *compression* (**ftp.cso.uiuc.edu directory: /doc/pcnet/compression**). This document (which, happily, is uncompressed) lists the ways files might be compressed and tells you where to go to get the proper software for decompressing.

In a Windows environment, you can use a utility called WinZip to decompress many different kinds of compressed files. WinZip is shareware; you will need to register your copy if you are going to use it regularly. You can obtain a copy to try from **ftp://FTP.deakin.edu.au** .

Common file formats

The kind of file you are dealing with can usually be identified by its file extension, or the letters following the filename. For example, a document prepared in WordPerfect might have the file extension .wp. Here are some common file extensions.

.txt	Text or ASCII file
.exe	Executable file; performs a task when you double-click on it. Sometimes it will unpack other files.
.ps	PostScript file (must be printed on a PostScript printer)
.gif	A photo or picture file
.jpg	Another type of graphical file
.wav	Sound file
.au	Sound file
.mpg	Moving picture file
.uue	File that has been coded for transfer through e-mail
.hdx	BinHex; a Macintosh compressed file
.sit StuffIt	Macintosh compressed file
.sea	Macintosh compressed file that unpacks itself when you double-click on it
.arc	DOS compressed file
.zip	Zipped file
.tar	Unix file
.Z	Unix compressed file
.gz	Unix compressed file

The Teacher's Complete & Easy Guide to the Internet

Locating files using Archie

Archie is the program that has been designed specifically to find files located on FTP servers. While it is possible to use telnet to access one of a number of sites that offer an Archie service, Archie searches can be performed more easily on the World Wide Web. A number of Web sites offer Archie browsers that prompt you to provide specific pieces of information and then allow you to search one or more Archie servers for the file you are looking for.

You can access a Web-based Archie search at **http://hoohoo.ncsa.uiuc.edu/archie.html** . At this site, you can check out a FAQ document about Anonymous FTP, and you will also find the Monster List of Files. You can even use these resources to access lists of files for downloading at particular sites.

To use this Web-based Archie service, access the site with your Web browser. Type in the name or partial name of the file you're searching for in the field provided. You can select the Archie server you prefer from the list of servers on the screen. (In Lynx, press **enter** on the highlighted term to see the range of options.) Read the search form carefully to take advantage of any special features, and note the cautionary message that the search may take awhile. When you are sure that you have completed the form correctly, begin your search by selecting Submit. The server will return to you a list of FTP sites (called *hosts*) and subdirectories where you can find the item you're searching for. Since the Archie search was performed on the Web, you can immediately link to the location where the file was found.

Figure 7-3
Initiating an Archie search

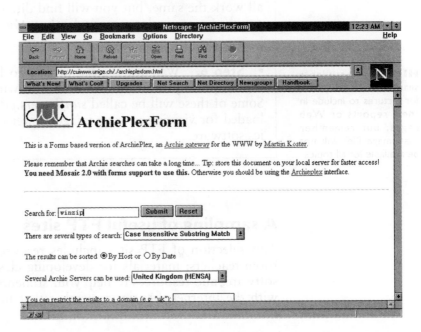

HINT You can search for software and graphics at the All-in-One Search Page:

http://www.albany.net/allinone

GETTING STARTED

... with FTP, Part I

Teacher exercise: Finding files

Although finding a file you're searching for at an FTP site sometimes requires that you have the exact filename, you can sometimes locate files on a topic just by entering a name that makes sense. In this exercise, you can try this technique and learn about Archie searches at the same time.

Let's say that you're searching for an image file of Van Gogh's painting, *Sunflowers*.

- **Step 1.** Use your Web browser to access **http:// hoohoo.ncsa. uiuc.edu/archie.html** .

- **Step 2.** Move to the line specifying "What would you like to search for?" Click on the field or line provided for typing in your term.

- **Step 3.** Type the word *sunflowers*.

- **Step 4.** View the available Archie servers. To do this with a graphical browser, use the scroll bar. In Lynx, highlight the server selection line and press **enter**. You can select any of the servers listed, but it is sometimes recommended that you select one nearest you geographically. Theoretically, the servers should all work the same, but you will find differences based primarily on when a particular server's database was last updated.

- **Step 5.** Click on **Submit**.

- **Step 6.** Wait for the list of files to be returned. Your list should point you to a number of sites with sunflower pictures. Some of these will be called *sunflowers.gif*. These can be downloaded for viewing in your image viewer or for use with graphics software.

HINT Have students search Archie to search for pictures to include in their reports or Web pages, but remember that image files will not be available for all topics.

A sampling of useful FTP sites

This selection of FTP sites includes resources of interest to classroom teachers: materials for developing class projects, educational software, and resources to help your students become more familiar with the Internet. (Again, remember that Internet sites can change daily.)

HINT For a lengthy list of FTP sites of interest to educators, access **ftp://tcet.unt.edu** . In the *pub/telecomputing-info/IRD/* directory, you'll find the document *IRD-FTP-archives.txt.*

AskERIC FTP Site   The resources available at AskERIC through their Web site or Gopher site can also be accessed through FTP. The site includes AskERIC InfoGuides, lesson plans, and information on such subjects such as grants and total quality management.
ftp://ericir.syr.edu

Clearinghouse for Microsoft Windows Software   This is a major computer shareware site, with over 300 Mb of public domain software and shareware. Here you will find a good selection of programs for educators, including math tutors, marking programs, and more.
ftp:// FTP.cica.indiana.edu
(Also try: ftp://oak.oakland.edu/pub/msdos)

Computer Mediated Communications Resources   This site provides directions to information resources and services about the Internet, networking, and about computer-mediated communication (CMC). Check the subdirectories *pub/communications/internet-cmc.*
ftp://fpt.rpi.edu

EASI Archive   An archive of text files related to disabilities.
ftp://um.cc.umich.edu

Exploratorium   FTP resources from the Exploratorium Museum.
ftp://ftp.exploratorium.edu

Gatekeeper   This is a major site with files on a wide variety of subjects. The pub directory contains over 3C subdirectories and includes resources ranging from maps to full-text books.
ftp://gatekeeper.dec.com

Internet Information   A range of resources about the Internet, including FAQs (Frequently Asked Questions) from Usenet newsgroups.
ftp://rtfm.mit.edu/pub/

HINT   Many good sources for using FTP in a Macintosh environment are available from
http://144.174.149.2/mac-ftp-list.html .
Check out these Macin-tosh sources as well:
Technical Support FTP Server
ftp://ftp.support.apple.com/pub
Brian's Repository of Macintosh Information
http://www.cs.wisc.edu/~tuc/mac
MacUser Magazine
http://www.ziff.com:8007/~macuser/
The TSO Macintosh Web Page
http://tso.cin.ix.net/user/fo/fostbt/mac.html
The Well Connected Mac
http://www.macfaq.com/

Kidsnet Teacher Contact Files A repository of information on Kidsnet networking projects. A subdirectory contains lists of useful telnet sites, Gophers, FTP sites, and bulletin board services.
ftp://ftp.vt.edu

Macintosh Archives There are a number of excellent FTP sites for Macintosh computers. These sites include HyperCard stacks, modem software, graphical tools, and QuickTime software and movies. Look in the Mac subdirectory.
ftp://mac.archive.umich.edu

Online Book Initiative Extensive collection of full-text book resources.
ftp://FTP.std.com

SchoolNet The software included here has been selected particularly because of its value to educators. A selection of general software is available here, also—Web browsers, viewers, and utilities such as PKUnzip for unzipping compressed .zip files.
ftp:// schoolnet.carleton.ca

Texas Center for Educational Technology Many documents are available here related to using the Internet in the classroom. Explore the *pub* subdirectory to access these.
ftp:// tcet.unt.edu

Wuarchive This is one of the biggest FTP sites on the Internet. It is known as a *mirror site*, which means that it provides copies of other FTP sites, such as the Stanford University Macintosh archives.
ftp://wuarchive.wustl.edu

A sampling of learning software available from SchoolNet

MACINTOSH

Chain-Stor-Eaze HyperCard stack for creating "chain stories" (each student writes one paragraph).

crazy Aces Simple card game that focuses on mathematics and multiplication.

EarthPlot Allows the Earth to be drawn from any perspective above its surface.

Function Master Algebraic function graphing and manipulating software.

GravSim Simple demonstration of gravity's action on an object near the Earth's surface.

Gravitation 4.0 Excellent simulation of gravitation in a solar system.

Journal Writer Simple application for making daily journal entries.

Mac FAQs Questions (and answers) regarding the Macintosh.

Whales HyperCard stack providing textual information on whales.

DOS

Creativity Package A three-part set to stimulate students' creativity.

Adventure Math An excellent shareware learning experience from the makers of Jill of the Jungle. Solve addition and subtraction problems.

ABC-Talk 2.5 Uses a human voice that teaches children to talk, learn the alphabet, read, spell, and work with a computer.

Animated Clock A program for children from preschool through third grade that teaches them to tell time in a variety of ways. This life-skill program helps children convert digital time to analog time and vice versa.

PERSONAL FAVORITES

Use this page to make notes on your own favorite FTP sites.

Site: ―――――――――――――――――――――――――――――

Description: ―――――――――――――――――――――――――――

Note files: ―――――――――――――――――――――――――――

Site: ―――――――――――――――――――――――――――――

Description: ―――――――――――――――――――――――――――

Note files: ―――――――――――――――――――――――――――

Site: ―――――――――――――――――――――――――――――

Description: ―――――――――――――――――――――――――――

Note files: ―――――――――――――――――――――――――――

Site: ―――――――――――――――――――――――――――――

Description: ―――――――――――――――――――――――――――

Note files: ―――――――――――――――――――――――――――

Site: ―――――――――――――――――――――――――――――

Description: ―――――――――――――――――――――――――――

Note files: ―――――――――――――――――――――――――――

Site: ―――――――――――――――――――――――――――――

Description: ―――――――――――――――――――――――――――

Note files: ―――――――――――――――――――――――――――

Site: ―――――――――――――――――――――――――――――

Description: ―――――――――――――――――――――――――――

Note files: ―――――――――――――――――――――――――――

Site: ―――――――――――――――――――――――――――――

Description: ―――――――――――――――――――――――――――

Note files: ―――――――――――――――――――――――――――

GETTING STARTED

... with FTP, Part II

Teacher exercise: Decompressing files

This exercise will give you practice accessing and downloading a file using FTP. In this case, the file is WinZip, a Windows-based program that you can use to decompress zipped files. WinZip is shareware. You will need to register your copy if you intend to use it.

• **Step 1.** Use your Net browser to access: **ftp://ftp.deakin.edu.au** . Notice that the subsequent display lists a series of filenames and directories, as well as dates and the size of individual files.

• **Step 2.** Click on the *pub* directory. When it appears, use your scroll bar to move to the *pc-net* subdirectory. Select this by clicking on it.

• **Step 2A.** *Only* if you do not already have a copy of PKUnzip, access the *dos* directory. Locate and click on *pkunzip.exe.* Select the **Save to Disk** option from the **Unknown File Type** window. This file will be needed to unzip the WinZip program. Now you will need to use the back arrow key to move to the previous directory. Continue with step 3.

• **Step 3.** Now you can access the Windows directory. Use your scroll bar to locate the *winzip* directory. Click on the directory name.

• **Step 4.** Click on *Winzip50.zip*. When the **Unknown File Type** dialog box appears, click on **Save to Disk** and use the Windows **Save** options for specifying the filename and location.

• **Step 5.** Once you have downloaded the file, establish the directory in which you want it to reside if you have not already done so. Next, use *pkunzip.exe* to unzip your copy of WinZip.

HINT RFC (*Request for Comment*) files are usually technical documents. Two that are of particular interest to teachers are **RFC1578** (*FYI on Questions and Answers to Commonly Asked Primary and Secondary School Internet User Questions*) and **RFC1709** (*K–12 Internetworking Guidelines*). You can access these and other RFCs from

ftp://ds.internic.net/rfc or from

ftp://nis.nsf.net/ internet/documents/rfc

Telnet

Telnet is the application that lets you navigate anywhere on the Internet and actually log on to remote computers. Although telnet is not used nearly as frequently as it used to be, there remain some resources that are simply not available any other way. One common use for telnet is to log on to a computer where you have a second account. Some teachers may have a school account and a separate personal account with an access provider. At a conference or on your summer vacation, you can sometimes find someone who is willing to log you on to their account so that you may telnet to your home account and not have to dial in long distance. There are also some special Internet services, such as MOOs, that are still available only through telnet. (MOOs are described later in this chapter.)

To use telnet, you will need some type of telnet client software. It is possible to telnet using a Web browser, but only if you have set up a telnet helper application in advance. In this case, when you put in the URL for a telnet site, your telnet client will be automatically activated. Once you've finished the telnet session, you will be returned to your Web browser.

In some instances, when you want to run telnet, you may call up your telnet client as a separate application. The main thing that a telnet client will do for you is to allow your smart computer to pretend that it is a dumb terminal. If you configured your own communications software, you may recall the term *terminal emulation*. Large mainframe computers generally require you to "dumb down" your personal computer before they will recognize you. Some common terminal emulation types are VT100, VT102, ANSI, and TTY. On the Internet, VT100 is the most frequently used terminal emulation, so you will probably want to set this as a default on your telnet software.

Your access provider should have given you a copy of some sort of telnet software. In a Macintosh environment you can use NCSA/BYU Telnet; in Windows you may use WinTel, QVTTerm, or another of the available telnet clients. If your service provider has not provided you with telnet software, you can obtain this from Stroud's Consummate Winsock Applications Page at **http://cwsapps. texas.net** (look under *Terminal Apps*). Helper applications for the Macintosh are available from a number of sites. Access **http://www.netscape.com/assist/helper.apps/machelpers.html** for a listing. With any telnet program, you will use the basic menu choices to configure the software and access a site. Remember that you will need to be logged on to your service provider for these applications to work.

If you are dialing in to a Unix computer, you can call up telnet simply by typing **telnet** at the system prompt. You can discover the basic telnet commands by typing **help** at this point. The two basic commands used in telnet are

open followed by the address of the site you wish to go to and **quit** to exit telnet.

The basic information needed for a telnet session is

- the *address* for the site that you want to connect to (e.g., compuserve.com to telnet to a CompuServe account)
- the *logon information* for the site. This could be your name and password for a personal account, or it could be a public logon, such as *bbs* on a telnet site that has been set up for public access.

Hytelnet

Telnet is invaluable if you know where you are going and what you want to do after you get there. Unfortunately, this is not often the case with most users. There are hundreds of specialized computer bulletin boards that can be accessed using telnet, and they are all different. Library catalogs can differ considerably and be difficult to navigate and exit once you have logged on. Be aware that what you see on your computer screen once you've logged on to a telnet site will be very different from the user-friendly Web pages.

> **HINT** Watch carefully for logging off instructions when you are telnetting to a site. On many systems, typing the **Control C** key combination or **Control]** (Control right bracket) may break the connection. You can also exit your telnet client, though it is highly preferable to log off from a site before doing so.

This is where Hytelnet comes in. Hytelnet is available through Gophers and through the World Wide Web as a kind of semiauto-

Figure 7-4
Hytelnet welcome screen

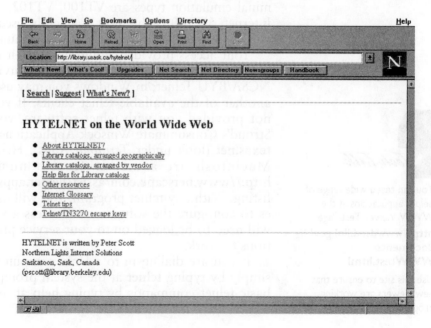

The Teacher's Complete & Easy Guide to the Internet

HINT You can use Hytelnet to gateway to Big Sky Telegraph, which offers teacher resources and lesson plans. Alternatively, you can telnet to **192.231.192.1** Login : bbs

mated telnet function. Hytelnet lists a great many telnet sites, tells you a little bit about them, including how to log on and log off, and allows you to link to a given telnet location. Better yet, you don't require separate telnet software to use the Gopher/Web versions of Hytelnet.

You can access the Web version of Hytelnet at **http:// library.usask.ca/hytelnet** . If you want to sample some telnet resources, use your Web browser to access this site. Select a library, database, freenet, or bulletin board that interests you. The Web site will describe the resource and provide a gateway to the telnet site.

Figure 7-4 shows what the initial Hytelnet screen looks like.

Hytelnet is an excellent way to locate library catalogs on the Internet. It also points you in the direction of many specialized bulletin boards and databases. However, more and more of these databases are moving onto the World Wide Web.

If you choose to sample some of the resources available through Hytelnet, be aware that once you have logged on to a system, it's easy to get lost. Teachers who have previously used online bulletin boards will have a better idea of what to expect. Some systems walk you through a lengthy registration process before you can use them. Generally, you need to watch the screens very carefully to find your way around. Be sure to note any special directions on how to access **Help** information. Most importantly, make note of any special instructions on how to log off from a system. Hytelnet generally provides this information before you log on.

New users will probably want to put unknown telnet sites toward the bottom of their list of new things to explore, but the basic telnet function is essential when you need to access and log on to a remote computer.

A sampling of useful telnet sites

CARL (Colorado Association of Research Libraries)   This site provides a number of interesting databases. Of particular interest is the Uncover service, which lets you search for and order magazine articles. There is a cost involved in having articles sent to you, but you might want to use this resource to get references to articles that might be obtainable through your local library's interlibrary loan service. (This is an outstanding service that school librarians should be aware of.)

telnet:// database.carl.org

Distance Education Database at the UK Open University   An international database for distance learning resources. Includes research and course listings.

telnet://acsvax.open.ac.uk (Username: ICDL; Account code: <Enter a valid country name>; Password: aaa)

National Distance Learning Center   An electronic information source for distance learning programs and resources. Elementary, secondary, and postsecondary continuing education courses are included in this database.

telnet://ndlc.occ.uky.edu (Login: ndlc)

SENDIT K12 Educational Telecommunications Network   This resource offers many online resources for K–12 school teachers.

telnet://sendit.nodak.edu (Login: bbs; Password: sendit2)

Telnet Services Gateway   From this location, you can access more than 150 other telnet sites. Brief descriptions of each site are included.

telnet://library.wustl.edu (To log in at this site, hit return to access the main menu.)

MOOs

MOO stands for *Multiuser Object-Oriented*. One teacher has suggested that MOOs should really be called MUHLs (pronounced "mules"), for *Many Unpleasant Hours Learning*. Indeed, MOOs can be confusing and frustrating to master. But they have the potential to bring such excitement and interest to the classroom that many teachers feel they are worth learning about. MOOs allow you to use the Internet to carry on a real-time conversation with people around the world. They are a bit like a telephone conference call, except that the conversations appear as text on the screen.

MOOs got their start as MUDs (Multi-User Dungeons), an online form of the game Dungeons and Dragons. MUDs are still quite popular on the Internet. But there are some differences between MOOs and MUDs. Perhaps the most important difference, from an educator's perspective, is that MOOs can have a more serious purpose.

An example of how a MOO can be used in an educational context is Diversity University (DU). DU is a MOO that has been set up as a resource for distance education and learning. Distance educators offer courses that use the MOO for professor–student interaction or class discussion. A group of geographically dispersed teachers get together once a week at Media MOO for something called *Netoric Cafe*, during which they discuss their common interest in using computers for writing. On the Canadian SchoolNet MOO, students can work together on group projects even though their classrooms are separated by great distances.

Because MOOs are text-based, they can seem cumbersome and unnatural compared with the World Wide Web. Another reason MOOs can be challenging to master is that they usually rely on the

PERSONAL FAVORITES

Use this page to make notes on your own favorite telnet sites.

Site: _____

Description: _____

Notes: _____

Site: _____

Description: _____

Notes: _____

Site: _____

Description: _____

Notes: _____

Site: _____

Description: _____

Notes: _____

Site: _____

Description: _____

Notes: _____

Site: _____

Description: _____

Notes: _____

Site: _____

Description: _____

Notes: _____

Site: _____

Description: _____

Notes: _____

metaphor of an actual physical location, so that one MOO might include a "foyer," a "study hall," a "lounge," or a "grassy knoll." In order to join in the conversation, you first need to find your way around. Finally, there is the issue of your identity as you enter a MOO. Even though you can often log on as a guest, some MOOs present you with a series of questions—such as what you would like to be called during your visit. (Made-up names are not considered a problem here; in fact, MOO culture encourages you to assume a "character.") Some MOOs will ask you to identify your gender (though the choices frequently include "neutral" and even "royalty"!). Once you have managed to log on to a MOO, you need to use a set of cryptic commands to move about and make yourself heard.

Undoubtedly, there is a considerable learning curve, but many teachers feel that MOOs are worth learning about. For students, the notion of talking to people online generates excitement and a sense of empowerment. They also gain language skills, including the ability to converse in a foreign language. (There are German, Spanish and French MOOs.) Students learn to express themselves clearly, to consult directly with tutors, and generally to "think on their feet." One teacher who has used a MOO to help students improve their writing skills pointed out that students must learn to use language much more precisely in a MOO environment, where the usual auditory and visual clues are not available. On some MOOs you can even establish your own learning space (known as "digging a new room"). Students can work with teachers to design a project and to manage the group consultation process.

Such learning experiences can be rewarding. But teachers planning to use a MOO with students should expect to spend at least fifteen hours familiarizing themselves with the MOO environment. Additional hours will be necessary to plan to manage the experience in the classroom. Students need careful preparation, including instructions about MOO netiquette. Considerable class time is involved, as well. If you're ready to try a MOO—or even if you've decided to save the MOO experience for next year—you can learn more about MOOs by using your Web browser to link to

http://tecfa.unige.ch/edu-comp/WWW-VL/
eduVR-page.html#Contents

Here you can learn how MOOs can be used, what specific client software is available, where to access educational MOOs, and other helpful information for getting started. The linked document for MOO Central (http://www.pitt.edu/~jrgst7/MOOcentral.html) includes a tip sheet for teachers. Some of the links available from this site will allow you to connect to a MOO.

The Teacher's Complete & Easy Guide to the Internet

Basic MOO commands

If you want to try logging on to a MOO, the best advice is to read everything displayed on the screen very carefully. If necessary, read it twice.

connect guest   A common logon. You may need to type this in rather than wait for a login prompt.

@quit   To log off

@who   To see who is currently logged on and in which room, within the MOO, they are located

@join <character name>   To join a character you have found by using the @who command. This can be a quick way to navigate to a room.

look   You can use this command to figure out where you are and what is around you. You can also type **look <object>** to obtain a description of some meaningful item in the room. If the object might convey information, you can type **read <object>** (e.g., read newspaper).

@go   To go to a particular area. You can often navigate using directions, such as **@go north**.

"   Use a quotation mark to precede anything you want to say to the group in your room.

say   This command is the same as the quotation mark in some MOOs.

whisper"<message>" to <character name>   Use this command if you want to speak only to one person in the room.

page <character name> "<message>"   To talk to someone who is not in the room you are in

help   For general help

help index   To view a list of items for which help is available

Be aware that commands can differ slightly from one MOO to the next. The most user-friendly MOOs give you specific prompts at the bottom of each screen to help you move elsewhere. Most MOOs also offer an online tutorial, so watch for these.

HINT MOOs are easier to use with a MOO client (such as TinyFugue for Unix) rather than straight telnet. To find out about clients that run on your platform, access the MOO Client FAQs at

http://info.desy.de/pub/uu-gna/moo/FAQ.txt

"One student who became interested in our MOO expressed a wish to recreate her family's cabin in the mountains, complete with the treehouse and paths that are so dear to her. Her descriptions are beautiful testaments to her love for her family cabin. Now, anyone who logs on to our MOO can see them, and she can show off 'her' place while 'talking' to visitors."

Andrew Smallman, Director, Puget Sound Community School, Seattle, WA, USA

HINT While MOOs can provide a useful learning experience, MUDs and MUSHes (*Multi-User Shared Hallucinations*) are unsuitable for classroom use. Teachers need to be aware that these areas exist online. Once you have introduced students to the techniques for using a MOO, be sure that they respect your rules.

A sampling of MOOs

Daedalus MOO   The focus of this MOO is computer-assisted work in composition.

   telnet://logos.daedalus.com:7777

DU (Diversity University)   Here, teachers and their classes can visit either by using the built-in MOO facilities or by assuming a character and setting up their own classroom at DU.

   telnet://moo.du.org 8888

FredNet MOO   This Web site invites K–12 school projects. Here you'll find a classroom, an American history project, cultural projects, and other inviting activities.
   http://fred.net/cindy/moo.html

Internet Public Library MOO   From your Web browser, select MOO. On the next screen, click to access the MOO. Follow the screen instructions carefully. The two most important commands are <connect guest> and <@quit>. A good place to practice!
   http://ipl.sils.umich.edu/

Media MOO   The focus here is on media and journalism. The MOO help sheet can be obtained from *http://www.cs.bsu.edu/ homepages/siering/netoric.html* .
   telnet://purple-crayon.media.mit.edu8888

MicroMuse   At the MicroMuse prompt, type <connect guest>.
   telnet://michael.ai.mit.edu (Login: guest)

Puget Sound Community School   A totally online school for students age ten to eighteen. Access *http://www.speakeasy.org/ ~pscs/tour.html* for more information. To experience the MOO:
   telnet://speakeasy.org7777 (Login: connect guest)

Regina DUisa k-12   For students and teachers.
   telnet://du.unibase.com 8888

Virtual Online University   Focus on distance learning. Also, check out VOU's Web home page at *http://www.iac.net/~billp/* .
   telnet://brazos.iac.net 8888

> "Puget Sound Community School is unique. ;) We don't have a school site; instead, we hold classes in libraries, community centers, and other public places. All our students have dial-up Internet accounts from their home (we help families without computers to get them). We do a lot online; besides our MOO, students also create their own home pages, and a team of students creates home pages for local organizations in exchange for free meeting space."
>
> *Andrew Smallman, Director, Puget Sound Community School, Seattle, WA, USA*

Online chat

IRC (*Internet Relay Chat*) allows real-time conversation with people from around the globe. This has not been an ideal tool for educators because (1) most IRC discussion groups don't have an educational focus and (2) discussions are not easily monitored. However, with the advent of improved tools for online real-time discussions, this technology is becoming more feasible for classroom applications. Software clients to enable online chat are now easier to use, even for "non-techies." In addition, some of the more sophisticated

HINT To find out about the latest chat software, search Yahoo (**http://www.yahoo.com**) using the keyword *chat*.

chat products include the opportunity to integrate graphics and sound. Some are also incorporating three-dimensional elements into chat events.

Regular chat events are held that can provide excellent opportunities for professional development. For example, universities and commercial agencies often sponsor tutorial sessions. As well, some schools are running their own chat servers.

Find out more about online chat technology by investigating either of the following two sites.

Prospero Research   This site has an effective graphical interface for connecting, and conversing, with others on the Internet. Such chat technology promises to be a useful tool for distance learning. Learn about global chat by attending regularly scheduled presentations. Chats include open discussions on current political topics, as well as question-and-answer sessions with technology experts.

http://www.prospero.com/globalchat/schedule.html

The Palace   A unique Internet-based multimedia chat that might be described as a cross between IRC and HyperCard. Chat servers are available for both Macintosh and Windows. Some chat clients let you visit other people's sites. To find out more about this software, use your Web browser to access

http://www.thepalace.com/

To learn more about Internet Relay Chat, access **http://www2.undernet.org:8080/~cs93jtl/IRC.html** .

Figure 7-5
Real-time discussion using chat software

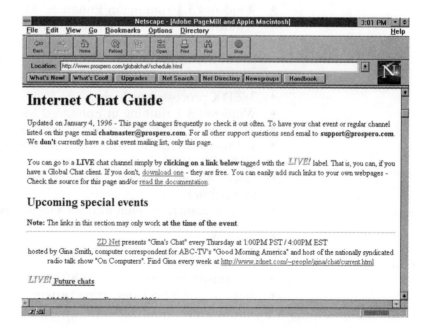

CU-SeeMe

CU-SeeMe is a software program that can be used for video-conferencing over the Internet. CU-SeeMe allows simultaneous conferencing with more than one site. With some versions, participants can exchange text and slides. Best of all, CU-SeeMe is available free. Ultimately, video-conferencing over the Internet will be a major means to deliver distance education courses.

For the time being, however, this type of application is, for many schools, a luxury. That's because video-conferencing requires specialized equipment. While the conferencing software is free, you will also need a microphone, a video camera or camcorder, and a frame grabber (a piece of equipment that connects the video camera to the computer). Once this connection is in place, whatever is captured in the lens of the camera is digitized and transmitted to the computer. You will also need a direct connection to the Internet, and your modem must transmit data at 14.4 kbps or faster.

CU-SeeMe runs on both Macintosh and Windows platforms. With this software, you will have the option to send and receive video, or just receive.

Here are specific hardware and software requirements for desktop video-conferencing using each of these platforms.

Windows

To receive only:
- 386SX processor or higher
- Windows 3.1 running in Enhanced Mode
- Windows Sockets-compliant TCP/IP stack
- a 256-color (8-bit) video driver at any resolution (640x480, 800x600, 1024x768, or higher).

To send and receive:
- 386DX processor or higher
- Windows 3.1 running in Enhanced Mode
- Windows Sockets-compliant TCP/IP stack
- a 256-color (8-bit) video driver at any resolution (640x480, 800x600, 1024x768, or higher)
- video capture board that supports Microsoft Video for Windows (see below)
- a video camera to plug into the video capture board.

Macintosh

To receive only:
- Macintosh platform with a 68020 processor or higher
- System 7 or higher operating system (it may run on system 6.0.7 and above)

- ability to display 16-level grayscale (i.e., any color Mac)
- an IP network connection
- MacTCP
- current CU-SeeMe application
- Apple's QuickTime, to receive slides with SlideWindow.

To send and receive:
- the specifications to receive video, listed above
- QuickTime
- a video digitizer (with VDIG software) and camera.

The simplest way to establish a video-conferencing setup for your school is to purchase a complete video-conferencing package from an appropriate vendor. You can download a copy of the CU-SeeMe software from the Web page for the CU-SeeMe Project (**http://cu-seeme.cornell.edu/**). Another very good source for information about CU-SeeMe is Michael Sattler's Web page (**http://baby.indstate.edu/msattler/sci-tech/comp/CU-SeeMe/**).

Once you have obtained the necessary hardware and software, you can connect to a site that is currently sending. CU-SeeMe send sites are also called *reflectors*, and the video segments are called *events*. One early event that received considerable press was a Rolling Stones concert. Other events have included online interviews with politicians, poets, and scientists. Teachers should begin to think about how they might use this technology to have classrooms interact across the Net.

Here are some other examples of events that have taken place. Note that the references for events include a reflector site address and/or URL for accessing the video presentation, and the time the event takes place.

> **HINT** To find out about school-related CU-SeeMe events, access
> **http://gsn.org/gsn/cuseeme.schools.info.html** .
> You can access a Web site that lists current CU-SeeMe events at
> **http://www.umich.edu/~johnlaue/cuseeme/csmlist.htm** .

Willie Nelson from Farm Aid   04:00 PM05:00 PM GMT-6 TBAUSA http://justicerecords.com/facbrcst.htm Willie Nelson live from the 10th Anniversary Farm Aid. Benefit for the American family farmer.

Third meeting of MEDIUM(MacUG)   18:0018:30 GMT 8133.24.188.13 Japan http://www.id.yamagata-u.ac.jp?index.html CU-SeeMe demonstration.

University of Nebraska/Omaha   00:00 PM00:00 PM GMT-6 See Web page http://137.48.3.211/ Twenty-four hour, seven-days-per-week multimedia presentation.

CU Connect   00:00 PM23:59 PM GMT-8 Canada http://www.
prairienet.org/~scaletti/cuConnect.html 3-7 Sept. 1995.
Connect with others on the WWW via CU-SeeMe.

HINT To connect to a CU-SeeMe site automatically from a Web page, you can use Go CU-SeeME Go (GCG), which is available for Windows. With this software, you can set up a Web page with links to your favorite CU-SeeMe locations and simplify access for students. For more information about Go-CU-SeeMe Go!, access **http://www.umich.edu/~johnlaue/cuseeme/gocusmgo.htm**

HINT The article, "Guidelines for an Effective CU-SeeMe Conference" is available from **http://www.gsn.org/gsn/articles/article.cuseeme.html**

Summing up

Because the Internet is constantly developing, there will undoubtedly be other kinds of software available for audio- or video-conferencing on the Internet. If you feel that some of the applications discussed in this chapter are too challenging for a novice to tackle, be reassured that none of these are necessary to make good use of the Net. It's worth repeating that the real power of the Internet is as a tool for human communication, and although such applications as MOOs and CU-SeeMe are interesting technologies for classroom learning, much can still be accomplished with a simple e-mail connection. Telnet and FTP will allow you to access some additional Net resources, but most users will probably find that the World Wide Web provides sufficient access to the resources that will be most useful to schools.

The real power of the Internet is as a tool for human communication.

Bringing the Internet into Schools

"So much can go wrong—a password typed incorrectly, server crashes, pornographic or illegal material. Yet, so much can go right. I can think of a hundred reasons not to get kids involved with the Internet, and I can think of a thousand reasons to get them actively participating. I am willing to put up with the small problems in order to achieve the results that I know will make my students self-motivated, critically thinking, lifelong learners."

— ROBERT STEENWINKEL, TEACHER, MARY BUTTERWORTH SCHOOL, EDMONTON, AB, CANADA

Change is rarely easy. As this book has suggested, the Internet is presenting educators with changes that are both exciting and necessary. As a result, school administrators, librarians, computer teachers, and classroom teachers all face the challenges of implementing this new technology. Problems are inevitable; in fact, we can't learn without them. When teachers discuss using the Internet in education, the hurdles of time, motivation, money, and technical training are mentioned time and time again.

This chapter will explore some of the ways in which schools are overcoming these barriers. It will help you plan for change in your school, and will suggest sources of funding to help make change a reality.

Chapter goals

■ **To provide guidelines for Internet implementation planning**
■ **To examine teacher training opportunities and procedures**
■ **To explore sources of funding**

The implementation plan

A well-developed strategic school plan for implementing or expanding Internet use addresses current equipment and its present utilization, how and why these technological learning resources and their management need to be improved, who will be responsible for which aspects of the improvement, and how the school will evaluate its progress. Planning committees can include administrators, teachers, parents, and students. The committee will require help from individuals with curriculum, technological, and administrative expertise.

A good plan includes

- the names and contact information of committee members
- a brief philosophy and mission statement
- a list of anticipated beneficial student outcomes
- proposed changes to current technology and its usage
- a hardware/software purchase plan, including proposed time of acquisition, cost, and sources of funding
- a detailed budget that includes costs of teacher training and support materials such as paper, duplication, and computer disks
- strategies to address upgrades, obsolescence, and maintenance
- the source and cost of ongoing technical support
- the role of each person involved in the implementation, and timelines for their actions
- an explanation of how the project will sustain itself over time
- a description of how the project will be evaluated, including review dates.

Since the plan will probably be used to solicit funding, it must be easy to understand. Thus, keep technical and educational jargon to a minimum. Prepare a brief summary as a handout. It's a good idea to have a catchy name and a student-designed logo for your package. If you have an opportunity to present your plan in a format other than print, try to use the very technology that you are advocating.

HINT An excellent resource for overall technology planning is *The Switched-On Classroom*, a technology planning guide developed for the public schools of Massachusetts, USA. This 250-page book outlines a twelve-step technology plan and implementation process, describes case studies of successful technology implementation, and includes an extensive listing of resources to help schools in their strategic planning efforts. It can be found at the World Wide Web site **http://www.swcouncil.org/switch2.html** . Other good examples and guidelines for technology planning are located at

The British Columbia Ministry of Education
http://www.etc.bc.ca/provdocs/disttech/home.html

The Pitsco Technology Education Web Site
http://www.pitsco.com

Training

Motivation

As a teacher who has chosen to read this book, you must already be motivated to learn more about using the Internet in your classroom or school. You may now be wondering: How can you excite and motivate your colleagues to join you?

When asked what moved them to get involved in using the Internet in their classrooms, many teachers cited the availability of accounts at low (or no) cost, either through discounts from vendors, local or national grants, or pilot projects. Such advantages tended to trigger acquisition and implementation. Some teachers mentioned that their prior involvement with computers made using the Internet a natural evolution. Others found that a personal interest (such as planning a vacation, researching a hobby, or communicating with a family member) got them started on the Internet. In many cases, the enthusiasm of a friend, relative, fellow teacher, or student provided the motivation; a team approach eased the learning curve. The availability of a central resource, such as Canada's SchoolNet, EduCom, Global SchoolNet, or EdWeb, was also helpful. Most importantly, all the teachers' comments reflected excitement and enthusiasm about the educational possibilities of the Internet.

> "Our school district purchased thirty accounts and distributed them to person-nel who were willing to volunteer twelve to fifteen hours of training time to the project. Its success has made some other teachers wish they had invested the time. The initial group will train others in Internet usage."
>
> *Carol Willard, Teacher, Troy Junior High School, Troy, MO, USA*

Training yourself

A common response from teachers when they see the educational possibilities of the Internet is, "This looks great, but there's so much to learn. Where do I begin?"

Start by examining the opportunities within your own school. Once you are committed to becoming Internet literate, look for learning partners and mentors among your colleagues. It's more fun, and more productive, to learn in collaboration than in isola-tion. Many schools hold inservice sessions, both during the day and after school. "Brown bag" meetings held during the lunch period offer an opportunity for users to share experiences, frustrations, and discoveries. You can save time by sharing lists of educational sites among colleagues who have visited them.

> "We [twenty to thirty teachers] got together for Internet training using an LCD panel two separate times for four weeks, two hours a week. Our librarian did the training and each week provided us with practice activities that forced us to use our newly acquired skills. It was a great experience, and humbling, too. We felt 'dumb' at times, just as our students sometimes do when we present them with new information."
>
> *Carol Willard, Teacher, Troy Junior High School, Troy, MO, USA*

Your school and/or district probably has resource people who can assist you in a variety of ways. Ideally, resource people would be located in your own school so that they are available when need-ed. However, with the realities of today's shrinking budgets, this isn't always possible. Reach out for whatever services are available from these resource people, such as

- offering workshops for groups of teachers, parents and/or students
- working cooperatively with you and your students on a project
- finding useful Internet sites to fit your curriculum
- putting you in touch with a focus group of interested teachers in other schools
- helping with technical problem solving
- recommending resource books, training manuals, and magazines
- providing lists of conferences and courses
- arranging a visit to another school or site.

"We have given demonstrations to entire staffs as an introduction to the Internet. We have also given workshops for small groups of teachers who are interested in learning more about the Internet. This approach has worked well because it allows us to offer more one-to-one help. In addition, I have also been busy helping teachers who want to be connected at home. I go to their homes, set up their computers, and give them one-to-one tutoring. ... Teachers who are comfortable enough to connect at school and at home will in turn help others in their own schools."

Bonnie McMurren, Teacher, Stony Mountain Elementary School,
Stony Mountain, MB, Canada

Many school districts have established their own bulletin board system. Though these may not have Internet access, you can use such local bulletin boards to learn and practice the skills of sending and receiving e-mail, uploading and downloading files, general navigation, and netiquette. They also provide forums through which you can exchange resources and ideas with other teachers. And there are Internet discussion groups you can join.

"Our school board features a mobile computer lab, the Micromobile. It travels from school to school, offering students and teachers opportunities to learn and use computer skills in a state-of-the-art facility. ... Each school now has an Internet account and a Net manager—a teacher who is given a computer to take home for the summer to get comfortable with the Net. The Net manager then becomes an on-site trainer for other staff. We also have a school board BBS that provides access to, and help with, Internet and other computer-related topics."

Peter K McLeod (1995, June 22), "Training."
Classuse@schoolnet.carleton.ca

University courses in educational technology, including the Internet, are numerous today. Many of these focus on practical classroom applications. The advantage of taking a course during the school year is that you can try out new strategies immediately in your own classroom.

"One teacher from each school that has Internet access was sponsored for an Internet course for new users, offered through the University of Calgary. Weekly assignments forced us to practice what we had learned. After five sessions we each had to present our project. This was excellent because each of us took on something entirely different. It gave us ideas for student projects and provided us with a list of resources that we could use in the classroom."

Sharon Lewis, Teacher, Red Deer, AB, Canada

Conferences such as those offered by the International Society for Technology in Education (ISTE), the National Education Computing Conference (NECC), and the Educational Computing Organization of Ontario (ECOO) offer sessions for both beginners and advanced Internet users.

HINT When you attend a computer conference, look for sessions that focus specifically on classroom use for the age of students you teach. That way, you'll come away with ideas to try in your classroom right away. If you're a beginner, avoid highly technical sessions.

Some private agencies, such as Internet service providers and computer stores, also offer short workshops and longer training sessions. Though they may not deal specifically with educational applications of Internet resources, these can introduce you to general Internet tools and allow hands-on practice time.

Many teachers prefer to schedule their Internet training in a more flexible manner. You don't have to leave home to learn how to use the Internet; you can access distance education courses, tutorials, reference books, and Internet guides on the Internet itself.

Here are some useful starting points on the World Wide Web.

Artsedge   Although this site is primarily a valuable resource for arts information, it is noted here because of its comprehensive pointers to documents to help teachers learn about the Internet.
   http://artsedge.kennedy~center.org

Australian Capital Territory Internet Help for Educators   This site contains links to basic Internet information sure to be of help to the hundreds of educators who come online every month. How do you decompress files? What are listservs? What resources are available for elementary and secondary school teachers? Many such questions are sure to be answered here.
   http://actein.edu.au/acteinnew/help.html

Electronic School Tour   Take a guided tour of the World Wide Web with the Electronic School. Developed specifically for educators, this site offers many educational resources, including the Library of Congress and the Louvre. This is also a good place to sample such sites as AskERIC and the Cisco Systems Meta-library of elementary and primary school Internet links.
   http://www.access.digex.net/~nsbamags/tour.html

Internet School Networking (ISN) The goal of this site, produced by the ISN group in the User Services Area of the Internet Engineering Task Force (IETF), is to list the questions most commonly asked about the Internet by elementary and secondary school educators, and to provide pointers to sources that answer those questions. It is directed at teachers, school media specialists, and school administrators who have recently connected to the Internet, who are accessing the Internet via dial-up or means other than a direct connection, or who are considering an Internet connection as a resource for their schools.

http://www.cusd.claremont.edu/www/people/rmuir/ric15/rfc1578

John December's Web Site This site is intended for those getting started with the Internet. It lists pointers that describe the Net and computer networks, and that identify and explore issues related to computer-mediated communication, including the technical, social, cognitive, and psychological aspects. For those who are more experienced, the site concisely summarizes sources of information. The author assumes that readers have access to e-mail, the Web, Gopher, telnet, FTP, and Usenet newsgroups, and know how to use these tools.

http://www.ucla.edu/htbin/finger?decemj@rpi.edu

Quest: Home of NASA's K-12 Internet Initiative This site includes many links for finding online training on the Net, along with curriculum-related resources, technology planning, and funding.

http://quest.arc.nasa.gov/net-learning.html

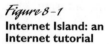

Figure 8-1
Internet Island: an Internet tutorial

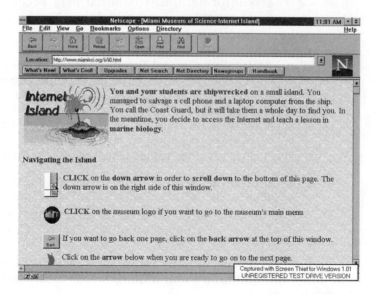

Other good Internet tours
are available at:
Internet Island
**http://www.miamisci.
org/ii/default.html**

Teacher's Guide to the
Internet
**http://quest.arc.nasa.
gov/teach/toc.html**

Global Village Tour
**http://www.
globalcenter.net/
gcweb/tour.html**

The Internet Pearls Index
**http://www.execpc.
com/~wmhogg/
beginner.html**

Appendix B contains more site addresses and descriptions of
what is available.

> "The Internet is like an elephant: you can eat it, but you have to take it one
> bite at a time!"
>
> *Christiane Dufour, Teacher, Small Schools Network,*
> *Quebec City, PQ, Canada*

Training others

Teachers, like their students, must see the relevance of what they are
to learn or they are not interested. Thus, the Internet needs to be
both understood and used in terms of its relevance to curriculum.
Once the educational applications are apparent, teachers are motivated to take the time to learn how to use it. If you are training
other teachers, offer them a choice of opportunities to see the
Internet in action, so that they can select the presentation that best
fits their timetable.

You'll need to have a computer system available after school for
teachers' use, with a co-trainer to attend when needed. Offer specific topic sessions, and build Internet awareness activities into scheduled meetings. After a brief introduction to the Net, encourage people to browse on their own. Stay close by to answer questions and
give suggestions. Find out each teacher's interest, and then locate
sites on the Internet that pertain to these. Show each teacher how he
or she might use the Internet in the classroom—and remember what
it was like for you when you were just beginning. The Internet is
still not terribly easy to use. Experienced users may accept such
inconveniences as dropped lines or unavailable sites, but small irri-
tations can be big roadblocks for people who are new to this technology.

> "I believe in 'just in time' training—that is, teaching people to use tools as they
> relate to projects they want to do now. Teaching Internet tools in the abstract
> is too overwhelming. But handing teachers a specific tool to do something they
> want to do makes learning easier."
>
> *Christiane Dufour, Small Schools Network,*
> *Quebec City, PQ, Canada*

Teachers who have had experience with Internet training courses
recommend the following strategies.

- Tie training to practical classroom needs.
- Reinforce learning by having teachers complete a project in conjunction with their training.
- Pair teachers with others in the school who are knowledgeable
  about the Internet.
- Provide hands-on experience. The only way to learn something
  is to do it.
- Ensure a low instructor-to-student ratio to allow for individual
  assistance.

- Plan short instructional sessions followed by lots of practice time.
- Schedule ongoing training over a period of time rather than a one-shot inservice.
- Reward participants with certification or a recognized credit of some sort.

> **HINT** A sample workshop for librarians interested in learning about the World Wide Web can be found at
> **http://homepage.interaccess.com/~wolinsky/jintro.htm** .
> This site includes a handout entitled 101 Sites to See.

Staying current

With the pace of change today, it's a continuing challenge to keep up to date. The Internet is no exception; in fact, it's the fastest growing technology around. The Internet is always changing. We asked some teachers how they keep abreast of new developments. Here are their suggestions.

- Read magazines such as *Internet World*, *Web Week*, *Net Guide*, and the *Journal of Teaching and Learning with Technology*.
- Use the Internet as often as possible. Explore on your own, and do searches of topics that interest you.
- Subscribe to listservs that discuss issues relevant to technology in education, such as:
  wwwedu@kudzu.cnidr.org,NET
  Netsurfer Digest,editor-bounce@netsurf.com,NET
  KIDSPHERE@vms.cis.pitt.edu,NET
  ednet@lists.umass.edu,NET
- Take a distance education course on the Internet.
- Have discussions with other teachers and individuals already involved in using the Internet.
- Search for tools or help to answer questions about practical needs that arise.
- Use the buddy system.
- Get involved in assisting other teachers to take advantage of the potential of the Net.
- Devote some time each day to surfing the Internet in order to discover new sites that might be useful at school. When a URL is recommended, view the site immediately, and if you like it, add it to your bookmarks. (Then, of course, share your bookmarks with others!)

Funding

In today's economy, money matters more than ever. But this is a good time to be seeking funds for Internet projects. With the

HINT Nicholas Mailer's document, "Preaching to the unconverted: Why should I put my school onto the Internet?" addresses such questions as: What will I find on the Internet? How much does the information cost? How do I get my school online? You can access it at

http://www.demon.co. uk/koekie/pubs/ why/pr.html

emphasis on educational reform, global communications, and technology, you'll find there are a variety of sources of funding available. Designate several members of your planning team to pursue funding opportunities. Consider local community businesses, large corporations, private foundations, charitable organizations, provincial/state government agencies, and national projects that support technology in education.

The responsibility for finding sources of funding generally rests with your school administration and the school board or district. If you don't presently have Internet access, ask a local service provider or university to allow you to use their account for a demonstration to administrators. Once they see the Internet in action, particularly in graphical format, they will be more likely to pursue funding.

The best way to convince the decision makers of the educational benefits of the Internet to is to have students demonstrate their learning and excitement. Invite trustees, parent councils, administrators, and community leaders to attend school technology fairs. Show them videos and slides of students at work using the Internet, and try to maintain a high profile for your technology projects. Collect a file of clippings about educational use of the Internet, and reserve a bulletin board for displaying current magazine and newspaper articles.

HINT Kid Wide Web: A Guide to the Internet for Teachers is a Danish site that illustrates some ways in which kids are using the World Wide Web today. The international nature of its links makes this an excellent site to show to decision makers. Visit it at

http://www.algonet.se/~bernadot/teachers/teachers.html

School fund raising

Many schools raise money for their projects through such efforts as fun fairs, technology fairs, school plays, bake sales, plant sales, math-a-thons, garage sales, and barbecues. You won't make a lot of money this way, but you might be able to buy a computer or install a dedicated phone line.

Corporate funding

Many large companies set aside funds specifically for community and educational projects. In the United States, these funds are often distributed through non-profit foundations. In Canada, they are usually controlled by the Community or Public Affairs Branch of the national office of the corporation. In both cases, you'll find formal selection policies and application procedures.

Your first step is to list all the corporations in your area that might be interested in your project. Technology-related corporations are the most likely choice, particularly telecommunications companies; but don't limit yourself. Remember that the benefits to

HINT You can find ideas for alternative sources of funding in the *Grassroots Funding Journal*, available from

GFJ
P.O. Box 11607
Berkley, CA 94701

Possible corporate sponsors

Some U.S. foundations include:

Apple Partners in Education
20525 Mariani Avenue
Cupertino, CA 95014

AT&T Foundation
1301 Avenue of the Americas
New York, NY 10019

Computer Learning Foundation
P.O. Box 60400
Palo Alto, CA 94306

Ford Foundation
320 E. 43rd St.
New York, NY 10017

Gifts in Kind
700 North Fairfax St.
Alexandria, VA 22314

Toshiba America Foundation
1251 Avenue of the Americas,
Ste. 4100
New York, NY 10020

Xerox Foundation
800 Long Range Road
P.O. Box 1600
Stamford, CT 06904

HINT You can find some good links to international telecommunications companies at the World Wide Web site **http://www.spp.unich.edu/companies.hmtl** .

learners are the driving force, not the technology itself. Your community library may have a reference guide to corporate funding that includes contact information. The magazine *Classroom Connect* also includes a monthly section on U.S. grants and funding sources and ideas.

Once you've identified possible sponsors, the next step is to find out what types of projects they support and what types of donations they provide. Ask them to send their application procedures and funding guidelines. Corporations generally prefer to donate to schools in their local area and may be more willing to contribute products or services than cash. You might approach them for donations such as telephone lines, equipment, or technical expertise. Corporate sponsors also tend to prefer to be the only ones of their kind involved in a specific project, so if you obtain significant funding from one source, don't solicit funds from competing companies in the same field. Consider establishing levels of sponsorship, each with a set amount—for example, founding sponsors, $1000; major sponsors, $500; contributing sponsors, $100. Explain in your application how the sponsors will be given credit for their assistance.

Some smaller hardware and software companies may give in-kind donations or offer reduced costs to schools. In-kind donations might include use of training facilities, printing and copying, surplus equipment, personnel for technical advice, or planning expertise.

Communicate directly and personally with appropriate companies in your neighborhood. Don't hesitate to approach your school's parent community for assistance from local businesses, both large and small. Parents are often your best connections and are more than willing to assist when your planned initiative directly benefits their own children.

Business–education partnerships

Establishing a business partnership is different from asking a business for a grant or donation. True business-education partnerships are cooperative relationships in which partners share values; human, material, or financial resources; and roles and responsibilities, in order to achieve desired learning outcomes. For example, a local Internet service provider might give your school reduced access charges if teachers enroll in their training courses.

> "Canadian employers and educators support business-education partnerships that:
> - enhance the quality and relevance of education for learners;
> - mutually benefit both partners;
> - treat fairly and equitably all those served by the partnership;
> - provide opportunities for all partners to meet their shared responsibilities toward education;
> - acknowledge and celebrate each partner's contribution through appropriate forms of recognition;
> - are consistent with the ethics and core values of all partners;
> - are based on the clearly defined expectations of all partners;
> - are based on shared or aligned objectives that support the goals of the partner organizations;
> - allocate resources to complement and not replace public funding for education;
> - measure and evaluate partnership performance to make informed decisions that ensure continuous improvement;
> - are developed and structured in consultation with all partners;
> - recognize and respect each partner's expertise;
> - identify clearly defined roles and responsibilities of all partners; and
> - involve individual participants on a voluntary basis."
>
> *The Education Forum, Conference Board of Canada (1995),*
> *"Ethical guidelines for business–education partnerships."*

Partnerships can be formed with individual companies, colleges, and universities, or with groups of individuals representing several related businesses. For a school, the benefits of forming a business partnership might include leadership from experts in a particular technology, gifts or loans of equipment, opportunities for student internships, and/or the provision of support services. You'll find that many of the grants and award programs available today require evidence of one or more business partnerships. Here are some tips for finding a potential business partner.

- Identify companies in your local area and companies whose products you are already using.
- Explore personal contacts, such as parents within your school.
- Find out as much as possible about potential partners and their needs.

- Establish credibility by showing people from the business community some of the great things that are already happening in your school through the use of technology. Proposals in which the school raises a portion of the money and the business matches the amount raised are often successful.
- Generate as much publicity as you can for your venture. Try to establish your school as an innovative leader. Everyone likes a winner.
- Provide a detailed plan of your project and its benefits to all parties.[1]

HINT You might wish to show interested parties some of the exciting initiatives already taking place in school partnerships. One good source is a massive educational technology project known as the K–12 Internet Testbed (**http://edweb.cnidr.org:90/testbed.home.html**). The Testbed creates Internet-based educational networking projects around the U.S. in the hopes of exploring the potential of student electronic publishing in the classroom. The K–12 Internet Testbed utilizes the experience of local public broadcasters, universities, museums, and other community institutions as the driving force behind each project's development. A total of 15 local partnerships make up the K–12 Internet Testbed, with sites in Indiana, California, Colorado, New Mexico, Arkansas, New Hampshire, Kansas, Virginia, Pennsylvania, Wisconsin, and New York. This Web site will serve as a home to the Testbed and its activities at the local and national level, providing details of each project, as well as links to station home pages and other related documents.

Government grants and awards

Individuals and schools can apply for government-sponsored grants and awards at both the national and provincial/state levels.

The U.S. Department of Education (ED) awards grants and contracts to schools, school districts, researchers, and others to implement new methodologies, research effective practice, and implement educational reform. The Department's World Wide Web site (**http:/www.ed.gov**), offers documents explaining the grants and contracts processes and rules. The section "What Should I Know About ED Grants?" is designed to de-mystify the grants process within the Department. The "Guide to U.S. Department of Education Program" provides, in concise form, the information necessary to begin the process of applying for funding from individual federal education programs. It includes a brief description of each of the Department's more than 200 programs, specifies who is eligible to apply, and gives the office and telephone number to contact for more information. This Web site features the latest announcements about funding opportunities, as well as the Department's "Combined Application Notice," which lists upcoming grant competitions. In some cases, the application packages are available for downloading. The site also provides directions to ED Board, an electronic bulletin board sponsored by ED's Grants and Contracts Service, which often contains additional information on contracts and grants. Alternatively, you can get this information by gophering to: **gopher.ed.gov** or writing to:

U.S. Department of Education
Office of Educational Research and Improvement
555 New Jersey Avenue, NW, Room 214
Washington, DC 20208-5725

Although education is not the direct responsibility of the federal government in Canada, schools can apply for government grants and awards sponsored by other federal departments. You can find out about these in the *Handbook of Grants and Subsidies of the Federal and Provincial Governments for Non-Profit Organizations*. The aim of this document is to keep citizens informed of all governmental assistance available. Funding opportunities include Education and Research, Cultural Affairs, Health and Social Services, and Employment and Development. The handbook and monthly updating service are available from:

Canadian Research and Publications Centre (CRPC)
33 Racine
Farnham, PQ J2N 3A3
(In Quebec, 1-800- 363-8304. In all other provinces,
1-800-363-1400.)

Don't limit yourself to grants specifically designated for technology. Be creative in showing how the Internet will benefit at-risk, disabled, and gifted students, and workplace preparation programs. The time spent in writing a proposal is well worth it. Once you have prepared one funding application, you can easily modify it to meet the criteria of others. Apply well in advance of the anticipated launch of your initiative, and be patient as you wade through the red tape and bureaucracy.

HINT The Pitsco Technology Education Web site includes an extensive list of links to sources of grants and funding:

http://www.pitsco.com

Most state and provincial departments of education have recently created funds for technology initiatives. There are too many to list here, and they change yearly, so contact your local school district or school board to get the details of these programs for your area.

Time

Finding time is one of the challenges to using the Internet most often articulated by teachers:
- time to learn Internet tools
- time to teach their use to the students

- time to find appropriate usable resources relating to the curriculum
- time to collaborate with other teachers on how to use the Internet in the classroom
- time to implement, given many user groups and limited access to computers
- time to re-think well-worn teaching strategies.

> "I believe the biggest challenge is time and training. We must first learn how to use the technology. Then we must fit it to our curriculum in meaningful and appropriate ways. Next, we need to figure out how best to teach our students the power of the tool. We must also cut down the amount of 'surfing' time, and devise ways to move right into classroom use."
>
> *Dave Lehnis, Teacher*

You don't have to master Internet tools before you start using the Net with your students. The overview provided in this book and some hands-on experience are all you need. Your ongoing training should focus on specific project needs. Rather than head out on your own, join an existing project such as those described in Chapter 3. Start small. If you run into a problem, you'll find that help is easy to get from the project leaders.

Nor do your students have to master many Internet tools before they begin. They'll learn to use the Internet within the context of their projects. This is authentic learning for a purpose. Arrange training for a few students, and then let them take the lead in training others so that you can move into the role of facilitator. Let parents, teachers-in-training, or older students work with small groups on the Internet while you manage the rest of the class.

> "An ironic downside is that [the students] would rather be on the Net than in the book or attentive to the teacher. So we change the teaching style, relinquish the direct power role, and become facilitators of their learning. I think 'what's wrong with the schools today' boils down to too much teaching and not enough learning."
>
> *Elizabeth S. Dunbar, Teacher, Baltimore City College High School, Baltimore, MD, USA*

The solutions to the challenge of finding time to locate useful resources on the Internet do not lie solely with the teacher. Such institutions as Canada's SchoolNet and its equivalents organize material in such a way as to make it easy for a teacher to find curriculum-related material and entry-level projects. When you begin, adopt a favorite general site, such as Canada's SchoolNet, EdNet, Global SchoolNet, Classroom Connect, or EdWeb, and stick with it rather than spending a lot of time sifting through the huge volumes of information on the Internet. You'll find that your horizons will broaden naturally as time passes and you become a more experienced user. One of the great benefits in collaborating with other teachers is the time saved by sharing specific useful sites among the group. You'll also save time by using Appendix B, which provides a wide variety of specific, reliable educational sites.

Rather than viewing Internet use as an add-on to your already heavy burden of curriculum, use it to replace more traditional methods. When you carefully document the learning outcomes you expect from your Internet project, you'll see how it accomplishes the goals of other activities you might have done in the past. As soon as you're confident that students will learn as well or better, abandon the old in favor of the new. You can also use your Internet resources as an alternative to more traditional tools. For example, in a research project, have some students use books as information sources while others use Internet resources. In a project requiring communication, have some students use telephone or postal services while others use e-mail.

Summing up

With effort, creativity, and commitment, you can find the time, money, and resources you need to travel the information highway with your students. Because the educational reform movement advocates change and encourages schools to use new technologies such as the Internet, there are literally thousands of funding sources available for technology-related projects. The energy and inspiration you need will come from the collaboration and support of colleagues, students, parents, and the community.

Ten tips for teaching teachers

1. Trainers should be part of the existing social network of the school or district, available for long-term support, and seen as contemporaries rather than as technology "gurus."
2. Ensure that teachers have access to tools before teaching them how to use them.
3. Provide access to many different types of Internet resources.
4. Introduce participants to e-mail and conferencing first, since these tools most closely resemble communication forms with which they are already familiar.
5. Introduce other tools such as Gopher, Archie, telnet, FTP, and the World Wide Web once participants are interested and motivated.
6. Provide written documentation that is clear, concise, friendly, and useful.
7. Provide online practice activities that are structured, enjoyable, relevant, and achievable.
8. As soon as teachers are comfortable with the tools, use curriculum-based activities.
9. Encourage the use of resource guides for listings of educational sites so that teachers don't have to spend time "surfing."
10. Fully support motivated teachers to grow. Don't mandate participation.[2]

Epilogue

"I want my students to know how to live satisfying, productive lives. Technology is an increasingly important part of living and working and playing in the world today. The essential role for teachers, as I see it, is to introduce students to some of the possibilities of this new culture, to give students the opportunity to participate and to belong."
— JOHN GRAVES, PARENT HOME SCHOOLER, SAN DIEGO, CA, USA

What will schools look like in the twenty-first century? We cannot predict this exactly, but as we plan for the future, it helps to have some idea of current trends. Some of the most pervasive trends in educational reform of the 1990s include

- inclusion of all learners
- students taking responsibility for their own learning
- a shift from all students learning the same things to students learning different things individually
- learning outcomes and performance assessment
- education for global stewardship facilitated by communications technologies
- collaboration, communication, and the integration of visual and verbal thinking
- the changing role of teacher from expert to facilitator, mentor, and partner in learning.

These changing parameters give us some vision of schools in the years ahead.

Imagine the role that technology, and specifically the Internet, can play in helping to integrate these trends into daily learning. It's not technology that will create change in education, but rather the power of technology that will *allow* teachers and students to make necessary changes.

Through the power of telecommunication, traditional hierarchies are broken down and education becomes the responsibility of *communities* of learners—students, teachers, and parents. Students now have access to a wide variety of information resources. They can be more involved in designing learning outcomes as part of functioning teams in which people change roles all the time, just as they do in the real world. This kind of teamwork sees students assuming leadership roles as well as being part of the team.

As we approach the excitement and challenge of exploring the educational potential of the Internet, we have the opportunity to be lifelong learners, and by doing so we set an example for the students with whom we work. Communication and collaboration skills are enhanced when both students and teachers are engaged in authentic learning.

Much experimentation is required to figure out the practical aspects of transforming teaching and learning, and it is sometimes difficult not to be overwhelmed by the technology itself. Improvements happen not suddenly, but over time. Continuous reflection and evaluation are critical to the process of change. At some point, teachers will undoubtedly view the Internet as an integral tool for professional growth and learning. Today, our challenge is not to master it, but rather to discover what is most important and most useful for learning, and how to reorganize classroom practices to take advantage of these aspects.

The Internet is a dynamic environment that can sweep students into a sea of constant change. In the midst of this dynamic activity, teachers will establish the islands where students can pause, reflect upon and share their learning experiences on their way to discovering the future.

"When my computer teacher asked what I will demand in the future, I started thinking... . I will expect more in middle school and in high school. I will expect to be able to communicate with anybody in the world. I will demand to continue to challenge and encourage us, and I will want the future to be even better than the present."

Meredith Geremia, Student, Grade 6, West Windsor Plainsboro Upper Elementary School, Plainsboro, NJ, USA

Glossary

Anonymous FTP   One of the Internet's main attractions is its openness and freedom. FTP (File Transfer Protocol) Internet sites let you access their data without registering or paying a fee.

Archie   A search tool that helps you locate information stored at hundreds of anonymous FTP sites around the Internet.

ASCII (Ask-ee)   *American Standard Code for Information Interchange*, plain text without formatting that's easily transferred over networks. (Got a question? Just ASCII.)

Backbone   The main communication line that ties computers at one location with those at another. Analogous to the human nervous system, many smaller connections, called *nodes* or *remote sites*, branch off from the backbone network. (Don't slip a disk!)

Bandwidth   An indication of how fast information flows through a computer network in a set time. Bandwidth is usually stated in thousands or millions of bits per second. see Ethernet.

Baud   Unit of speed in data transmission; maximum channel speed for data transmission.

Bit   The basic unit of data. It takes eight bits (a byte) to represent one character (e.g., a letter or number) of text.

Bounce   Return of e-mail that contained a delivery error.

Bozo filter   A program that screens out unwanted and irritating incoming messages. (Both messages and filter can be breaches of netiquette.)

Byte   The memory space required for storage of one character — eight bits.

kilobyte (KB) = 1,024 bytes of data
megabyte (MB) = 1,048,576 bytes
gigabyte (GB) = 1,000 megabytes
terabyte (TB)= 1,024 gigabytes

CCITT   The Consultative Committee for *International Telegraph* and *Telephone* makes technical recommendations concerning data and telephone communications systems.

CD-ROM   Compact *Disk* Read-Only Memory. CD-ROM can hold the equivalent of 1,500 floppy disks. It is the most popular carrier of interactive multimedia programs that feature audio, video, graphics, and text.

Chat and Talk   A chat program lets you electronically "converse" online with many people simultaneously. A talk program is like a personal telephone call to a specific cybernaut — only in text. See IRC (Internet Relay Chat).

CIX   Commercial *Internet* eXchange, a group of companies providing a range of specialized services, such as financial data, for a fee.

Client   A desktop personal computer that communicates with other PCs and larger computers, called *servers* or *hosts*.

Client/server computing
Combining large and small computers in a network so data are readily available when and where they are needed. For example, in a retail store, information is collected from customers at point-of-sale terminals. Then it is directed to a server in the store and forwarded to a larger enterprise server for inventory management and other functions.

CNRI   Corporation for *National Research Initiatives*, an organization that is exploring different ways to use a national information highway.

Computerphobe   Someone who is afraid of using computers. (Now, who could that be?)

Copyright   The legal right granted to a copyright owner to exclude others from copying, preparing derivative works, distributing, performing, or displaying original works of authorship of the owner. Copyrighted works on the Internet are protected under national and international laws. Examples of copyrighted works include literature, music, drama, pictures, graphics, sculpture, and audiovisual presentations.

Cybernaut   Someone who explores the vast world of cyberspace where only the brave dare venture.

Cybernetics   In 1948, Norbert Wiener coined this term to describe the "entire field of control and communication theory, whether in the machine or in the animal." *Cyber-* has become a popular prefix for many Internet terms: cyberlingo, cyberwonk, cybercast. (What hath Norbert wrought!)

Cyberspace   Word coined by William Gibson in his 1984 sci-fi novel, *Neuromancer*. Refers to all the sites that you can access electronically. If your computer is connected to the Internet or a similar network, then it exists in cyberspace. Gibson's style of fiction is now called *cyberpunk*.

Daemon   Web software on a UNIX server; a program running all the time in background, providing special services when required.

Dedicated line   A telephone line that is leased from the telephone company and used for one purpose. In cyberspace, dedicated lines connect desktop systems to servers.

DES   The *Data Encryption Standard* represents a set of criteria for providing security for transmitted messages. Standards like this lay the groundwork for electronic commerce over the Internet.

Dial-in connection   A way to access a computer on the Internet using a PC, telephone line, and modem. Slower than connecting directly to the Internet backbone, but provides accessibility from many sites and does not require specialized equipment.

Domain   The system of organizing the Internet according to country or type of organization, such as educational or commercial. For instance, an educational institution such as The Franklin Institute Science Museum in Philadelphia, USA would have ".edu" as a suffix to its domain name (sln.fi.edu). Other typical suffixes include ".com" for commercial organizations and ".org" for non-profit groups.

Domain Name System (DNS)   The scheme used to define individual Internet hosts.

Download   When you transfer software or other information from the Internet to your PC. *Upload* refers to transferring content to a server from a smaller computer or a PC.

E-mail   Electronic mail. The term has several meanings: the network for sending messages; the act of sending a message electronically; and the message itself. It all comes down to using a computer network to send electronic messages from one computer user to another. Fortunately, all the electronic junk mail you receive is environmentally friendly since it generates no paper—unless you print it.

Electronic commerce   Buying and selling products and services over the Internet.

Ethernet   (Not an illegal fishing device.) A common type of network used in corporations. Originally limited to 10 million bits of information per second, technical improvements have raised Ethernet bandwidth (how fast information flows through a computer network in a set time) to 100 million bits of information per second—in concept, enough speed to transfer the entire contents of the *Encyclopaedia Britannica* in one second.

E-Zine   A Web-based electronic publication.

FAQ   List of *Frequently Asked Questions* (and answers) about a particular topic. FAQs can usually be found within Internet discussion groups that focus on specific topics. Read FAQs before asking a question of your own—the answer may already be waiting.

Finger   A program that provides information about someone connected to a host computer, such as that person's e-mail address.

Firewall   A mechanism to keep unauthorized users from accessing parts of a network or host computer. For example, anonymous users would be able to read documents a company makes public but could not read proprietary information without special clearance.

Flame   rude or ludicrous e-mail. Advice: Don't reply to flames, just extinguish them by deleting.

Freenet   A community computer network, often based on a local library, that provides Internet access to citizens from the library or sometimes from their home computers.

FTP   *File Transfer Protocol* is a program that lets you transfer data from an Internet server to your computer.

Gateway   A system that connects two incompatible networks. Gateways permit different e-mail systems to pass messages between them.

Geek A person who is so involved with computers and the so-called "virtual world" as to have only a tenuous hold on the real world. (But then again, what is reality?). Similar terms: nerd, propeller head, and techie.

Gigabyte A unit of data storage that equals about 1,000 megabytes. A CD-ROM holds about two-thirds of a gigabyte (650 million bytes). That's enough space to hold a full-length motion picture. (Don't forget the popcorn.)

Gopher A system that uses menus and special software on host computers so that you can more easily navigate around the Internet. The area of navigation is referred to as *GopherSpace*. See Jughead and Veronica.

GUI *Graphical User Interface*, software that simplifies the use of computers by letting you interact with the system through graphical symbols or icons on the screen rather than coded commands typed on the keyboard. Microsoft Windows and the Apple Macintosh operating systems are the two most popular GUIs.

Hacker The best reason of all to put up a firewall. Originally some of these pranksters breached computer security systems for fun. Computer criminals have created chaos on computer networks, stealing valuable data and bringing networks down for hours or days. See DES (Data Encryption Standard).

Home page Document displayed when first accessing a Web site.

Host A server computer linked directly to the Internet that individual users can access.

Hotlists Frequently accessed URLs (*Uniform Resource Locators*) that point to Web sites. Usually organized around a topic or for a purpose, e.g., a hotlist of museums on the Web.

HTML *HyperText Markup Language*; the codes and formatting instructions for interactive online Internet documents. These documents can contain hypertext, graphics, and multimedia elements, including sound and video.

Hypermedia Multimedia and hypertext combined in a document.

Hypertext An electronic document that contains links to other documents offering additional information about a topic. You can activate the link by clicking on the highlighted area with a mouse or other pointing device.

Information Highway Also referred to as I-Way, Internet, Infobahn, Autostrada, National Information Infrastructure (NII), Global Information Infrastructure (GII). The network is currently "under construction" to make existing computer systems more efficient at communicating and to add new services, such as electronic commerce, health information, education, polling—just use your imagination.

Infrastructure   The base on which an organization is built. It includes the required facilities, equipment, communications networks, and software for the operation of the organization or system. But most important, it includes the people and the relationships that result.

Internet   An interconnection of thousands of separate networks worldwide, originally developed by the U.S. federal government to link government agencies with colleges and universities. Internet's real expansion started recently with the addition of thousands of companies and millions of individuals who use graphical browsers to access information and exchange messages. See Mosaic.

InterNIC   The *Internet Network Information Center*. This NIC is run by the U.S. National Science Foundation and provides various administrative services for the Internet.

IP   *Internet Protocol* is the communications language used by computers connected to the Internet.

IRC   *Internet Relay Chat*, a software tool that lets you hold keyboard conversations. See Chat and Talk.

ISDN   The *Integrated Services Digital Network* defines a new technology that delivers both voice and digital network services over one "wire." More important, ISDN's high speed enables multimedia and high-end interactive functions over the Internet, such as video-conferencing.

Jughead   A system that lets you restrict your search of GopherSpace to a particular area. See Gopher.

Knowbots   An intelligent program or "agent" that you can instruct to search the Internet for information about a particular subject. While still in their infancy, these agents are the focus of intense software research and development.

LAN   *Local Area Network*, a collection of computers in proximity, such as an office building, that are connected via cable. These computers can share data and peripherals such as printers. LANs are necessary to implement client/server computing since the LAN allows communication to the server.

Listserv; Listserver   An electronic mailing list used to deliver messages directly to the e-mail addresses of people interested in a particular topic, such as education.

Luddite   Person who believes that the use of technology will diminish employment.

Lurking   The practice of reading about a newsgroup in order to understand its topics and tone before offering your own input.

Mbone   Multicast back*bone* is an experimental system that sends video over the Internet.

MIME   (*Not* Marcel Marceau.) *M*ultipurpose *I*nternet *M*ail *E*xtensions, an enhancement to Internet e-mail that lets you include non-text data, such as video and audio, with your messages.

Mosaic   This sophisticated, graphical browser application lets you access the Internet World Wide Web. After the introduction of Mosaic in 1993, the use of Internet began to expand rapidly.

Multimedia   Multiple forms of communication including sound, video, video-conferencing, graphics, and text delivered via a multimedia-ready PC.

Net surfing   The practice of accessing various Internet sites to see what's happening. (A whole new world for the Beach Boys!)

Netiquette   Standards of behavior and manners to be used while working on the Internet. For example, a message in ALL CAPS can mean the sender is shouting.

Network   People connected via computers to share information.

Newbies   Newcomers to the Internet.

Newsgroup   The Internet version of an electronic discussion group where people can leave messages or post questions.

Newsreader   A program that helps you find your way through a newsgroup's messages.

Newsserver   A computer that collects newsgroup data and makes it available to newsreaders.

NFS   The *N*etwork *F*ile *S*ystem lets you work with files on a remote host as if you were working on your own host.

NNTP   *N*etwork *N*ews *T*ransport *P*rotocol, an extension of TCP/IP protocol; describes how newsgroup messages are transported between compatible servers.

NSFNet   Large network run by the U.S. National Science Foundation. It is the backbone of the Internet.

Packet   A collection of data. Packet switching is a system that breaks data into small packets and transmits each packet independently. The packets are combined by the receiving computer. (Danger! We may have crossed over into geek-space.)

Point Of Presence (POP)   A method of connecting to an Internet service locally. If a service company has a POP in your area, then you can connect to the service provider by making a local call. POP is also used for *Post Office Protocol*.

Postmaster   The person at a host who is responsible for managing the mail system.

PPP   *Point-to-Point Protocol* connects computers to the Internet using telephone lines; similar to SLIP, but not as widely used.

Protocol   Rules or standards that describe ways to operate to achieve compatibility.

Public domain software   Computer programs you may use and distribute without paying a fee. *Shareware* is distributed at no cost, but you are expected to pay the author a fee if you decide to keep and use it.

Resource hog   A program that eats up a large amount of network bandwidth.

Router   A device that acts as a traffic signal to direct data among different networks. Routers often have enhanced processing capabilities that enable them to send data on an alternative path if one part of the network is busy.

Server   Equivalent to a host, a machine that works with client systems. Servers can be anything from PCs to mainframes that share information with many users.

Service provider   A company that provides a connection to the Internet.

SIG   *Special Interest Group.* (Also nickname of Wagnerian opera hero.)

SLIP   *Single Line Internet Protocol* is a technique for connecting a computer to the Internet using a telephone line and modem. Also called Serial Line Internet Protocol. See PPP.

Smiley   Manipulating the limited potential of keyboard characters to show goodwill, irony, or other emotions with a "smiley face." There are a number of text-based effects, for example, (–: and ;–).

SMTP   *Simple Mail Transport Protocol*, the Internet standard for transmitting electronic mail messages.

Sneakernet   The 1980s way of moving data among computers that are not networked, by storing data on floppy diskette and running the disks from one computer to another. (Very good for the cardiovascular but not the information system.)

SNMP   *Simple Network Management Protocol* is a standard of communication of information between reporting devices and data collection programs. It can be used to gather information about hosts on the Internet.

Spamming   Indiscriminately sending a message to hundreds or thousands of people on the Internet, e.g., unsolicited junk mail. Not good netiquette.

Streaming   Audio, video, and text available for viewing on your computer even as it is in the process of downloading to your system from a Web site.

T1   Telecommunications lingo for digital carrier facility used to transmit information at high speed. (T1 is to the Web what passing gear was to the '64 Cadillac.) If you want to turbocharge your network backbone, many companies are expanding to the even faster T3 service.

TCP/IP   *Transmission Control Protocol/Internet Protocol*; communication rules that specify how data are transferred among computers on the Internet.

Telnet   Software that lets users log on to computers connected to the Internet.

Token ring   Featured on LANs (Local Area Networks) to keep control messages (tokens) moving quickly among the users.

UNIX   Software operating system that provides the underlying intelligence to Internet servers. Mosaic and other browser programs have helped increase Internet usage by hiding the complexities of UNIX from the average cybernaut.

URL   Abbreviation for *Uniform Resource Locator*, the Internet addressing system. (What's your URL?)

Usenet   *User Network*, an array of computer discussion groups, or forums, that can be visited by anyone with Internet access.

Veronica   Program that lets you explore GopherSpace. *Jughead* restricts your search of GopherSpace to a particular area.

Virus   Destructive computer program that invades by means of a normal program and damages the system.

WAIS   *Wide Area Information Servers* search through the Internet's public databases for specific information. For instance, you could locate information about a particular medical breakthrough by searching through the research libraries of teaching hospitals connected to the Internet.

The Teacher's Complete & Easy Guide to the Internet

Web site   A sequence of related Web pages normally created by a single company or organization.

Webster   Habitué of Web sites and other cyberplaces.

White Pages   Because they remind people of the old telephone book, services that list user e-mail addresses, telephone numbers, and postal addresses.

Winsock   *Win*dows *Sock*et, an extension program designed to let Windows applications run on a TCP/IP network.

Worm   this computer program replicates itself on other systems on the Internet. Unlike a destructive virus, a worm passes on useful information. (Maybe we're fishing too deeply.)

WWW   The World Wide Web is a hypertext-based collection of computers on the Internet that lets you travel from one linked document to another, even if those documents reside on many different servers.

Sample Acceptable Use Policy

Internet Use Agreement for K–12 Students, Lafayette County School District and Mississippi Center for Supercomputing Research
April 12, 1995
Please read this document carefully before signing.

I. Introduction

Internet access is now available to students and teachers in the Lafayette County School District (LCSD) through access to computing facilities at the Mississippi Center for Supercomputing Research (MCSR). We are very pleased to bring this access to the LCSD and believe the Internet offers vast, diverse, and unique resources to both students and teachers. Our goal in providing this service is to promote educational excellence in schools by facilitating resource sharing, innovation, and communication.

II. What Is the Internet?

The Internet is an electronic highway connecting thousands of computers all over the world and millions of individual subscribers. Students and teachers have access to:

- electronic mail communication with people all over the world;
- information and news from national and international research institutions (e.g., NASA) and the opportunity to correspond with the scientists at these research institutions;
- public domain software and shareware of all types;
- discussion groups on many topics ranging from Chinese culture to the environment to music to politics;
- many on-line University Library Catalogs, the Library of Congress and ERIC.

With access to computers and people all over the world also comes the availability of material that may not be considered to be of educational value in the school setting. LCSD and MCSR have taken precautions to restrict access to controversial materials. However, on a global network it is impossible to control all materials, and an industrious user may discover controversial information. We firmly believe that the valuable information and interaction available on this worldwide network far outweigh the possibility that users may obtain material that is not consistent with the educational goals of the District.

III. Terms and Conditions

Internet access is coordinated through a complex association of government agencies, and regional and state networks. The smooth operation of the network relies upon the proper conduct of the end users who must adhere to strict guidelines. These guidelines are provided so that you are aware of the responsibilities you are about to acquire. In general this requires efficient, ethical and legal use of the network resources. If a LCSD user violates any of these provisions, his or her account will be terminated and future access could be denied. Violations of this agreement will be referred to appropriate school officials for disciplinary action. Violations of state or federal law will be referred to the appropriate law enforcement agency. The signatures at the end of this document are legally binding and indicate parties who signed have read the terms and conditions carefully and understand their significance.

Parents: *It is important that you and your child read this agreement and discuss it together. When your child is given a login ID and is allowed to use the computers it is extremely important that the rules are followed. As a parent, you are legally responsible for your child's actions. You are responsible for supervision of your child's Internet use when not in a school setting.*

A. Acceptable Use

The use of your account must be in support of education and research and consistent with the educational objectives of the LCSD and MCSR. Use of other organizations' network or computing resources must comply with the rules appropriate for that network. Transmission of any material in violation of any U.S. or state regulation is prohibited. This includes, but is not limited to: copyrighted material, threatening or obscene material, or material protected by trade secret.

B. Privileges

The use of the Internet is a privilege, not a right, and inappropriate use will result in the cancellation of those privileges. (Each student who receives an account will be part of a discussion with a LCSD faculty member about the proper use of the network.) MCSR officials will deem what is inappropriate use, and their decision is final. Also, MCSR officials may close an account any time as required. LCSD officials may request MCSR to deny, revoke, or suspend specific user accounts. MCSR expects the co-signing teacher to monitor the student accounts for which he or she is responsible. This may include random checks of files and/or e-mail to determine whether the accounts are being used in a manner that is consistent with this agreement. Students accepting MCSR accounts consent to such monitoring.

C. Responsibilities

You are expected to abide by the generally accepted rules of network use. These include (but are not limited to) the following:

- Do not use the network for any illegal activity (e.g., violating copyright or other contracts, gaining illegal access or entry into other computers).
- Do not use the network for financial or commercial gain.
- Do not interfere with the proper operation of MCSR systems and networks, as well as systems and networks accessible through the Internet.
- Do not use your account or the network in such a way that you would disrupt the use of the facilities by other users.
- Do not use MCSR computing and network resources in a wasteful or frivolous manner (e.g., tying up resources with computer-based game playing such as MUD, sending trivial or excessive messages, downloading excessively large files).
- Do not use an account owned by another individual.
- Do not share your account with another individual.
- Do not reveal your personal address/phone number or the personal address/phone number of a colleague.
- Vandalism will result in cancellation of privileges. Vandalism is defined as any malicious attempt to harm or destroy data of another user, Internet, or any of the above listed agencies or other networks that are connected to the Internet backbone. This includes, but is not limited to, the uploading or creation of computer viruses.
- If you feel you can identify a security problem on the Internet, you must notify a system administrator or your District official. Do not demonstrate the problem to other users.
- Respect the privacy of other individuals.
- Files/data belonging to others are to be considered private property unless explicit authorization is given by the owner of the files.
- Be polite. Do not be abusive in your messages to others. Use appropriate language. Do not swear, use vulgarities or any other inappropriate language.

MCSR and LCSD make no warranties of any kind, whether expressed or implied, for the service that is provided. MCSR and LCSD will not be responsible for any damages you suffer. This includes loss of data resulting from delays or service interruptions caused by its own negligence or your errors or omissions. Use of any information obtained via the Internet is at your own risk. No guarantee of complete privacy is made. LCSD specifically denies any responsibility for the accuracy or quality of information obtained through MCSR facilities.

IV. Agreement to Comply

User: *I understand and will abide by the LCSD/MCSR Internet Use Agreement. I further understand that any violation of the regulations above is unethical and may constitute a criminal offense. Should I commit any violation, (1) my access privileges may be revoked and (2) school disciplinary action and/or appropriate legal action may be taken.*

Specifically, the co-signing teacher has discussed each of the following points with me.

_____ Accounts for high school students are viewed as a privilege, not a right.

_____ Accounts are to be used for educational and research purposes only, consistent with educational objectives of LHS and MCSR. Misuse will result in loss of the account.

_____ MCSR asks that the co-signing teacher monitor high school accounts, including e-mail, to see that the accounts are being used for the stated purposes. For this and other reasons, e-mail is not private. Violations that may lead to revocation of the account include:

_____ Playing MUDs or other network intensive games, or using IRC

_____ Downloading excessively large files

_____ Sharing password with anyone besides the co-signing teacher

_____ Subscribing to inappropriate newsgroups

_____ E-mail correspondence inappropriate to educational purposes

_____ Any activity posing potential risks to myself or others

_____ Harassing other users (e.g., with unwanted e-mail messages)

_____ Illegal activity

_____ Revealing my or another's home address/phone number

_____ Vandalism of accounts or systems

_____ Using abusive, vulgar, or other inappropriate language

_____ Activities that would violate LHS handbook policy

_____ Failure to report known security problems

_____ Any other inappropriate use or misuse of the account

_____ MCSR officials will deem what is inappropriate use, and their decision is final. Accounts are monitored, and use of the account implies agreement to such monitoring. MCSR may close an account at any time for violations.

I understand the conditions for keeping this account.

User Name: _____

Signature: _____

Date: _____

Parent or Guardian: *(Parents/guardians of K–12 student users must also read and sign this agreement.) As the parent or guardian of this student, I have read the Internet Use Agreement. I understand that this access is designed for educational purposes. LCSD and MCSR have taken precautions to eliminate controversial material; however, I also recognize it is impossible for LCSD and MCSR to restrict access to all controversial materials, and I will not hold them responsible for materials acquired on the network. Further, I accept full responsibility for supervision if and when my child's use is not in a school setting. I hereby give permission to issue an account for my child and certify that the information contained on this form is correct.*

Parent or Guardian's Name: _____

Signature: _____

Date: _____

Sponsoring Teacher: *(Must be signed if the applicant is a K–12 student) I have read the Internet Use Agreement and agree to promote this agreement with the student. Because the student may use the network for individual work or in the context of another class, I cannot be held responsible for the student's use of the network. As the sponsoring teacher I have instructed the student on acceptable use of the network and proper network etiquette (see checklist).*

Teacher's Name: _____

Signature: _____

Date: _____

Curriculum Links: Online Resources

Introduction

The following list is a selection of useful links to curriculum resources on the Internet. Although the list is not comprehensive, it provides a sampling of curriculum resources available in a range of specific subject areas.

Be sure also to check the many curriculum and general resources included in the text. Some of the very best resources are identified in the text as favorite sites, or along with project ideas. Not all resources identified in the text are duplicated here. In addition to the specific links to curriculum subject areas, this list includes a list of special needs resources on the World Wide Web, additional sites for kids, and additional sites of professional interest to teachers. Finally, a number of sites for Australia and the U.K. have been included in this Appendix.

How to Use This Appendix

With so many sites to choose from, it's easy to get lost. As you sample the sites both here and in the text, use a highlighter to flag your favorites. Ours are marked with a star (★). Following is a list of the curriculum area resources included in this Appendix.

1. General Activities and Resources — Here you will find general pointers to educational sites as well as references to those sites that are of interest in a number of curriculum areas.
2. Art
3. Music
4. Computers and the Internet — Watch for Internet tutorials, references to Acceptable Use Policies and information on creating Web pages, along with many general references for using computers in the classrooms.
5. Dictionaries, Glossaries, and Other References
6. English Language and Literature
7. Non-English Languages and English as a Second Language
8. The Environment
9. Geography
10. History and Current Events
11. News
12. Mathematics
13. Native Education

14. Science Activities
15. Astronomy and Space
16. Biology
17. Chemistry
18. Geology
19. Physics
20. Miscellaneous Science Resources
21. Special Needs
22. Additional Links for Kids — Here you will find children's activities and sites.
23. Additional Links for Teachers

You will also find pointers to resources at *The Teacher's Complete & Easy Guide to the Internet* Web site: **http://www.ingenia.com/trifolium/** .

1. General Activities and Resources

http://www.snowcrest.net/freemanl/index.html
A general K–12 resources site for teachers.

★ **http://badger.state.wi.us/agencies/dpi/www/WebEd.html**
An excellent general classified list of resource links for teachers.

http://pc2.pc.maricopa.edu/
The Pueblo Project: this collaborative effort involves two schools and Xerox PARC. Descriptive material on projects and publications.

http://education.indiana.edu/cas/tt/tthmpg.html
Teacher Talk: an online publication for secondary teachers which deals with current issues such as sexuality, AIDS, classroom management style, cultural diversity, violence, and the generation gap.

http://execpc.com/~dboals/boals.html
An excellent resource that includes map making, Canadian geography, art, history and electronic texts.

gopher://ericir.syr.edu/11/Lesson
AskERIC Lesson Plans. More Lesson Plans from ERIC.

gopher://bvsd.k12.co.us/11/Educational_Resources/ Lesson_Plans/Big%20Sky
Big Sky Lesson Plans.

gopher://kids.ccit.duq.edu/11/classrooms/lessons
KidLink Lesson Plans.

gopher://ericir.syr.edu:70/77/Lesson/.lesson/lessons
Index to Lesson Plans: a searchable Gopher index using keywords. You'll be prompted for a search term.

★ http://www.nptn.org/cyber.serv/AOneP/
Academy One: an international online educational resource for students, educators and parents. Grades K–12. Includes:

> http://www.nptn.org/cyber.serv/AOneP/internet.html
> Favorite Educational Resources on the Internet listed by curriculum area. Includes:

> http://www.nptn.org/cyber.serv/AOneP/academy_one/teacher/cec/curr-exch.html
> The Curriculum Exchange: contains over 500 lesson plans written by teachers. Grades K–12.

★ http://sunsite.unc.edu/cisco/schoolhouse.html
The CEARCH Virtual Schoolhouse. Includes:

> http://www.cs.cmu.edu:8001/afs/cs.cmu.edu/user/clamen/misc/Canadiana
> Canadiana Resources Server: a huge site that offers information on several curriculum areas.

http://sunsite.unc.edu/cisco/horizon/pointers/
Educational On-Ramp: links to other valuable sources of information about education, available on the World Wide Web.

http://www.csulb.edu/gc/
The Global Campus: WWW project that contains educational materials such as the Global Campus of Fine Arts.

★ http://schoolnet2.carleton.ca/english/
Canadian Schools on the Internet: links to SchoolNet and a large number of educational resources.

http://www.ucalgary.ca/~dkbrown/rteacher.html
Links to resources and lesson plans on a wide variety of subjects.

★ http://www.kidlink.org/
KidLink: Global Networking for Youth 10–15. A grassroots project in global dialogue that includes classroom topics and projects.

> gopher://global.kidlink.org/00/arc/KIDLINK.GENERAL
> Information for all people interested in the KidLink Project.

http://www.ed.uiuc.edu/exchange/
Links to learning resources for ESL, world cultures, and world news and events.

http://www.csu.edu.au/education/library.html
World Wide Web Virtual Library: Education. Resources listed by education level, site, resource.

http://www.w3.org/hypertext/DataSources/bysubject/Overview.html
The World Wide Web Virtual Library: Subject Catalogue.

http://www.packet.net/schoolhouse/Welcome.html
Latitude 28 Schoolhouse: a project designed to make educational materials accessible to students of all ages. Links to resources on art, math, science, and reading.

★ http://www.yahoo.com/Education/On_line_Teaching_and_Learning
Education: online teaching and learning. Includes:

> http://www.yahoo.com/Education/
> Education.
>
> http://www.ncsa.uiuc.edu/Edu/Classroom/classroom.html
> Internet Resources for the K–12 Classroom. Includes physical science and social science.
>
> http://mentor.external.hp.com/
> Hewlett Packard E-mail Mentor Program: to encourage K–12 students in their education by providing encouragement for their dreams, goals and interests.
>
> http://www.syllabus.com/
> SyllabusWeb: covers technologies of interest to educators in high schools, colleges, and universities. Includes free subscription to *Syllabus Magazine*.
>
> http://www.pomona.edu/visual-lit/intro/intro.html
> The On-Line Visual Literacy Project: learn about dot, line, shape, direction, value, hue, texture, etc.

http://www.screen.com/streetcents.html
Street Cents Online: a great Canadian program for youth consumers.

http://www.uml.edu/Babylon-Enc/enc.html
The Unofficial Babylon 5 Encyclopedia. A complete glossary of characters, races, ideas, groups, and terms.

★ http://www.cochran.com/theosite/KSites.html
Berit's Best Sites for Children: links to selections about animals, art galleries, astronomy, dinosaurs, history, science, and more.

http://www.bbcnc.org.uk/education
BBC TV and radio resources covering English, geography, science, music, sex education, and history.

http://www.tc.cornell.edu/Kids.on.Campus/WWWDemo/
Hands-on WWW Demonstration: includes planets and space, fingerprinting, writing and reading, things to try, and more.

> http://www.swarthmore.edu/~sjohnson/stories/
> Storytelling resources on the Web.

http://www.comenius.com/keypal/index.html
E-mail pen pal connection: links native English speakers and students of English from around the world. An avenue for learning about different cultures.

★ http://www.scri.fsu.edu/~dennisl/CMS.html
Cyberspace Middle School, Grades 6–9. Includes Educational Resources for Teachers; Topics of Interest — activities and information.

http://www.ex.ac.uk/~gjlramel/edulink.html
Links to a large number of educational resources.

http://ics.soe.umich.edu/#menu
WebICS (Interactive Communications and Simulations): interactive, educational telecommunications exercises, e.g., the Arab-Israeli Conflict Simulation.

http://Educ.QueensU.CA/index_can_page.html
Points North: Canadian K–12 Resources. Includes Education in the Provinces, National Treasures, and The Newsstand (*Globe & Mail*, *Maclean's*, *Saturday Night*, and *International News Sources*).

gopher://nysernet.org:3000/11/
Empire Internet Schoolhouse (K–12): resources for K–12, discussion groups and an invitation to join Internet projects.

★ http://gsn.org/
Global SchoolNet Foundation Home Page. Includes:

> http://gsn.org/gsn/gsh.home.html
> Global Schoolhouse.
>
> http://gsn.org/gsn/geogame.home.html
> Geogame: students use atlases, maps, and other references to solve a geography puzzle, as well as research local information to create a geography puzzle. A simple first project for beginning telecommunications.
>
> http://gsn.org/gsn/ggl.home.html
> Global Grocery List: students record prices of grocery items and share them with participating classes all over the world. Data can be used for math, social studies, health classes. A good project for telecomputing beginners.
>
> http://gsn.org/gsn/newsday.home.html
> Newsday: students write articles and post them on the Newsday Newswire, download articles from other students, and create a newspaper.
>
> http://gsn.org/gsn/roger.home.html
> Where on the Globe is Roger? Students learn about history, culture, and geography as they travel electronically along with Roger Williams while he drives around the world.

http://www.npac.syr.edu:80/textbook/kidsweb
Kidsweb: A World Wide Web Digital Library for School Kids and Teachers. Links to the arts the sciences, social studies, and more.

★ http://www.gatech.edu/lcc/idt/Students/Cole/Proj/K-12/TOC.html
Website for Busy Teachers. Includes sources materials and lesson plans on art, mathematics, science, and more.

http://www.indiana.edu/~eric_rec/comatt/links.html
Links to Other Educational Resources. Includes Web sites, newsgroups, listservers, and other information.

★ http://ericir.syr.edu/collections.html
AskERIC's Collections (Educational Resources Information Centre). Includes AskERIC, an Internet-based question-answering service for teachers and others involved in education, and AskERIC Virtual Library (resources for education).

http://pen.k12.va.us/~cfifer/treasures.shtml#E
Education Treasures on the Internet.

★ http://www.classroom.net/
Classroom Connect on the Web: newsletter for educators using the Internet in the K–12 classroom. Links to educational resources and lesson plans.

http://www.classroom.net/classroom/whatnew.htm
Look here for new links recently added.

★ http://gnn.com/gnn/meta/edu/index.html
GNN Education Center Home Page (Global Network Navigator). Goals include helping to navigate the vast Internet resources; building partnerships; enhancing curriculum with projects and ideas; delivering current articles and K–12 resources.

http://www.coreplus.calstate.edu/KALEIDO/Nav.html
K–12 Kaleidoscope. Links to art, science, current events, education information, teachers, social studies, kids' resources, language arts, and more.

http://solar.rtd.utk.edu/friends/home.html
Friends and Partners: Russian–American Information Server. Information system developed to promote better understanding of peoples and cultures. Includes economics, art, history, science, and education.

http://www.sas.upenn.edu/African_Studies/Home_Page/
AFR_GIDE.html
K–12 Electronic Guide for African Resources on the Internet. The aim of this guide is to assist K–12 teachers, librarians, and students

in locating online resources on Africa that can be used in the classroom, for research and studies.

http://www.fie.com/www/us_gov.htm
List of WWW servers: a massive list of U.S. Federal and state sites. For example: Departments of Education, Energy, Health and Human Services, Army, Defense, Agriculture, Commerce.

★ **http://www.ed.gov/**
U.S. Department of Education. Includes national education goals, department-wide initiatives (e.g., Goals 2000), and a teacher's guide to the U.S. Department of Education.

http://www.swcouncil.org/switch2.html
The Switched-On Classroom: offers an online technology planning guide, outlining a 12-step technology planning and implementation process for public schools. Includes instructive narratives, case studies, and listing of resources.

http://www.whitehouse.gov/
White House Server. Includes About the First Family, tours, and:

★ **http://www.whitehouse.gov/White_House/Publications/html/Publications-plain.html**
Publications such as speeches, the budget, NAFTA and GATT.

★ **http://www.cs.cmu.edu:8001/Web/Unofficial/Canadiana/README.html**
Canada: the Canadian Resources Page. Includes news, facts and figures, travel and tourism, government services and information, law, politics, and history.

http://www.webcom.com/~larkin/LW/LWWelcomePage.html
LearnWorld: promotes ongoing education, conversation, and publicly accessible lists of texts. LearnWorld readers arrange their own study around selected texts, which are arranged by topic and pathways.

http://glef.org OR gopher://glef.org
The George Lucas Educational Foundation. Edutopia, the foundation's newsletter, focuses on effective educational practice and technology integration into the teaching/learning environment.

★ **http://www.cochran.com/TT.html**
Preschool interactive story connected to the Canadian children's television series, *Theodore Tugboat*.

http://scholastic.com:2005/public/Store-Page.html
An online store selling K–12 educational materials.

★ **http://www.exploratorium.edu/**
Exploratorium: a collage of interactive exhibits in the areas of science, art, and human perception.

http://gnn.com/gnn/meta/edu/features/archive/andy.html
A view of K–12 Education on the Web.

http://media1.hypernet.com/oees.html
Equal education for the sexes.

http://www.stolaf.edu/network/iecc/
Intercultural E-Mail Classroom Connections.

http://www.pulver.com/netwatch/topten/tt3.htm
Netwatch Top Ten: Education.

http://www.classroom.net/cgi/rofm/eduFind.html
Search the Grades Educational Library.

http://bvsd.k12.co.us/docs/research.html
Research sources for students.

http://www.tiac.net/users/lewkaren/student-teaching.html
K's Resources for K-6 Student Teachers.

★ http://www.elibrary.com/id/2568/fiesty.htm
Electric Library makes available 150 newspapers, 900 full-text magazines, 2,000 complete works of literature, etc.; it is updated daily. There is a modest cost, but a free trial subscription is available.

★ http://ics.soe.umich.edu/#menu
DeweyWeb: an experiment in online global education. Includes background on a number of learning projects and the DeweyWeb Library, developed with classroom goals in mind.

http://www.ed.uiuc.edu/Activity-Structures/
Judi Harris' Network-Based Educational Activities: a collection of 236 exemplary network-based educational activities, including projects for writing, social action, tele-fieldtrips, and many more.

http://execpc.com/~dboals/k-12.html
K–12 Sources: curriculum and lesson plans.

★ http://io.advanced.org/ThinkQuest/
ThinkQuest: an annual contest created by Advanced Network & Services, Inc. for students in grades 7–12. ThinkQuest challenges students to work in teams with their teachers, as coaches, to build educational tools and materials for the Internet that can be shared with other students.

★ http://pitsco.inter.net/pitsco/
Pitsco Educational Technology Web Site: a first-rate resource for teachers. Click on "one stop Internet resource for teachers" to access an excellent set of links to curriculum resources, grant information, acceptable use policy information, and much more.

http://life.anu.edu.au/education.html
ANU Hypermedia Educational Resources: pointers to educational resources from the Australian National University.

http://ewu66649.ewu.edu/WAC.html
Writing across the curriculum page.

★ http://www.csu.edu.au/links/education.html
Educational Web servers in Australia.

http://www.kn.pacbell.com/wired/
Wired Learning in the Classroom and Library. This site includes a searchable index of Internet learning applications.

http://gnn.com/gnn/meta/edu/index.html
Education Center Home Page: K–12 curriculum ideas, projects, contacts for networking and instructional support. GNN has been a pioneer in K–12 online learning.

★ http://www.chaos.com:80/learn/
Electronic Learning Lab: a resource from Neteach News, a pioneer publication on classroom networking.

http://www.usa.net/~pitsco/pitsco/ask.html
Worldwide Ask-an-Expert Web links.

http://actein.edu.au
Australian Capital Territory Education Information Network includes helps for teachers in Australia and pointers to educational sources.

http://www.dpi.state.nc.us/Curriculum/Computer.skills/compcurr.html
Many Ask-an-Expert World Wide Web links from North Carolina Department of Public Instruction.

★ http://sln.fi.edu/qanda/qanda.html
InQuiry Almanack is a delightful resource from the Franklin Institute that identifies lots of new and interesting Net happenings for kids.

http://www.collegeview.com
The CollegeView Web Edition: a database of 3,300 two- and four-year colleges, featuring multimedia "tours."

http://www.csun.edu/~vceed009/
Excellent collection of resources and lesson plans for K–6. Resources include creative classroom projects, interactive activities, visits to museums, and trips around the USA and other countries.

★ http://www.etc.bc.ca/~tcoop/index.html
Network Nuggets: good selection of educational links with a keyword-searchable index. Sites are categorized by curriculum area to allow easy browsing.

http://www.websys.com/cyberschool/home.html
Cyberschool: links created by Susan J. Hendricks, a grade 2 teacher.

http://www.saschools.edu.au/
South Australia's Schools Net.

http://www.schnet.edu
SchoolsNET is an Australian organization dedicated to providing Internet access and online educational resources to schools.

http://www.demon.co.uk/koekie/
Good resource for information about educational resources and connectivity in the U.K.

http://www.neosoft.com/~dlgates/uk/ukindex.html
United Kingdom Pages.

http://rdz.stjohns.edu/kidopedia/
Kidopedia: Global Children's Encyclopedia.

http://www.nosc.mil:80/planet_earth/Library/edu_room.html
Planet Earth Education Room.

http://www.scholastic.com/public/Learning-Libraries.html
The path included in the review is correct, but you can also use the following URL to access the Scholastic Gopher:

> **http://www.nosc.mil:80/planet_earth/Library/edu_room.html**
> Education Room.

http://www.mts.net/~jgreenco/jerdeb.html
Jerome and Deborah's Big Page of Education Links: many curriculum resources for teachers, Internet projects, references, special education, counseling, and more.

http://www.yam.regulus.com
Internet Classroom Home Page. In the subfile The KidsSAY Center, you will find a series of "input forms" for kids to complete and submit to the database. The data are then collected and summarized for teacher use.

★ **http://www.nas.nasa.gov/HPCC/K12/edures.html**
Online Educational Resources list

http://www.comlab.ox.ac.uk/archive/other/museums.html
Museums.

http://www.igc.apc.org/iearn/
I*EARN is an international educational network that has a strong focus on social and environmental issues from local, national and global perspectives. Through I*EARN, students and teachers work collaboratively on curriculum-based projects that make a meaningful difference in the world.

http://dune.srhs.k12.nj.us/WWW/ACUP.HTML
A cyberlibrary and interesting Internet projects for high school.

★ http://schools.sys.uea.ac.uk/schoolnet/index.html
SchoolNet UK: includes pointers to U.K. schools on the Web.

http://schools.sys.uea.ac.uk/
Schools' server from University of East Anglia in Norwich, England.

http://www.cs.ucl.ac.uk/misc/uk/intro.html
U.K. Guide: links to broadcasting, government information, news, and more.

http://mbhs.bergtraum.k12.ny.us
Interesting school resource (Murry Bergstraum High School) with some well-developed Internet projects.

http://ivory.lm.com/~mundie/DDHC/CyberDewey.html
David Mundie's CyberDewey Page: Dewey Decimal access to subjects.

http://fox.nstn.ca/~nbarkhou/avshome.html
Innovative K–12 Web site search.

★ http://www.tc.cornell.edu:80/Edu/MathSciGateway/about.html
The Cornell Theory Center Arts and Social Sciences Gateway provides links to language arts, foreign languages, the fine arts, social studies, and history. It is aimed at "all K–12 students and educators," and was created by elementary and high school librarians, with help from the Theory Center Information Group.

http://www.web.net/crc/
Education & Youth Homepage: free software from Microsoft; early maps of Canada from Canada Map; your school homepage on the Internet.

http://www.gsa.gov/staff/pa/cic/cic.htm
U.S. Government Consumer Information Centre. Provides information useful for class projects.

http://www.pacificrim.net/~mckenzie/museum/oldies&goodies.html
The School Museum List and Site. Includes a museum how-to and a list of pointers to museums around the world.

http://www.cccnet.com
Curriculum on the Web: curriculum resource from CCCnet.

★ http://www.info.apple.com/education/
Apple Education.

★ http://k12.cnidr.org/gsh/gshwelcome.html
Global Schoolhouse Home Page.

http://www.yam.regulus.com/
Young Author's Magazine: classroom publication for teachers and students.

http://www.csun.edu/~vceed009/
Resources and lesson plans for K–6.

http://www.clark.net/pub/journalism/kid.html
KID List: anchors to sites that children and their parents might enjoy. Museums, games, children's literature resources and much more are included.

http://www.usa.net/~pitsco/pitsco/ask.html
Ask-An-Expert World Wide Web links.

http://www.smartpages.com/worldlink/worldlink.html
Good educational resources, including projects, Web Weaver monthly highlights for K–12, and Ten Tips for Webmasters.

http://www.tenet.edu/depot/main.html
Texas Education Network.

http://www.techware.com/JOBCITY/
Job City: a multimedia learning system that teaches career awareness for grades 4 to 8. Includes printed activities and experiments in reading, writing, social studies, fine arts, math, and science. Teachers can download a Macintosh or DOS version of the software.

http://www.gu.edu.au/aeres/
Australian Educational Resource: Australia's largest and most comprehensive Internet site for Australian educational information. Topics include primary, secondary, tertiary, and technical fields of study.

★ http://www.scri.fsu.edu/~dennisl/CMS.html
The Cyberspace Middle School. Note in particular the Middle School Teacher Resource Center.

http://tiger.coe.missouri.edu/Resource.html
An extensive list of K–12 educational resources on the Internet, including mathematics, science, and technology.

http://www.rogerswave.ca/wave/
WAVE for Schools: Rogers Cablesystems initiative directed at students from K–12.

http://ericir.syr.edu/
AskERIC Home Page.

http://ics.soe.umich.edu/ed712/DeweyHome.html
The Dewey Web.

http://pixel.cs.vt.edu/melissa/projects.html
Projects designed by an educator.

★ http://sunsite.unc.edu/cisco/edu-arch.html
Cisco Educational Archive and Resources Catalog.

http://netspace.students.brown.edu/eos/main_image.html
Educational Online Sources.

http://www.io.org/~dbower/
David Bower's Educational Marketplace. David Bower is a secondary school science teacher (physics), and his Web page is intended to provide a site where teachers can share ideas and resources.

http://www.socialstudies.com.
Social studies projects and links to social studies sites and curriculum materials.

2. Art

http://www.pomona.edu/visual-lit/intro/intro.html
The On-Line Visual Literacy Project: Learn about dot, line, shape, direction, value, hue, texture, etc.

http://rubens.anu.edu.au/
ArtServe: a variety of image collections and small presentations, all of which deal with art history.

http://www-lib.haifa.ac.il/www/art/
MYTHOLOGY_WESTART.HTML
Mythology in Western art.

http://sgwww.epfl.ch/BERGER/index.html
World art treasures.

http://sunsite.unc.edu/cisco/art.html
The Art Room. Links to museums, exhibits, and art-related subjects.

http://www.uky.edu/Artsource/artsourcehome.html
ArtSource is a popular set of links to art and architecture resources worldwide. Includes bibliographies, electronic exhibitions, online art journals, architecture resources, and more.

http://solar.rtd.utk.edu/friends/art/art.html
Includes Paul Gauguin and the Russian avant garde exhibition, an electronic photo gallery, and Muscovy Imports (about Russian art).

http://www.lib.virginia.edu/dic/colls/arh102/index.html
Images of Renaissance and Baroque architecture; architectural history.

http://www.msstate.edu/Fineart_Online/art-resources/
A jumping-off place for people interested in art and relationships between art and technology.

http://www.concourse.com/wwar/default.html
Art resources on the Internet. Includes a searchable index, publications, galleries, and exhibitions.

http://superdec.uni.uiuc.edu/departments/finearts/art/artspace/
uniartspace.html
Art Space: the first-ever high school online art gallery.

http://www.ncsa.uiuc.edu/SDG/Experimental/vatican.exhibit/
Vatican.exhibit.html
Vatican Exhibit. Includes history, music, and an object index.

http://www.comlab.ox.ac.uk/archive/other/museums.html
Links to museums, art galleries, and exhibits.

http://sparta.schenley.pps.pgh.pa.us/library/700_.html
The Arts. Includes virtual exhibitions and music resources.

http://fox.nstn.ca/~puppets/activity.html
Puppets Page.

http://rsc2.carleton.ca/NSTW/
Canadian Students' Creative Art Project.

http://www.artsednet.getty.edu/
More than 250 pages of free lesson plans and resources for arts
educators.

http://www.crayola.com/art_education
The Crayola Art Education site.

http://www.awa.com/artnetweb/
ArtNetWeb Projects Section.

★   http://artsedge.kennedy-center.org/artsedge.html
Artsedge: a major site for art education materials.

http://www.herron.iupui.edu/faculty_html/larmann/chlk1.html
Art Student/Teacher Resource: online resource for artists from the
Indiana University's Herron School of Art.

3. Music

http://www.music.indiana.edu/misc/music_resources.html
Music Resources on the Internet. A vast (60 pages) resource of
Gopher, telnet, FTP, and WWW sites, all related to music.

http://syy.oulu.fi/music.html
Music: links to many resources.

★   http://www.yahoo.com/Entertainment/Music
Yahoo Music List.

http://www.teleport.com/~celinec/music.shtml
Internet Music Resource Guides.

http://athena.athenet.net/~wslow/index.html
The Music Educator's Home Page: an Internet resource for music

educators from the Fox Valley Regional Music Technology Center, Kaukauna, WI, USA.

★ **http://sln.fi.edu/tfi/hotlists/music.html**
A hotlist for music education designed to help both music specialists as well as generalist teachers who teach music.

4. Computers and the Internet

http://chs.cusd.claremont.edu/www/people/rmuir/rfc1578.html
Frequently Asked Questions (and Answers) about K–12 Internetworking.

gopher://gopher.anes.rochester.edu/1roadmap.70
Roadmap to the Internet Training Workshop. Complete at your own pace.

★ **http://www.microsoft.com/k-12/mainpg.htm**
Microsoft Focus on K–12. Leads to activity guides and curriculum ideas.

http://artsedge.kennedy-center.org
A comprehensive and well-organized set of links to Net tutorials and tools. Also links to education and arts education-related lists, sites, programs, organizations, projects, curriculum, resources, etc.

http://www.missouri.edu/~wleric/help.html
Computer and Network Help. Links to a wide variety of help files and FAQs about the WWW, Gopher, mailing lists, mailer software, etc.

http://pclt.cis.yale.edu/pclt/default.htm
PC Lube and Tune. General resource for coping with PC computers, such as tutorials on key problems.

http://gagme.wwa.com/~boba/tips1.html
Tips on building your home page; detailed practical help.

http://web66.coled.umn.edu/
★ A K–12 World Wide Web project. Goals include helping educators set up their own Internet servers and helping to locate appropriate resources on the WWW. Includes:

> **http://web66.coled.umn.edu/Cookbook/contents.html**
> The Classroom Internet Server Cookbook: explains how to set up a Web server in your classroom.

http://www.cis.ufl.edu/help-system/big-dummy/
Big Dummy's Guide to the Internet.

http://www.rpi.edu/Internet/Guides/decemj/text.html
Online tutorial for the Internet by John December.

http://www.ncsa.uiuc.edu/Edu/Tutorials/TutorialHome.html
Internet Tutorials: learn how to create your own HTML documents.

http://www.teleport.com/~vincer/starter.html
School Education Resources Page. Created to introduce students and teachers to the internet. Includes pointers to K–12 resources for the humanities, social studies, mathematics, science, and schools on the Internet.

http://www.stfx.ca//people/stu/x94emj/bookmark.html
Ron MacKinnon's Netscape Bookmarks. Especially for educators; provides content areas to search plus links to nearly all Web general reference search tools. Includes:

http://hillside.coled.umn.edu/others.html
Web sites of schools around the world. Includes a clickable map of North America which is further broken down into states and provinces.

http://www.ncrel.org/ncrel/sdrs/pathwayg.htm
Pathways to School Improvement. Includes Plugging In; Choosing and Using; Educational Technology.

http://www.utexas.edu/cc/micro/microlib
Microlib Software Archives. Microcomputer freeware, shareware, and freely distributable software.

http://www.screen.com/understand/explore.html
Another very good Internet tutorial. This one includes information on basic connectivity (including how to setup Winsock), specific electronic mail packages and other basic tools, where to find Internet software, and how to create your own home page.

★ **http://www.primus.com/staff/peggy/provider.html**
Internet Providers List. Identifies Internet providers in the U.S. and links to an international providers' list.

http://www.pacificrim.net/~mckenzie/fnomay95.html
This back issue of From Now On discusses the topic of creating broad policies for student use of the Internet.

★ **http://www.sendit.nodak.edu/k12/**
Pointers to K–12 schools on the Internet.

http://www.mailbase.ac.uk:8080/ife/
A course originating in the U.K. for Internet beginners.

http://www.tcm.org/
The Computer Museum. Computer fun at Boston's famous computer museum.

http://www.dsiegel.com/tips/
Tips for writers and designers of Web pages.

http://www.kww.com/cool/
The Cool Doctor: a free Internet and WWW magazine. Its purpose is "to help folks know more about computers, software, the Internet, and the World Wide Web."

http://www.ot.com/%7Edmills/share.html
Links to shareware, including Macintosh software.

http://www.dpi.state.nc.us/Curriculum/Computer.skills/compcurr.html
North Carolina Department of Public Instruction computer skills curriculum.

http://weber.u.washington.edu/~jgurney/java/
The Java Boutique. Java is an exciting programming language for the Web that brings animation to Web pages. This site offers a collection of nearly 40 working examples of downloadable Java applications, including their source codes and how to use them.

http://www.svi.org/guidelines.html
Smart Valley Technical Guidelines for Schools: a collection of suggested minimum specifications created by industry experts for local and Wide Area Network designs that will accommodate distributed multimedia Internet access, cable TV and satellite feeds, and security requirements.

http://edweb.sdsu.edu/edfirst/edfirst.html
This HyperCard tool guides schools through the creation of a school home page, personal home pages for staff and students, and indexes for the personal pages.

http://freenet.msp.mn.us/~drwool/webconf.html
Conferencing on the World Wide Web. A guide to software that powers discussion forums on the Web.

http://www.pacificrim.net/~mckenzie
From Now On: The Educational Technology Journal.

http://www.rpi.edu/~decemj/cmc/mag/current/toc.html
Computer-Mediated Communications Magazine.

http://www.training.ibm.com/usedu
Education and Training Information from IBM. This site includes material of interest to the K–12 community and resource for school networking.

ftp://ftp.classroom.net/wentworth/Classroom-Connect/aup-faq.txt
A Frequently Asked Questions file relating to the creation of Internet Acceptable Use Policies in a K–12 setting. Written and regularly updated by the staff of *Classroom Connect*.

http://www.isd77.k12.mn.us/resources/dougwri/internet.rub.html
The Mankato Rubrics is a self-assessment for teachers to determine their level of Internet knowledge and skill.

http://www.shareware.com/
Virtual Software Library (VSL) search engine. Can be used to search for, browse, and download freeware, shareware, demos, fixes, patches, upgrades. The site also offers an e-mail newsletter to keep current on new additions.

http://www.webcom.com/impulse/list.html
New Webpage Resource for Listserv Lists. Another all-in-one resource for learning about, finding and subscribing to e-mail discussion groups/lists.

http://www.smartpages.com/worldlink/worldlink.html
Helping Educators Navigate the Net.

★ **http://gsn.org/gsn/**
Internet Projects Registry Archive Services from the Global SchoolNet Foundation. Key resource for locating online projects that can be registered on a monthly calendar.

http://www.cs.yale.edu/homes/sjl/clipart.html AND
http://www.eecs.wsu.edu/~rkinion/lines/lines.html
Clip art sources.

http://web66.coled.umn.edu/
Web66 Registry of K–12 Schools on the Web.

http://www.oise.on.ca/~mwronski/aup1.html
AUPs (Acceptable Use Policies) from nine different schools; also useful guide on what issues an AUP should cover.

http://dune.srhs.k12.nj.us/WWW/ACUP.HTML
Southern Regional High School (NJ) Acceptable Use Policies. This site includes sample policies, contracts, parental waivers, and links to other policies.

gopher://riceinfo.rice.edu:1170/11/More/Acceptable/
Rice University also has a large collection of policies at its Gopher site.

http://www.ed.uiuc.edu/Guidelines/
Guidelines for Educational Uses of Networks.

http://www.ucalgary.ca/~mueller/hanson.html
This site was developed for a presentation at a Telecommunications conference. It addresses ethical, technical, social, personal, and supervision issues. Also note the pointer to Sally's Home Page which contains an excellent set of links to school-related telecommunications projects.

http://www.iworld.com
iWorld is on online publication from Mecklermedia, the publishers of *Internet World*. The publication will particularly interest computer teachers and school librarians.

http://www.internetvalley.com/top100mag.html
Top 100 Computer Magazines. Links to the top 100 computer- and software-related Web magazines.

http://www.ziff.com:8007/~macuser/
MacUser Magazine.

http://www.faulkner.com
FaulknerWeb: an award-winning technology electronic magazine (e-zine), free shareware downloads (all programs are reviewed on the site), and other features.

http://www.gsn.org/gsn/cuseeme.schools.info.html
Key resource for schools using CU-SeeMe video-conferencing. Includes information about the CU-SeeMe mailing list.

http://www.dana.edu/~dwarman
A densely packed, tightly organized resource, designed to help the WWW user to locate the resources needed to make efficient use of the vast number of sites on the Web. Includes a primer for new users.

http://www.zdnet.com/~macuser/
MacUserWeb: for Macintosh users.

http://uu-gna.mit.edu:8001/uu-gna/text/internet/notes/
Introduction to the Internet: class notes.

http://www.execpc.com/~jeffo/webdes/frefavmn.htm
Freeware Favorites Newsletter.

http://http://www.ultranet.com/~mills/
LOGO language where you can find Microsoft WinLOGO for Windows and Windows '95.

http://www.cwru.edu/help/introHTML/toc.html
Very good introductory HTML tutorial from Case Western Reserve.

http://www.mcp.com/general/workshop
Macmillan HTML Workshop: has links for experienced Web authors, as well as an online style guide for beginners.

http://www.edu.yorku.ca/~tcs/~rfouchaux/index.htm#html
This site is a good starting point for learning HTML. It includes links to tutorials from beginner to advanced, clip art, graphics, and shareware for writing HTML.

http://info.med.yale.edu/caim/StyleManual_Top.HTML
Web style manual.

http://www.cris.com/~jmm/collegehill.html
Beginners Guide to Setting Up Web Sites. Includes an online tutorial that explains some of the basics of setting up your own Web site.

gopher://isaac.engr.washington.edu:70/11/software/instruct
http://users.aol.com/myridia1/myridia1.htm
http://www.dnai.com/~dunda/products.html
Shareware for educators.

http://www.cnet.com/Resources/Download/
Free educational software, including programs for math, sciences, English, and more.

http://vsl.cnet.com/
Index source for many software archives.

http://scwww.ucs.indiana.edu/mlarchive/
Majordomo, Listproc and Listserv electronic discussion groups' master list. A searchable database of some 13,000 mailing lists.

http://www.netskills.ac.uk
Internet for Everyone: a course that provides a thorough introduction to the Internet and the skills needed to use it.

http://www.nauticom.net/www/future21/create1.html
http://www.cs.biu.ac.il:8080/cgi-bin/createPageM
World Wide Web Authoring and Internet On the Fly Server are sources to help you create a home page.

http://snowwhite.it.brighton.ac.uk/~mas/mas/courses/html/html.html#LOGIC
HTML guide from the U.K.

http://www.missouri.edu/~c588349/colormaker-tutorial.html
Color tutorial.

http://tso.cin.ix.net/user/fo/fostbt/mac.html
The TSO Macintosh Web Page.

http://www.macfaq.com/
The Well-Connected Mac.

http://www.macplay.com
MacPlay.

http://www.dartmouth.edu/pages/TidBITS/TidBITS.html
TidBITS Mailing List Archives.

http://www.cs.wisc.edu/~tuc/mac
Brian's Repository of Macintosh Information

http://www.best.com/~myee/ultimate_mac.html
Ultimate Macintosh List.

http://asearch.mccmedia.com/macintosh.html
Macintosh-related information.

http://www.k14.peak.org
The Oregon State University Computer Science Outreach Services
has several K–14 related activities.

http://oeonline.com/~tomk/MacMagazine
MacMagazine, a monthly WWW magazine for Macintosh users.

5. Dictionaries, Glossaries, and Other References

http://www.nosc.mil/planet_earth/books.html#b105
Dictionaries, thesaurus, acronyms plus libraries, publishers, and more.

http://www.eecis.udel.edu/dictionaries.html
Dictionaries, including an acronym dictionary and *The Free On-line
Dictionary of Computing*.

http://www.princeton.edu/Main/refwww.html
Dictionaries, bibles, and other reference works on the Web.

http://tuna.uchicago.edu/forms_unrest/ROGET.html
A searchable forms-based *Roget's Thesaurus*.

http://www.c3.lanl.gov/mega-math/gloss/gloss.html
The MegaMath Glossary and Reference Section.

http://edweb.cnidr.org:90/dic.html
The EdWeb Dictionary. A glossary of telecommunications terms.

http://www.wiltel.com/glossary/glossary.html
Wiltel Telecommunications Glossary. Contains over 700 terms.

gopher://nceet.snre.umich.edu/00/.g-i/glossK6.clres
Environmental Glossary for grades K–6.

gopher://nceet.snre.umich.edu/00/.g-i/gloss712.clres
Environmental Glossary for grades 7–12.

http://rdz.stjohns.edu/kidopedia/
A global Children's Encyclopedia, written by kids for kids.

http://mlab-power3.uiah.fi/EnglishFrench/avenues.html
English–French Dictionary.

http://mlab-power3.uiah.fi/EnglishFrench/FE.html
Dictionnaire Français–Anglais.

http://tuna.uchicago.edu/forms_unrest/FR-ENG.html
French–English Dictionary.

gopher://wiretap.Spies.COM/00/Library/Document/shake.dic
Early Modern Europe: Shakespeare Glossary.

http://www.mit.edu:8001/afs/athena.mit.edu/user/g/a/galileo/
Public/WWW/galileo.html
The Biographical Dictionary. Provides concise facts about figures
from ancient times to present day.

★ http://www.loc.gov/
Library of Congress World Wide Web Home Page includes Exhibits
and Events, e.g., Scrolls from the Dead Sea; African-American
Culture and History; Services and Publications. Digital Library
Collections.

http://thorplus.lib.purdue.edu/reference/index.html
Virtual Reference Desk.

http://www.nara.gov/
The U.S. National Archives Document Service contains valuable
permanent records of the U.S. government, including nine presidential libraries.

http://k12.oit.umass.edu/rref.html
Librarians' Ready Reference Guide Using the Internet.

http://sparta.schenley.pps.pgh.pa.us/library/dewey.html
Virtual Library compiled and maintained by Linda Savido and
Kathy Olesak. Internet guide to hot topics; uses the Dewey Decimal
Classification System.

http://www.cc.columbia.edu/acis/bartleby/bartlett/index.html
Bartlett's *Familiar Quotations*.

★ http://ipl.sils.umich.edu
Internet Public Library.

http://www.slac.stanford.edu/~clancey/refs.html
General Reference Resources: a quick resource list of reference
materials.

http://www.tricky.com/liz/
NBNSOFT: Net Encyclopedia. Extensive resources on the Internet,
featuring the very best of what's new.

6. English Language and Literature

gopher://bvsd.k12.co.us/11/Educational_Resources/Lesson_Plans/
Big%20Sky/language-arts
K–12 Language Arts Lesson Plans: an excellent resource of over 60
lesson plans on vocabulary, writing, grammar, literature, and poetry.

http://www.indiana.edu/~eric_rec/
ERIC Clearinghouse on Reading, English, and communication: a
site dedicated to providing educational materials, services, and
coursework to parents, educators, students, and others interested in
the language arts. Includes:

http://www.indiana.edu/~rugs/webdem.html
The Web Demo.

http://english-www.hss.cmu.edu/langs.html
Languages and Linguistics Archive: holds works on language, linguistic theory, and structural linguistics. Includes dictionaries, grammar, and much more.

http://www.cogsci.princeton.edu/~wn
WordNet 1.5 online lexical reference system. Free copy for downloading. English nouns, verbs, adjectives, and adverbs in synonym sets from Princeton University.

http://www.willamette.edu/~tjones/Language-Page.html
The Human Languages Page. Extensive collection of dictionaries and language home pages.

http://www.missouri.edu/~wleric/writehelp.html
Writing Resources. Includes handouts, online writing labs, and many other useful writing links.

http://gsn.org/gsn/newsday.home.html
Newsday. Students write articles and post them on the Newsday Newswire, download articles from other students, and create a newspaper.

http://scholastic.com:2005/public/PressReturn/Press-Return.html
Press Return: this site gives young writers, poets, and journalists the chance to collaborate with professional editors and have their work read by a worldwide audience.

http://riceinfo.rice.edu/armadillo/Owlink/Lessons/rigginsles.html
Writing for Real. A writing exercise.

★ http://www.cs.cmu.edu/Web/booktitles.html
Books Online. Includes title and author search.

gopher://wiretap.Spies.COM/11/Books
Electronic Books at Wiretap. A large range of books for all age groups.

★ http://english-www.hss.cmu.edu/
Carnegie Mellon University's English Server. Humanities texts published on the Internet.

http://the-tech.mit.edu/Shakespeare/works.html
The complete works of William Shakespeare.

http://english-www.hss.cmu.edu/Poetry.html
Poetry. Many poems and poetry resources, including:

> http://english-www.hss.cmu.edu/Poetry.html
> The Internet Poetry Archive. Makes poems from contemporary poets accessible to new audiences.

http://www.wordsmith.org/
Provides a word a day; users may subscribe. For high school students.

http://www.wwa.com/math/puzzles/preposterousWords/PuzzleOfTheWeek
Provides an unusual word with a multiple choice answer. For high school students.

http://www.swarthmore.edu/~sjohnson/stories/
Storytelling resources on the Web. Includes tales from other cultures, folk tales, stories by children, and links to other resources such as the Children's Literature Web Guide.

★ http://www.ucalgary.ca/~dkbrown
Children's Literature Web Guide. Internet resources related to books for children and young adults. An extremely good resource.

http://www.docker.com/~whiteheadm/yaread.html
Reading lists and book reviews for high school students.

http://www.packet.net/schoolhouse/reading.html
Resources of reading lists, an on-line writing lab, and poems.

★ http://owl.trc.purdue.edu/writing-labs.html
List of online writing centers, resources, and writing labs on the Internet.

http://owl.trc.purdue.edu/
A Virtual Writing Laboratory. Includes parts of speech, spelling, ESL, and general writing concerns.

http://www.cs.yale.edu/HTML/YALE/CS/HyPlans/loosemore-sandra/froggy.html
Frogs: songs, stories, pictures, sounds, and science activities.

★ http://en-garde.com/kidpub/
Kidpub WWW Publishing. For early- to middle-grade students and teachers.

http://ipax.apana.org.au/~itisus/index.html
Ozlit: Australian literature page.

http://ipax.apana.org.au/ozlit
OzLit, the Australian Literature Internet Site. Includes:

> http://ipax.apana.org.au/ozlit/ozkidz.html
> Australian Children's literature page.

http://lrdc5.lrdc.pitt.edu/awad/home-txt.html
A Word-A-Day Home Page.

http://www.cas.usf.edu/english/walker/mla.html
Citations of electronic resources (MLA style).

http://www.wilpaterson.edu/wpcpages/library/ref.hm
A Guide for Citing Electronic Information; gives examples.

http://www.uvm.edu/~xli/reference/estyles.html
Another reference source for citing electronic sources.

http://english.ttu.edu/kairos/1.1/index.html OR
http://english.ttu.edu/acw/
Kairos, an electronic journal sponsored by the Alliance for
Computers and Writing, is on a server at Texas Tech University and
the Alliance's home page. Valuable Internet writing links.

http://www.literature.org/Works
Extensive resource for online electronic books, including many classic works of literature.

http://www.columbia.edu/acis/bartleby/strunk/
Strunk & White's *Elements of Style* in electronic format.

http://www.nova.edu/Inter-Links/reference.html
Writer's General Reference.

★ http://www.parentsplace.com/readroom/childnew/index.html
The Children's Literature Home Page: designed to enhance children's literacy by helping adults find the best books available.
Reviews of hardback books, electronic books, and multimedia products.

http://mgfx.com/Kidlit/
KidLit Children's Literature Web site, featuring quality children's literature.

http://www.users.interport.net/~hdu/
Books for children and writers' tips.

http://sunsite.unc.edu/ibic/IBIC-homepage.html
World Wide Web Virtual Library: literature source.

http://web.syr.edu/~fjzwick/twainwww.html
Mark Twain on the Web. Complete compilation of Mark Twain quotes, booklists, and hotlinks.

http://www.pd.astro.it/local-cgi-bin/kids.cgi/forms
The Children's Page: offers book suggestions by and for kids.

http://www.nation.org/~krishnar/ananse.html/
Ananse site: An archive of Ananse (Spider) stories.

http://www.li.net/~scharf/author.html
Author! Author!: A good starting point for finding information or texts by many authors.

http://the-tech.mit.edu/Classics/
The Tech Classics Archive: another premier classical literature resource; offers 375 works by 30 classical authors, in English translation.

http://www.halyon.com/ahcool/home.html
Cool Writers' Magazine: publishes student writing.

http://www.comenius.com/index.html
The Virtual English Language Center.

http://www.comenius.com/fable/index.html
Resource for fables.

http://www.imgnet.com/auth/index.html
Authornet: many English and American authors.

http://spider.netropolis.net/slummit/
Slummit: a language-arts instructional magazine.

7. Non-English Languages and English as a Second Language

http://teleglobe.ca/~leo/french.html
French Lesson Home Page. Includes eight lessons, additional vocabulary, French expressions and idioms.

http://www.yahoo.com/Humanities/Linguistics_and_Human_Languages/Languages/Spanish/Weekly_Spanish_Lessons_by_Tyler_Jones/
Weekly Spanish lessons by Tyler Jones.

http://sparta.schenley.pps.pgh.pa.us/user/fougeres/isix1.html
Lesson plans for German classes, developed by Regine Fougere.

http://www.ed.uiuc.edu/edpsy-387/rongchang-li/esl/
Starting point for ESL students who want to learn English through the World Wide Web. Includes links to listening/speaking, reading, writing, ESL sites on the Web and other resources.

http://www.comenius.com/
The Virtual English Language Centre: resources for ESL students and teachers. Includes:

> http://comenius.port.net/fable/index.html
> Fluency Through Fables; True & False. Also vocabulary; written exercises.

http://deil.lang.uiuc.edu/exchange/
Exchange: an electronic magazine for English Second Language students.

http://www.ed.uiuc.edu/exchange/contributions/learning/learning.html
ESL resources, including learning tips and a grammar tutorial.

http://www.rpi.edu/dept/llc/writecenter/web/text/esl.html
ESL: Use of articles "a," "an," and "the."

http://www.cc.utah.edu/~coj6886/jltc.html
The Joint Language Training Center Home Page: a large collection of links to various Web resources for many foreign languages.

http://www.ncbe.gwu.edu/
National Clearinghouse for Bilingual Education.

http://www.willamette.edu/~tjones/Language-Page.html
The Human Languages Page: links to resources in language, literature, linguistics, and language learning sources.

http://www.pacificnet.net/~sperling/ideas.html
ESL Cafe: projects and ideas for English as a Second/Foreign Language.

ftp://ftp.dartmouth.edu/pub/LLTI-IALL/365german-news/tw/index.htm
Downloadable crossword puzzles for foreign language learning.

http://thecity.sfsu.edu/~funweb
Frizzy University Network (FUN) Home Page: a collection of ESL-related sites on the Web.

http://www.hut.fi/~rvilmi/email-project.html
The Language Centre.

http://www.cortland.edu/www_root/flteach/flteach.html
Foreign Language Teaching Forum.

http://www.pvp.com/esl.htm
The ESL Virtual Catalog: online index to Internet resources available to students and teachers of ESL and EFL.

http://prairienet.org/community/esl/homepage.html
Hands On English.

8. The Environment

http://envirolink.org/enviroed/students.html
Environmental education resources for students.

★ http://www.envirolink.org/enviroed/envirok12.html
Environmental education resources for teachers of grades K–12.

http://wx3.atmos.uiuc.edu/
The Daily Planet. A good resource for learning about weather.

http://faldo.atmos.uiuc.edu/WEATHER/weather.html
The Weather Unit. Lessons and activities about the weather, taught from the perspectives of math, science, art, music, geography, etc. For grades 2–4.

http://mh.osd.wednet.edu/
High School Rainforest Workshop Home Page: lesson plans, activities, and further links.

http://mh.osd.wednet.edu/Homepage/Mammals.html
Animal awareness lesson plan and links to further information.

http://quest.arc.nasa.gov/livefrom/livefrom.html
Live From Antarctica. Includes teacher's guide and classroom activities, question and answer archive, field journals, and links to resources.

http://www.covis.nwu.edu/
Students study atmospheric and environmental sciences through inquiry-based activities, resembling the question-centered, collaborative practice of scientists. Grades K–12.

http://ellesmere.ccm.emr.ca/npri/clone/npri.html
National Pollutant Release Inventory: provides a list of substances and the ability to map pollutants. High school.

gopher://nceet.snre.umich.edu/
NCEET (National Consortium for Environmental Education and Training) Gopher menu. NCEET works to enhance and support effective environmental education for grades K-12. Includes:

> **gopher://nceet.snre.umich.edu/11/nceet**
> About NCEET: goals, funding, partners.

> **gopher://nceet.snre.umich.edu/11/toolbox**
> Environmental Education Toolbox. Includes Using Computers in Environmental Education; Getting Started: Bringing EE Into Your Classroom; and the EE Reference Collection.

> **gopher://nceet.snre.umich.edu/11/activities**
> Activities/lesson plans/programs for EE. Directories of lesson plans and activities are divided by grade level where possible.

> **gopher://nceet.snre.umich.edu/11/classres**
> Curriculum for EE: Bibliographies/catalogs/A-V/software. Includes:

> **gopher://nceet.snre.umich.edu/11/classres/SNAP**
> Includes an annotated bibliography of resources, such as activity guides, for teaching environmental education. Grades K–12.

> **gopher://nceet.snre.umich.edu/00/.g-i/glossK6.clres**
> An Environmental Glossary for grades K–6.

> **gopher://nceet.snre.umich.edu/00/.g-i/gloss712.clres**
> An Environmental Glossary for grades 7–12.

★   Also, check out the following NCEET Web sites:

> **http://www.nceet.snre.umich.edu/**
> EE-Link, the Environmental Education Server: to support and enhance environmental education with resources, activities and lesson plans for Grades K–12.

http://www.nceet.snre.umich.edu/classres.html#top
Classroom activities covering ozone, air quality and pollution, birds as indicators of environmental pollutants, global change, and more.

http://www.nceet.snre.umich.edu/EndSpp/Endangered.html
An extensive collection of information on endangered species. Current news, factsheets, images, a clickable map, government contact information, curricula, and current K–12 projects on endangered species.

http://www.globe.gov/
Global Learning and Observation to Benefit the Environment.

www.ran.org/ran/kids_action/index.html
Rainforest Action Network—Kids' Corner.

http://www.voyagepub.com/publish
Voyage is an online magazine that each month publishes 80 of the most interesting and relevant news stories on environmental issues. Stories are selected and summarized from over 500 sources.

http://www.etc.bc.ca/~tcoop/enviro.html
The Environment.

http://www.nwf.org/nwf/
National Wildlife Federation.

http://www.ran.org/ran/
Rainforest Action Network (RAN).

http://www.covis.nwu.edu/Geosciences/index.html
Geosciences Webserver: includes a wide variety of information about climatology, oceanography, and global warming, and some especially interesting interactive visualizers, such as the Greenhouse Effect Visualizer.

http://www.miamisci.org/hurricane/hurricane0.html
Hurricanes: Storm Science. A five-part resource on hurricanes; developed particularly for elementary students and teachers.

9. Geography

http://info.er.usgs.gov/education/teacher/what-do-maps-show/index.html
Lesson plans for four geography and map-reading lessons. Upper elementary and junior high school.

http://gsn.org/gsn/geogame.home.html
Geogame: students use atlases, maps, and other references to solve a geography puzzle, as well as research local information to create a geography puzzle. A simple first project for beginning telecommunications.

http://rowan.lib.utexas.edu/Libs/PCL/Map_collection/Map_collection.html
PCL Map Collection: over 230,000 maps covering every area of the world.

★ http://tiger.census.gov/
Tiger Mapping Service: provides a public resource for generating high-quality, detailed maps of anywhere in the United States, using public geographic data.

http://tiger.census.gov/cgi-bin/gazetteer
U.S. Gazetteer: identifies places to view with the Tiger Map Server and the 1990 Census Lookup. Searchable index. Includes Tiger Maps that let students zoom in and zoom out.

http://www.yahoo.com/Regional_Information/States/
Yahoo for the United States. Includes: Regional information (e.g., census report, business, government, Internet Access Providers) for each state.

http://www.yahoo.com/Science/Geography/maps
Yahoo Map Page. Leads to many map links and resources, including:

> http://fermi.jhuapl.edu/states/states.html
> Shaded relief maps of the U.S.

★ http://ellesmere.ccm.emr.ca/wwwnais/wwwnais.html
Gateway to Canadian Geography. Links to: Make a Map, Find a Geographical Name, List of Atlases, and:

> http://ellesmere.ccm.emr.ca/npri/clone/npri.html
> National Pollutant Release Inventory: provides a list of substances and maps pollutants.

http://wintermute.ncsa.uiuc.edu:8080/map-tutorial/image-maps.html
Graphical Information Map Tutorial: a step-by-step tutorial for designing and serving graphical maps of information resources.

http://www.webcom.com/~bright/petermap.html
Peter's Projection Map: tutorial to be downloaded.

http://www.ed.uiuc.edu/exchange/contributions/culture/culture.html
Human Geography: World Cultures. Information organized by topic (e.g. wedding ceremonies, male/female roles) or by country.

http://quest.arc.nasa.gov/livefrom/livefrom.html
Live From Antarctica in 1994–95: an electronic field trip. Includes teacher's guide and classroom activities.

★ http://gsn.org/gsn/roger.home.html
Where on the Globe is Roger? Students learn about history, culture,

and geography as they electronically travel along with Roger Williams while he drives around the world.

http://geog.gmu.edu/gess/jwc/bosnia/bosnia.html
The Bosnian Virtual Field Trip. Students prepare for their virtual journey by learning where Bosnia is. They view maps and pictures, obtain passports, and check travel advisories. Finally, they "go" to Bosnia.

telnet://martini.eecs.umich.edu:3000
The Geographic Name Sever.

http://www.interport.net/~ednorman/list.html
A guide to global culture.

http://spirit.lib.uconn.edu/ArcticCircle
The Arctic Circle Web site at the University of Connecticut provides information on the peoples and environment of the Arctic and Subarctic regions.

http://www.cs.ucl.ac.uk./misc/uk/intro.html
U.K. Guide.

http://www-nais.ccm.emr.ca/schoolnet
National Schoolnet Atlas from Canada with links to sites for many local Canadian cities.

10. History and Current Events

http://neal.ctstateu.edu/history/world_history/world_history.html
Gateway to World History. Current issues with an historical perspective. Includes documentary archives, world history online resources, reference works, and more. Grades K–12.

http://www.directnet.com/history/DirectoriesofHistoricalResources
Massive list of Web links to historical materials.

http://ukanaix.cc.ukans.edu/history/
Huge collection (97 pages) of links to areas related to history.

★ **http://english-server.hss.cmu.edu/History.html**
History and historiography, a directory of electronic documents and of further sites.

gopher://wiretap.spies.com/11/Gov/US-History
U.S. historical documents.

http://www.cwc.lsu.edu/
★ U.S. Civil War-related Web links. Includes books, information, memorials and monuments, letters and diaries, maps, newspapers, and much more.

http://www.msstate.edu/Archives/History/index.html
The Historical Text Archive. Includes:

http://www.msstate.edu/Archives/History/USA/usa.html
History of the United States. Covers the colonial period through WWI and WWII to the Gulf War.

gopher://gopher.house.gov:70/1
U.S. House of Representatives Gopher menu.

gopher://gopher.senate.gov:70/1
U.S. Senate Gopher menu.

http://info.ic.gc.ca/opengov/
Canadian government information.

http://neal.ctstateu.edu/history/world_history/archives/cuba.html
Latin America: History & Struggles of Cuba. Includes documents (e.g., Cuba Human Rights Practices, 1993), extracts from an interview of former U.S. Attorney General on the U.S. blockade of Cuba, and "The Gap between Underdeveloped and Developed Countries Is Getting Bigger," an address by Fidel Castro to the U.N. Summit, 1995.

http://www.ushmm.org/
Holocaust Memorial Museum, Washington, D.C. Includes background information, educational programs, a teacher's guide with brief history, and answers to frequently asked questions.

http://www.infomall.org/kidsweb/history.html
KidsWeb—History. Includes:

> http://rs6.loc.gov/amhome.html
> American Memory. Multimedia material relating to American culture and history. Includes special collections of the Library of Congress, such as Civil War photographs.

http://sunsite.unc.edu/expo/1492.exhibit/Intro.html
1492: An Ongoing Voyage. Focuses on the cultures of the early Americas, the Mediterranean (15th–16th C.), Christopher Columbus, and the European claims in the western hemisphere. Grades 7–10.

http://grid.let.rug.nl/~welling/usa/revolution.html
From Revolution to Reconstruction. An HTML text on American history from the colonial period until WW I.

http://www.usdoj.gov/ojp/rol/docs/un.html
United Nations Information Servers. Includes volunteer and development program information.

★ http://lcweb.loc.gov/exhibits/African.American/intro.html
Selections from the African-American Mosaic: a Library of Congress resource guide for the study of Black history and culture. Covers 500 years of the Black experience in the western hemisphere.

http://www.csulb.edu/gc/libarts/am-indian/nae/
The Native American Experience: photographs, drawings, maps, and short descriptions chronicling the experiences of the Native American population from pre-1600 to recent times.

http://riceinfo.rice.edu/armadillo/Owlink/Lessons/larryles.html
Explains how the close of the frontier threatened Indian civilization. Useful site for discussion of culture, racism, treaties/laws, Americanization, and ethnic groups. Grades 3–9.

http://arcturus.pomona.claremont.edu/
Indigenous Peoples: Ancient Cultures of the Western Hemisphere. Includes the cultures of the Inuit, Aztec, and Maya.

http://www.he.net/~archaeol/index.html
Archaeology Magazine: official publication of the Archaeological Institute of America. Reports all the latest archaeological discoveries. Includes news briefs and links to related Web sites.

http://orion.it.luc.edu/~sgerlac/links.html
My Guide to Classical Archeology: a well-organized site that includes museum links, academic classics departments, and related discussion group resources.

gopher://gan.ncc.go.jp/11/JAPAN/History
East Asia: Japan Information—History. Includes ancient times, feudal age, unity in isolation, restoration of imperial rule, the modern period, and 1945 to the present.

http://solar.rtd.utk.edu/friends/history/history.html
History of Our Nations. Includes Russian and American constitutions, history of Vikings in Russia, 1867 Treaty with Russia, and more.

★ http://www.loc.gov/
Library of Congress World Wide Web Home Page. Includes Exhibits and Events (e.g., Scrolls from the Dead Sea, African-American Culture and History), Services and Publications, and Digital Library Collections.

http://www.demon.co.uk/history/index.html
The World of Vikings. Includes research projects, educational resources, museums, and mailing lists. Focus on the years 800–1100 CE. Grades 7–10.

http://odin.nls.no/viking/vnethome.htm
The Viking Network. Includes an electronic mail project, quiz (see below), and information about the Vikings

http://www.mit.edu:8001/afs/athena.mit.edu/user/g/a/galileo/Public/WWW/galileo.html
The Biographical Dictionary: concise facts about figures from ancient times to the present day.

★ http://www.einet.net/galaxy/Social-Sciences/History.html
History resources on the Web.

http://thomas.loc.gov
Thomas Register: U.S. legislative information, including the Congressional Record.

http://www.fred.net/nhhs/html/election.htm
The U.S. presidential election of 1996.

http://haven.uniserve.com/~andreasn/chart/chart.html
An excellent example of a World History Time Line is available at this site.

http://www.pathfinder.com/reinventing
An online Reinventing America game, which offers players the chance to try their hand at balancing the federal budget.

http://www.tristero.com/alamo
The Alamo: Victory or Death: history of the Battle of the Alamo (1836) in San Antonio, TX.

http://www.seatimes.com/mlk/index.html
Developed by the Seattle Times, this site commemorates the life and legacy of Dr. Martin Luther King.

http://www.kaiwan.com/~mcivr/genesis.html
African Genesis: features information on African and African-American history, religion, music, news and commentary.

http://www.multied/history
MultiEducator site: includes photos, documents and links to other history-related sites. Subjects include Civil War, Aviation, Railroad, American History, JFK, FDR, and World History of the 20th Century.

★ http://www.kaiwan.com/~lucknow/horus/horuslinks.html
Horus' History Links: articles and links on every imaginable area of history.

http://odin.nls.no/viking/vnethome.htm
An intriguing site for those studying the Vikings.

http://www.access.gpo.gov/su_docs/aces/aaces001.html
Depository GPO Access sites. Documents are available in ASCII text; some are also available in Adobe Acrobat PDF format.

http://cobweb.utcc.utk.edu/~hoemann/warweb.html
American Civil War Home Page: diaries, bibliographies, timelines, battle information and more.

http://www.internexus.net/~paladine/immigration
American immigration research.

★ http://www.si.edu/start.htm
Smithsonian Institution site; includes the *Encyclopedia Smithsonian*.

http://www.exploratorium.edu/nagasaki/mainn.html
Nagasaki Memories: looks at the atomic bombings of Hiroshima and Nagasaki, and at the last days of WW II.

11. News

http://schoolnet.carleton.ca/english/events/index.html
Educational resources centered around current or special events.

http://ukanaix.cc.ukans.edu/carrie/news_main.html
Omnivore: a comprehensive daily news service designed to cover events around the world as they happen.

http://www.iisd.ca/linkages/un/youth.html
Youth of the World. Messages from youth from all over the world concerning such issues as Women and Girls, Poverty, The Environment, Human Rights, and Population.

http://www.vir.com/~sher/julian.htm
Current issues and resources for investigative journalists; interesting resource for the classroom.

http://www.vir.com/~sher/topics.htm
Story Topics. Resources covering health and medicine, the environment, justice, culture, racism and human rights, the military and spies, business, and the far right.

http://www.whitehouse.gov
White House information and publications.

http://www.canoe.ca
Canadian Online Explorer: Canadian media source including the Toronto, Calgary, and Edmonton *Suns*, the *Financial Post, Maclean's,* and *680News Radio.*

http://www.ed.uiuc.edu/exchange/contributions/news/news.html
News from Around the World. Articles by non-native English language users.

http://ayn-0.ayn.ca/PAGES/news.htm
Aboriginal Youth Network: information from across Canada and the world, including articles, sections of newspapers, and newsletters.

http://www.cs.vu.nl/~gerben/news.html
International News. Current events, news divided by geographic area, and news in languages other than English.

http://uttm.com/
CBS News Up To The Minute. Provides news coverage, Internet developments, movie reviews, women's health reports, parenting, and what's news in space.

★ http://www.pathfinder.com/
Pathfinder [Time Warner Publications]. Includes magazines focusing on current events (e.g., *Time, Asiaweek*), finance, technology, sports, arts and entertainment, home and hobbies, and "kids' stuff." Full-text search service for back issues of Time and other Time-Warner publications.

http://www.nyc.pipeline.com/edpub/e-papers.home.page.html
Online Newspaper Services Directory. Includes list of newspaper publishers with online services, and resources of interest to the newsmedia community.

http://www.umassd.edu/SpecialPrograms/ISN/KidNews.html
International Student NewsWire—KidNews. A news service for students and teachers around the world. Anyone may submit or use stories, or comment in the discussion sections.

http://nytimesfax.com/
The *New York Times* Web site: links to Sportsworld, Computer News Daily, and more. In Acrobat format; requires free Acrobat reader to view.

★ http://baretta.calpoly.edu/htmlpages/publications.html
Online Newspapers and Magazines. An excellent listing of daily national and international newspapers, including the *San Francisco Chronicle, London Daily Telegraph, St. Petersburg Express,* and *China News Digest.*

http://www.sjmercury.com/
San Jose Mercury News.

http://www2.nando.net/
Nando Times: News and Observer online news service.

http://www.cbc.ca/whatsnew/educat1.html
Educational resources from the Canadian Broadcasting Corporation.

http://www.ingenius.com
Children's news from Reuters and TeleCommunications Inc.

http://detnew.com/nie
Newspapers in education.

http://www.southam.com/nmc/index.html
Southam News on the Web: Canadian and international news, including links to local and regional news.

http://www.etc.bc.ca/~tcoop/world.html
Newslinks that have been featured in Network Nuggets.

http://www.kdtech.co.uk/uktoday/index.html
U.K. Today. Hourly updated U.K. newspaper on the Web, providing hourly updates, current headlines, stories, sports, and fun content.

http://www.lib.umich.edu/libhome/Documents.center/docnews.html
The University of Michigan Government Documents Center provides a Documents in the News page. Taken from official sources, this page has full-text documents on current events and subjects in the news, such as Bosnia, the Ebola Virus, and United Nations events.

★ http://www.newslink.org
NewsLink: a link to news sources, including a top 10 hotlist of the most frequently cited online news resources.

★ http://www.eg.bucknell.edu/~boulter/crayon/
CRAYON (CReAte Your Own Newspaper). Students select different sources of online news, then create a custom "newspaper" that can be saved as a file on your hard drive.

http://www.cnn.com/
CNN's interactive site.

http://www.bbcnc.org.uk/education
BBC Education Online: offers various educational services.

http://www.theatlantic.com
Atlantic Monthly Magazine's electronic edition on the World Wide Web.

http://www.uky.edu/Subject/current.html
WWW Resources—Current Events.

http://www.phlab.missouri.edu/~wlspif/news.html
Newspapers, magazines a news services on the Net.

http://www.hk.net/~drummond/milesj/china.html
The China News Page: provides links to sources of political, social and economic news about China and the far East.

http://www.tezcat.com/~top/NewsLink.html
NewsLink: links to a number of news sources, including U.S. Official News sources and NASA News.

http://www.well.com/user/niche/hometown.htm
Hometown Free Press.

http://www.trib.com/news/APwire.html
American Press Wire Service.

http://www.adnet.wsj.com
The *Wall Street Journal's* electronic edition on the Web.

★ http://www.iguide.com
News Corp./MCI: an all-purpose site for media. Includes useful material on Cyberspace and computing.

12. Mathematics

gopher://bvsd.k12.co.us/11/Educational_Resources/Lesson_Plans/
Big%20Sky/math
Mathematics Lesson Plans: over 40 math activities and lesson plans.

gopher://ericir.syr.edu/11/Lesson/Math
AskERIC Math Lesson Plans. More than 40 activities and lesson plans. Grades K–12.

http://sashimi.wwa.com:80/math/
MathPro: puzzles, problems and resources.

http://www.cam.org/~aselby/lesson.html
Lessons for math and logic. Includes links to further resources.

★ http://forum.swarthmore.edu/dr-math/dr-math.html
Ask Dr. Math: An interactive service where students can e-mail in their math questions.

★ http://forum.swarthmore.edu/mathmagic/
MathMagic: work with other students to solve math problems. Grades K–12.

★ http://www.tc.cornell.edu/Edu/MathSciGateway/
The Cornell Theory Centre Math and Science Gateway: links to resources in math and science for educators and students. Grades 9–12.

http://forum.swarthmore.edu/k12/k12.html
Geometry problems and solutions.

http://riceinfo.rice.edu/armadillo/Owlink/Lessons/geoms.html
A geometry lesson.

http://riceinfo.rice.edu/armadillo/Owlink/Lessons/bowardles.html
Comparing data sets using the T-test. Lesson plans, worksheets for grades 8 and up.

http://riceinfo.rice.edu/armadillo/Owlink/Lessons/Boward/pg8-9.html
Statistics orientation handout. Includes symbols, terminology, definitions, hypothesis testing, and descriptive statistics.

★ http://www.cs.uidaho.edu/~casey931/mega-math/
Mega-Math. Includes activities relating mathematics and knots, a glossary, problem-solving stories, and interesting links.

http://www.c3.lanl.gov/mega-math/gloss/gloss.html
The MegaMath Glossary and Reference Section.

http://www.uni.uiuc.edu/departments/math/glazer/fun_math.html
Fun Math Things. Includes paradoxes and logic puzzles.

http://mh.osd.wednet.edu/Homepage/AnteaterMath.html
Selecting and solving math problems; turns into a game of feeding the anteater. Elementary grades.

http://archives.math.utk.edu/k12.html
List of sites for teaching mathematics. Grades K–12.

http://archives.math.utk.edu/tutorials.html
Mathematics Archives—Lessons and Tutorials. Includes a calculus self-tutor.

gopher://ericir.syr.edu/00/Lesson/Math/cecmath.30
Grade 3 lesson plan focused on area and volume.

http://gauss.uni.uiuc.edu/
WAVE Project: provides math notebooks for high school.

http://kao.ini.cmu.edu:5550/bdf.html
Blue Dog Can Count. Type in a simple formula, and Blue Dog will "bark" the answer back to you. A fun site for younger students.

http://www-cm.math.uiuc.edu/
Calculus and Mathematica Home Page. Computer-based calculus course designed for classroom use.

http://www.cam.org/~aselby/lesson.html
Exercise for math and reason at the high school and early college level.

http://www.cs.ubc.ca/nest/egems/home.html
E-Gems. Electronic games for math and science.

http://www.yahoo.com/Science/Mathematics/Numbers/PI/
All about pi.

http://www-cm.math.uiuc.edu/
These pages describe a new method of communication in mathematics teaching. Lessons are presented in the form of interactive texts running on computer.

http://jjj.mega.net/BEATCALC
Beat the Calculator Web Page.

http://www.cam.org/~aselby/lesson.html/
Appetizers and Lessons for Math and Reason: ideas for starters for math lessons; kindergarten to postsecondary.

http://www.wri.com/demo/
Interactive demonstration of Mathematica.

http://forum.swarthmore.edu/mathmagic/
MathMagic! Matematica, evidentemente (Mathematics: it is evident)

13. Native Education

http://kuhttp.cc.ukans.edu/~marc/
NativeWeb Home Page. Resources organized by subject, geographic regions, and nations/peoples.

http://www.fdl.cc.mn.us/~isk/
Fond du Lac Tribal College. Includes links to further resources.

http://hanksville.phast.umass.edu/misc/NAresources.html
Index of Native American Internet Resources. Includes cultural, art and educational resources.

http://www.io.org/~jgcom/aborl.htm
Aboriginal Links: Links to Internet resources about Aboriginal peoples around the world. A huge collection including maps of reserves, treaty information, newsgroups, art, and human rights issues.

http://ayn-0.ayn.ca
Canadian Aboriginal Youth Network. Includes news (see below), Internet sites, community events, and an Internet search.

http://www.fdl.cc.mn.us/~isk/maps.html
Aboriginal Canadian children tell about their culture: people, stories, natural features, animals, jobs, and myths.

http://hanksville.phast.umass.edu/~pgiese/
How to make Web pages and other computer resources for Native schools.

gopher://inspire.ospi.wednet.edu/11/Curr_Projects/Nat_Americans
Curriculum resources for learning about indigenous peoples. Includes an on-line Native project.

http://www.csulb.edu/gc/libarts/am-indian/index.html
American Indian Studies: includes The Native American Experience, Alcatraz, Aboriginal Art Gallery, and more.

http://www.cmcc.muse.digital.ca/cmc/cmceng/welcmeng.html
Canadian Museum of Civilization's Web site.

gopher://mercury.cair.du.edu/00/gophers/public_policy/
Native American Curriculum Resource Guide. An extensive bibliography. (Choose American Association for the Advancement of Core Curriculum, then Curriculum Resources, then Native American Studies.)

★ http://web.maxwell.syr.edu/nativeweb/
NativeWeb: a rich source of information and documents about

North and South American indigenous peoples. Future plans include developing the site to include Asia and Africa.

http://hanksville.phast.umass.edu/misc/NAresources.html
Index of Native American resources on the Internet.

http://indy4.fdl.cc.mn.us/~isk/
Web Pages and Other Resources for Indian Teachers and Students: an extensive site with much original material.

★ http://ipax.apana.org.au/ozlit/aborignl.html
Australia's indigenous people.

http://www.ota.gov
OTA Native American Resource Page.

14. Science Activities

gopher://bvsd.k12.co.us/11/Educational_Resources/Lesson_Plans/Big%20Sky/science
Science Lesson Plans: over 110 science activities and lesson plans for grades K–12.

gopher://ericir.syr.edu/11/Lesson/Science
Science-Based Lesson Plans: approximately 200 lesson plans for grades K–12.

http://ericir.syr.edu/Newton/welcome.html
PBS and You (AKA the Newton's Apple Educational Materials Resource): includes 26 lessons/activities, "Science Try It" experiments, and a quiz.

http://www.gene.com/ae/AE/WWC/1991/
Over 50 science activities for high school, such as predator-prey simulation, dusty air examination, and an experiential survival exercise.

gopher://ec.sdcs.k12.ca.us/11/lessons/UCSD_InternNet_Lessons
Lesson plans for biology, earth science, chemistry, physics.

gopher://ericir.syr.edu:70/00/Lesson/Science/cecsci.164
One Colour or Two?: hands-on activity to discover primary and secondary colors. Grade 2.

http://megamach.portage.net:80/~bgidzak/nick.html
A young student describes three successful projects that could be used as activities: Erosion; Battery Power; Soil Pollution. For elementary and middle schools.

http://www.bev.net/education/schools/mbeeks/ca/index.html
Christa McAuliffe Project: UNITES. A program that uses children's fictional literature to promote science, math, and technology education. Elementary and middle grades.

★ **http://quest.arc.nasa.gov/**
NASA K–12 Internet Initiatives. Links to interactive projects.

★ **http://actein.edu.au/Questacon/Act.html**
Simple hands-on activities for schools and families, using everyday materials. Includes soup as an elastic substance and Newton's law of opposing forces.

http://www.nbn.com/youcan/
Beakman & Jax Science Stuff. Games and experiments for students interested in science (and grossing out their friends or parents!).

http://www.cs.ubc.ca/nest/egems/home.html
Electronic educational games in math and science.

http://www.scicomm.org.uk/biosis/human/consent.html
Science Museum: offers information on genetic screening and genetics in general.

http://pharmdec.wustl.edu/YSP/MAD.SCI/MAD.SCI.html
Mad Scientist Network (MSN): answers the science questions of students of all ages every day over the Web.

http://ericir.syr.edu/Newton/welcome.html
Newton's Apple for the Teacher: derived from the PBS science show, this Web site offers hands-on science activities.

http://www.sci.mus.mn.us/sln
Thinking Fountain. A great collection of science learning activities.

http://www.ncsa.uiuc.edu/Cyberia/Expo/
Science for the Millennium. NCSA's Multimedia Online Expo offers an online show that covers a range of stimulating topics from black holes to the Big Bang.

http://www.sd68.nanaimo.bc.ca/schools/nroy/welcome.html
Highway to Science: an activities-based site developed by teachers for grade 4–7 science. Experiments and activities related to the digestive system. Click on Local Teachers' Site, then Science Sites.

http://www.usa.net/~pitsco/pitsco/curr.html
http://www.usa.net/~pitsco/pitsco/onactivities.html
http://www.usa.net/~pitsco/pitsco/lesson.html
http://www.usa.net/~pitsco/pitsco/sci.html
http://www.usa.net/~pitsco/pitsco/resource.html
Science sources and lessons for elementary school students.

http://www.sciencedaily.com/>
ScienceDaily: offers the latest discoveries and research projects in all fields from labs across North America. Includes links to science magazines, top-rated science sites, and interactive science centers.

http://www.kie.berkeley.edu/KIE.html
Knowledge Integration Environment: engages middle and high school students in such science activities as comparing theories, critiquing evidence, and designing solutions to real-world problems. Students use commercial and custom networking software to work with scientific evidence from the Internet.

http://www.nj.com/yucky/roaches/index.html
Science Fun: Science activities for elementary and middle grades.

http://www.miamisci.org/
Miami Museum of Science Web site.

http://www.miamisci.org/avocado/
Avocado Elementary School Home Page.

★ http://www.miamisci.org/sln.html/
Miami's Science Learning Network Hotlist.

[Each of the above three sites is affiliated with the Science Learning Network (SLN), a three-year project testing the implementation of the Internet and inquiry-based science learning into K–8 classrooms.]

http://world.std.com/~bunt/edu.html
New and innovative individualized science modules that guide children through a chain of adventures. Fosters curiosity about themselves and their environment.

http://192.239.146.18/
Many great activities for any type of science class.

http://www.scholastic.com/public/Learning-Libraries.html
Middle School Science Library—Science Lesson Plans: (Select: Middle School Science Library/ Doing Science Library/ Science Activities and Lesson Plans)

http://tigger.jvnc.net/~levins/hadrosaurus.html
http://tigger.jvnc.net/~levins/dinosaur.html
Dinosaur skeletons.

http://scitech.lm.com/index.html
Summer science activities.

15. Astronomy and Space

http://schoolnet.carleton.ca/english/astronauts/astronauts.html
Canadian Space Information: meet Canada's latest astronauts!

http://www-hpcc.astro.washington.edu/k12/astroindex.html
AstroEd: collection of pointers to resources related to teaching and learning astronomy. Includes Ask-an-Astronomer.

gopher://info.stemnet.nf.ca/00/K-12/prim/Lesson%20Plans%20and%20Curriculum%20Units/Science/Solar%20System
Planetary rotation and revolution activity for grades 2–3.

http://www.gettysburg.edu/project/physics/clea/CLEAhome.html
Contemporary Laboratory Exercises in Astronomy: computer exercises for Mac and PC with lab manuals at no charge. High school.

http://www-hpcc.astro.washington.edu/k12/astroed.html
AstroEd: astronomy hypertext documents, curriculum materials and online courses. Includes the StarChild Project, which connects NASA and the K–12 classroom.

http://www.hq.nasa.gov/office/pao/NewsRoom/today.html
Today at NASA. NASA's outlet for daily updates to its activities. Includes press releases, Internet happenings, information on upcoming missions.

★ http://quest.arc.nasa.gov/lfs-announce.html
Live From... The Stratosphere: an electronic field trip to study planets, stars, and galaxies.

http://www.nptn.org/cyber.serv/AOneP/academy_one/science/nesput.html
NESPUT (National Education Simulations Project Using Telecommunications): simulated real-life activities for educational purposes.

http://chico.rice.edu/armadillo/Simulations/simserver.html
Educational Space Simulations Project. Includes space simulation "starter kit" for educators, student activities and experiments for use in space, launch and landing scripts.

http://esther.la.asu.edu/asu_tes/TES_Editor/educ_activities_info.html
Arizona Mars K–12 Education Program: brings Mars into the classroom with reading lists, missions, Mars facts, and teacher's resources. Includes such useful links as educational resources at other WWW sites, planetary science and space Internet links, and more.

http://seds.lpl.arizona.edu/billa/tnp/
The Nine Planets: a multimedia tour of the solar system.

http://www.c3.lanl.gov/~cjhamil/SolarSystem/homepage.html
A solar system tour.

http://www.c3.lanl.gov/~cjhamil/SolarSystem/comet/toc.html
A text on comets.

http://www.c3.lanl.gov/~cjhamil/SolarSystem/education/index.html
Lesson plans, activities, science summaries and fact sheets on such topics as moon phases, comets, and eclipses.

gopher://ec.sdcs.k12.ca.us/11/lessons/UCSD_InternNet_Lessons/
Earth_Science/Space_Planets
Lesson plans about the planets.

http://oel-www.jpl.nasa.gov/basics/bsf.htm
A text about the solar system.

http://www.eia.brad.ac.uk/btl/
Earth and Universe: multimedia guide to stars and galaxies.

gopher://ericir.syr.edu/11/Lesson/Astronomy
Lessons on the stars, solar system, space research, and a list of projects.

http://marvel.stsci.edu/top.html
Space Telescope Electronic Information Service Home Page. A wide array of information and educational resources. See the "Public" section for support materials for teachers.

http://marvel.stsci.edu/pubinfo/Pictures.html
Hubble Space Telescope: public pictures.

http://www.tpoint.net/earthandsky
Star Facts—An Electronic Journal About the Universe: articles, guides to the current evening sky, and pointers to astronomical resources on the Internet.

http://oz.sunflower.org/~starwalk/current_sky.html
Que Tal: a monthly astronomy review.

http://www.skypub.com
Sky Online: the Web site of *Sky & Telescope* magazine; a good jumping-off point into astronomy.

http://tommy.jsc.nasa.gov/~woodfill/SPACEED/SEHHTML/
seh.html
Space Educators Handbook: space calendar, space quotes, space spinoffs, and more. Downloadable versions of everything are included at the site for Macs and PCs using runtime versions of HyperCard and ToolBook 1.5.

http://cyclops.pei.edu:8001/~briddlkc/sky_stuff/current_sky.html
Current sky information.

http://shuttle.nasa.gov/
NASA Shuttle Space Archives: all you need to know about the STS-69 mission including photos, videos, real-time data, experiments, and more.

http://seds.lpl.arizona.edu/nineplanets/nineplanets/
nineplanets.html#toc

http://www.c3.lanl.gov/~cjhamil/SolarSystem/homepage.html
Sites for planetary studies.

http://www.jpl.nasa.gov/galileo/
Galileo Educator's Resources: from Galileo's Educational Outreach Office.

http://www2.ari.net/home/odenwald/cafe.html
Astronomy Cafe. Developed by a professional astronomer, this site provides unusual information about the research scene, data collection, anatomy of a published research paper, Ask-an-Astronomer, and software suitable for science fair or classroom projects.

16. Biology

http://george.lbl.gov/ITG.hm.pg.docs/Whole.Frog/
Whole.Frog.html
Dissecting a frog using computer-based 3D visualization. High school.

http://www.cs.yale.edu/HTML/YALE/CS/HyPlans/
loosemore-sandra/froggy.html
Frogs: songs, stories, pictures, sounds and science activities.

gopher://ec.sdcs.k12.ca.us/11/lessons/UCSD_InternNet_Lessons/
Biology
Lesson plans for biology.

http://www.im.nbs.gov/bbs/
North American Breeding Bird Survey: includes maps of spatial trends and a bird quiz.

http://compstat.wharton.upenn.edu:8001/~siler/birding.html
Birding on the Web.

http://www.hcc.hawaii.edu/dinos/dinos.1.html
Tour a dinosaur exhibit.

http://www.bvis.uic.edu/museum/
Dinosaurs—Field Museum of Natural History: includes exhibit, teacher's guide, bibliography, and media page with movies and questions.

http://informns.k12.mn.us/wolf.html
Wolf Studies Project: includes lessons and worksheets.

http://www.ex.ac.uk/~gjlramel/welcome.html
A site for pupils and teachers focusing on bugs. Includes collecting and setting, evolution, anatomy, classification.

http://www.physics.helsinki.fi/whale/
Whale Watching Web: links to dolphin, whale, and shark resources.

http://wjh-www.harvard.edu/~furmansk/dolphin.html
The Dolphin Page: links to dolphin resources.

http://curry.edschool.virginia.edu/~kpj5e/Whales/
Whales. Includes teacher resources (lesson plans and teacher's guides), student activities, and Internet resources. Grades K–8.

http://turnpike.net/emporium/C/celestial/epsm.htm
Electronic Prehistoric Shark Museum.

http://www.actwin.com/WWWVL-Fish.html
Virtual Fish. Covers biology, aquariums, environmentalism, sport fishing, and aquatic creatures.

gopher://info.stemnet.nf.ca:70/00/k-12/prim/Lesson%20Plans%20and%20Curriculum%20Units/Science/Animal_Coverings
Drawing activity focusing on different types of animal coverings and movement. Grades K–5.

http://www.nlm.nih.gov/extramural_research.dir/visible_human.html
Visible Human Project: complete, anatomically detailed, 3D representations of the human body (female and male).

http://cwis.usc.edu/dept/garden/
Virtual TeleGarden: interactive garden filled with living plants. Students can plant, water, and monitor seedlings via a robotic arm.

www.bhm.tis.net/zoo/
The Birmingham Zoo.

http://netvet.wustl.edu/e-zoo.htm
Electronic Zoo.

http://www.ex.ac.uk/~gjlramel/welcome.html
Gordon's Entomological Home Page.

http://www.dnai.com/~hohealth
Hall of Health.

★ http://sln.fi.edu/TOC.biosci.html
Virtual Heart: anatomy lesson for elementary school teachers and pupils.

http://phylogeny.arizona.edu/tree/phylogeny.html
Tree of Life Project: collection of WWW pages containing information about various organisms: phylogeny, characteristics, phylogenetic relationships, references, and more.

http://aggie-horticulture.tamu.edu/kinder/index.html
KinderGARDEN: information about growing plants and vegetables indoors and out, composting, worms, gardening poems, slugs, mud, nutrients and even horticultural therapy — all with a classroom focus.

http://sln.fi.edu/tfi/hotlists/insects.html
Insect Hotlist.

http://sln.fi.edu/inquirer/inquirer.html
The Philadelphia Inquirer Health & Science Magazine: recent science topics include computer science pioneers, adult immunizations, the search for a cure for diabetes, and the debate among physicists over the mass of neutrinos. Check weekly for new science information.

★ **http://www.cs.yale.edu/HTML/YALE/CS/HyPlans/loosemore-sandra/froggy.html**
Froggy Page: Frog dissection.

http://www.nwf.org/nwf/
National Wildlife Federation Home Page.

http://biotech.chem.indiana.edu/pages/contents.html
The goal of this site is to educate those who lack experience in biology and biotechnology and to provide quick access to useful biology-related resources. Makes "biotech" as useful a tool to high school students as it is to postdoctoral fellows.

http://web.mit.edu/invent/
Invention Dimension: MIT's Web site devoted to American inventors, past and current.

http://whale.simmons.edu
WhaleNet.

http://www.scicomm.org.uk/biosis/human/consent.html
A set of interactive pages from the Science Museum to help students learn about genetics and genetic screening.

http://www.gene.com/ae
Access Excellence: biology project sponsored by Genentech and others.

http://turnpike.net/emporium/C/celestial/epsm.htm
The Electronic Prehistoric Shark Museum.

http://sln.fi.edu/tfi/info/current/dinosaur.html
The Dinosaurs of Jurassic Park: available from the Franklin Institute.

http://tigger.jvnc.net/~levins/hadrosaurus.html
Dinosaur skeleton site: takes visitors back in history and down into the 30-foot ravine in New Jersey, where the world's first nearly complete dinosaur skeleton was found in 1858.

17. Chemistry

http://www.rpi.edu/dept/chem/cheminfo/chemres.html
Internet chemistry information resources.

http://www.cchem.berkeley.edu/Table/index.html
Periodic Table of the Elements.

gopher://ec.sdcs.k12.ca.us/11/lessons/UCSD_InternNet_Lessons/
Physical_Science_and_Chemistry
Over 30 lesson plans for physical science and chemistry.

http://www-hpcc.astro.washington.edu/scied/chemistry.html
ChemEd: chemistry education resources.

★ http://rampages.onramp.net/~jaldr/chemtchr.html
Chemistry Teacher Resources: for high school chemistry teachers —
labs, demos, and a bibliography. Includes:

> http://rampages.onramp.net/~jaldr/item03.html
> Internet chemistry resources: information on the elements,
> ozone, nuclear and safety issues, molecular models, chemical
> images, and more.

http://riceinfo.rice.edu/armadillo/Owlink/Lessons/pattyles.html
Algebra/chemistry mixture problems. Activities and worksheets for
high school classes.

http://riceinfo.rice.edu/armadillo/Owlink/Lessons/monles.html
Hydrocarbons: lesson plan and activity for high schools.

http://helios.cr.usgs.gov/gips/aii-home.htm
Understanding Our Planet Through Chemistry: poster presentation
— composition of the earth's surface, chemistry behind issues such
as the economy, and more.

http://www-wilson.ucsd.edu/education/edu.revised.html
Physical chemistry with lots of graphics.

http://www.chem.ucla.edu/chempointers.html
Chemistry pointers via the WWW Virtual Library.

18. Geology (Earth Science)

http://walrus.wr.usgs.gov/docs/ask-a-ge.html
Ask-a-Geologist.

★ http://volcano.und.nodak.edu/
Volcano World: learn about volcanoes. Lesson plans, activities,
teaching suggestions, references, Ask-a-Volcanologist. Grades K–12.

gopher://ericir.syr.edu/00/Lesson/Science/cecsci.16
Earth's structure, location of continents, earthquakes. Elementary
grades.

http://pong.igpp.ucla.edu/pet/pet_intro.html
Petrographic Workshop: microscopic images of hundreds of rocks
and minerals, with textual descriptions.

gopher://ec.sdcs.k12.ca.us/11/lessons/UCSD_InternNet_Lessons/
Earth_Science
Lesson plans for earth science.

http://info.er.usgs.gov/education/teacher/what-do-maps-show/index.html
Map reading: a series of posters on how to read maps from the U.S. Geological Survey. Includes lesson plans and activity sheets.

http://www.usgs.gov/fact-sheets
Earth sciences booklets, fact sheets, leaflets and posters. Published by the U.S. Geological Survey. Includes:

http://internet.er.usgs.gov/fact-sheets/understanding_color-infrared_photographs/understanding.html
Understanding Color: infrared photographs and false-color composites.

http://www.usgs.gov/fact-sheets/finding-your-way/finding-your-way.html
Finding Your Way with Map and Compass: learn about scale, distance and direction, with an emphasis on topographic maps.

http://ucmp1.berkeley.edu/welcome.html
University of California Museum of Paleontology. Includes online exhibits and fossil specimen databases.

http://volcano.und.nodak.edu/
Volcano World: an excellent Web site for children and volcano experts alike. Offers up-to-the-moment information on currently active volcanoes, as well as information on inactive volcanoes. Includes resources and ready-to-teach lesson plans.

19. Physics

http://192.239.146.18/CESMERes.html
Downloadable activity manual for physical science teachers: measurement of mass, friction, recycling, acceleration, etc.

http://unite.ukans.edu/UNITEResource/783751281-447DED81.rsrc
A lab activity to calculate the impact points of an object fired off a table horizontally and one fired downward at an angle. Grades 9–12.

http://unite.ukans.edu/UNITEResource/783750776-447DED81.rsrc
Activity: experimentation of variables affecting movement. Other activities available to be downloaded. Elementary grades.

http://www.nptn.org/cyber.serv/AOneP/academy_one/science/a1mtpv.html
Practice concepts of power and force while challenging the Mouse Trap Powered Vehicle Hall of Fame.

http://ericir.syr.edu/Newton/Lessons/hangglid.html
Explores air currents and thermals using a model hang glider made from 8"x 10" paper. High school.

http://schoolnet.carleton.ca/english/worldinmotion/index.html
Learning kit of activities and lesson plans focused on motion.

★ http://www-hpcc.astro.washington.edu/scied/physics.html
Links to courses, lesson plans, organizations and other resources useful in teaching and learning physics.

http://www.phys.ufl.edu/~selman/Demo1.html
Online tutorial on optics. High school.

http://www.phys.ufl.edu/~deserio/simplens/simplens.htm
Laboratory experiment: imaging properties of a simple lens. Elementary through high school.

http://www.oulu.fi/~spaceweb/textbook/
Space Physics Textbook. High school.

http://telerobot.mech.uwa.edu.au/
Links to a robotics tutorial.

gopher://ec.sdcs.k12.ca.us/11/lessons/UCSD_InternNet_Lessons/Physics
Lesson plans for physics.

gopher://ericir.syr.edu/ORO-15254-/Lesson/NASA/Teachers/Glossary.txt
Physics Glossary available for download.

http://halliwell.phy.uic.edu/IP/instructions/*IP.html
For senior students, a university-level Introductory Mechanics course using the Interactive Physics application.

http://www.integratedconcepts.com/virtualprof
The Virtual Prof's Physics Shop: physics tutorial help, chat groups, bulletin board, and other useful materials.

http://uptown.turnpike.net/L/lindeman/physics_ub.html
Physics_Unbound: ongoing HTML textbook to which visitors may contribute. The purpose of the site is to encourage scientific authorship on the Web as well as physics education.

20. Miscellaneous Science Resources

http://www.demon.co.uk/eureka/
Eureka Children's Museum Home Page.

http://unite2.tisl.ukans.edu/
Explorer Home Page.

http://family.starwave.com/
Family Planet.

http://www.sptimes.com/aquarium/default.html
Florida Aquarium.

http://sln.fi.edu/
Franklin Institute Science Museum.

http://www.cs.cmu.edu/~mwm/sci.html
Hands-On Science Centers Worldwide.

http://www.nyu.edu/pages/mathmol
MathMol: K–12 mathematics and molecules.

http://www.wln.com/~deltapac/ocean_od.html
Ocean Odyssey: hands-on children's museum.

http://freenet.calgary.ab.ca/science/tyrrell/
Royal Tyrrell Museum of Palaeontology.

http://oberon.educ.sfu.ca/splash.htm
Safari Splash Home Page.

http://www.cgl.com/~laurel-travel/ClubMaritime/SDZoo.html
San Diego Zoo Home Page.

http://www.bev.net/education/SeaWorld/homepage.html
Sea World/Busch Gardens Home Page.

http://www.cfn.cs.dal.ca/Science/DiscCentre/welcome/virtual.html
Virtual Discovery Centre.

http://lsnt5.lightspeed.net/~whaletimes/
Whaletimes.

http://fas.sfu.ca/css/gcs/
Great Canadian Scientists.

http://www.packet.net/schoolhouse/science.html
Latitude28 Science Department: links to natural history, paleontology (fossils, dinosaurs), chemistry, biology, astronomy and space.

http://erasmus.biol.csufresno.edu/second.html
Secondary Science Education: direct connections to many resources.

http://www.csulb.edu/gc/science/index.html
Global Campus of Science. Includes:

> http://ucmp1.berkeley.edu/exhibittext/evolution.html
> Enter Evolution: Theory and History. Dinosaur discoveries, scientists from 17th-20th C., and *The Origin of Species* by Charles Darwin.

http://bang.lanl.gov/video/stv/arshtml/arstoc.html
Art of Renaissance Science: includes Renaissance Art and the Mathematical Perspective, From Human Architecture to Architectural Structure, and more.

★ http://www.osc.on.ca/
Ontario Science Centre Home Page.

http://jasper.stark.k12.oh.us
Cross-district, interdisciplinary, discovery-based learning through the use of StarkNet.

http://turnpike.net/metro/vollans/sci.html
School Science Home Page Software for IBM PC. This page provides useful links to other sites on school science.

http://www.websys.com/cyberschool/home.html
Cyberschool teacher resources and science links.

http://icair.iac.org.nz/education.html
Online educational resources about the Antarctic. Includes Ozone Depletion over Antarctica and other resources available for purchase.

★ http://www.tc.cornell.edu/Edu/MathSciGateway/about.html
A gateway that provides links to resources in math and science for teachers and students, grades 9–12. Includes museum and Ask-an-Expert links.

http://esther.la.asu.edu/asu_tes/TES_Editor/LINKS_2_OTHR_SITES/links_menu.html
Links to sites relevant to K–12 in planetary sciences and earth sciences.

http://inspire.ospi.wednet.edu:8001/
Project Athena: curriculum resources for grades K–12.

http://sln.fi.edu/tfi/hotlists/kid-sci.html
A WWW resource list by and for kids, grades K–8. Earth and life sciences, space, weather, political and computer sciences.

http://www.newscientist.com/
New Scientist Planet Science: outstanding science and technology site.

★ http://unite.ukans.edu/
Explorer curriculum resources for sciences and math. Plans are underway to develop this database to include other curriculum areas.

http://www-sci.lib.uci.edu/SEP/SEP.html
Fran Potter's Science Gems: physical sciences, earth sciences, health sciences. Well organized, with many resources broken down by grade level.

http://www.lookup.com/Homepages/37409/worksheets.html
Downloadable science worksheets.

http://www.webcom.com/~netspace
NetSpace Home Page.

http://www.exploratorium.edu/learning_studio/sii/
Science Information Infrastructure: a collaboration among teachers and scientists, this initiative is developing resources based on NASA images and data.

http://www.nj.com/yucky/roaches/index.html
Science Fun: learn interesting things at the site that calls itself the "yuckiest site on the Net."

http://www.lookup.com/Homepages/37409/worksheets.html
Secondary school science worksheets.

http://science.cc.uwf.edu
Science Education Home Page: links to most of the major science ed groups.

http://www.parentsplace.com/readroom/explorer/index.html
Parents' Science & Nature Newsletter: electronic version of *Family Explorer*, an activities newsletter for parents of 6- to 12-year-olds.

http://www-hpcc.astro.washington.edu/scied/science.html
Science and Mathematics Education Resources Group Home Page.

http://lmewww.mankato.msus.edu/ci/elem.sci.html
Elementary Science This Month.

★ http://cirrus.sprl.umich.edu/wxnet/
A wonderful weather resource.

http://ucmp1.berkeley.edu/
Museum of Paleontology.

http://cpmcnet.columbia.edu/dept/physio/
A good pre-college science education site.

http://turnpike.net/metro/vollans/sci.html
School Science Home Page. Useful links to school science sources.

http://www.mos.org/sln/toe/toe.html
Theater of Electricity from the Boston Museum of Science.

http://www.mos.org/sln/sem/sem.html
Scanning Electron Microscope.

http://www.omsi.edu/sln/ww/waterworks.html
A water resource.

http://sln.fi.edu/tfi/units/energy/wind.html
A wind resource from the Franklin institute.

http://www.miamisci.org/hurricane/hurricane0.html
Hurricanes—Storm Science: resource from the Miami Museum of Science.

21. Special Needs Resources

★ http://www.eskimo.com/~user/kids.html
Talented and gifted resources on the World Wide Web.

http://www.sped.ukans.edu/speddisabilitiesstuff/speddisabilities-welcome.html
Resources for research on disabilities from the Department of Special Education, University of Kansas. Includes some useful full-text resources.

gopher://val-dor.cc.buffalo.edu:70/1
Cornucopia of disability information.

http://home.earthlink.net/~masterstek/ASLDict.html
Basic Dictionary of American Sign Language Terms.

http://deafworldweb.org/deafworld/
Deafworld Home Page: provides a central Net point for information for about the deaf world. Includes culture and references.

http://www.blindcntr.org/bcc/
Blind Children's Center.

http://www.c-cad.org/ccad-tct.htm
Center for Computer Assistance to the Disabled.

http://curry.edschool.Virginia.EDU/insite/CONTENT/SPECIALED/
Special education resources from the Society for Information Technology and Teacher Education.

gopher://teach.virginia.edu:70/11/TEIS/Special%20Education
Special education Gopher.

★ http://www.hood.edu/seri/serihome.htm
SERI (Special Education Resources on the Internet): important collection that includes legal resources, special education discussion groups, and more.

★ http://schoolnet2.carleton.ca/~kwellar
Special Needs Education Network: comprehensive, well-developed site that provides services specific to parents, teachers, schools, and others involved in the education of students with special needs.

http://www.isc.rit.edu/~easi
EASI (Equal Access to Software and Information): this organization focuses on dissemination of information about access to computing and information technology for persons with disabilities. Includes some K–12 helps.

http://www.webcom.com/pleasant/sarah/teach/sped.html
Excellent set of links to information dealing with special needs in schools, including the needs of gifted students.

http://www.eskimo.com/~jlubin/disabled.html
A great list of Internet resources on disabilities developed by Jim Lubin, a person with quadriplegia who works nine hours a day at his computer.

★ http://web.webable.com/wedsites.html
Disability Web sites; an extensive listing.

http://weber.u.washington.edu/~doit
This site promotes the involvement of special needs individuals in math and sciences. The downloadable guide to disability resources on the Internet is particularly useful.

http://disability.com
Links to careers and jobs, as well as government information and assistive/adaptive technologies.

http://www.apple.com/disability/welcome.html
Disability resources, including shareware designed for kids and adults with disabilities.

22. Additional Links for Kids

http://www.onramp.ca/~lowens/107kids.htm
Canadian Kids Home Page.

http://www.pd.astro.it/local-cgi-bin/kids.cgi/forms/
The Children Page.

http://www.parentsplace.com/shopping/codys/ikidexcp.cgi
Cody's: Internet for Kids.

http://net.org/clubhouse/index.html
The Computer Clubhouse at the Computer Museum, Boston.

http://mack.rt66.com/kidsclub/home.htm
Cyberkid's Club.

http://www.woodwind.com/cyberkids/
CyberKids' Home Page.

★ http://sln.fi.edu/tfi/hotlists/kids.html
Hotlist by and for kids.

http://gil.ipswichcity.qld.gov.au/eetint1a.html
Internet Educational Resources: special sites for kids.

http://psych.hanover.edu/kidsweb/misc.html
Internet Kid's Web.

http://www.umassd.edu/SpecialPrograms/ISN/Kidnews3.html
ISN Kid News.

http://www.peinet.pe.ca/Kids/kids.html
Just for Kids.

http://fox.nstn.ca/~tmonk/kayskids/kay.html
Kay's Kid's Collection.

http://alexia.lis.uiuc.edu/~watts/kiddin.html
Kidding Around.

http://www.clark.net/pub/journalism/kid.html
Kid List.

http://www.en-garde.com/kidpub/
KidPub: WWW publishing.

http://pages.prodigy.com/ID/merit/meritkids.html
Kids and Parents Home Page.

http://www.spectracom.com/kidscom/index1.html
Kidscom Home Page.

http://www.primenet.com/~sburr/index.html
Kids' Web.

http://www.primenet.com/~hodges/kids_crambo.html
Kid's Crambo.

http://rmii.com/~pachecod/kidsnet/ckids.html
Kids' Crossing: Voice of Rocky Mountain Youth.

http://www.zen.org/~brendan/kids.html
The Kids on the Web.

http://www.nucleus.com/kids.html
Kids' Page.

http://www.islandnet.com/~bedford/kids.html
The Kids' Place.

http://plaza.interport.net/kids_space/
Kids' Space.

http://www.npac.syr.edu/textbook/kidsweb/
KidsWeb: a World Wide Web digital library for school kids.

http://www.ot.com/kids/
Oasis: Kids' Corner.

★ http://www.kidlink.org
Global networking for youth (10–15).

http://www.vividus.com/~infov/
Children's Internet: links to activities.

http://www.pegasus.oz.au/~futurecom/kids.htm
Kidscape (from Australia).

http://www.ozemail.com.au/~ctech/wps.htm
Another Australian site with fun and educational activities for children from Wangaratta Primary School.

http://www.ehche.ac.uk/%7Ewiredue/kidpub/
KidPub, U.K.

http://www.sara-jordan.com/edu-mart/
Edu-Mart Educational Resources for kids, parents, and teachers. Includes some good activities for kids.

★ http://www.mtlake.com/cyberkids/
CyberKids: a free online magazine for kids.

http://www.freenet.hamilton.on.ca/~aa937/Profile.html
Cyberhaunts for Kids: Includes many links for kids that are appropriate year round.

★ http://www.internet-for-kids.com/
The Internet for Kids: A well-designed Web site for young people, set up by Dr. Victoria Williams, a teacher, superintendent, and parent. Provides eight major links to different areas of interest.

http://www.sju.edu/~milliken/demos/hot-educ.html
More kids' sites.

★ http://www.tc.cornell.edu:80/Kids.on.Campus/
Kids on Campus.

http://www.spectracom.com/kidscom/
KidsCom: a communication playground for children ages 8–12. Kids can find keypals, get help with Internet questions, talk about what they'd like to be when they grow up, and explore links to other children's sites.

http://www.primenet.com/~hawaii
Kids' *Time Magazine*: for middle grades.

http://www.bizcafe.com/kidskorner
BizCafe's Kids' Korner.

http://www.texas.net/user/kidsport
Kids' Sports Network.

http://www.slip.net/~scmetro/citykids.htm
City Kids' Directory.

http://www.indirect.com/www/mcintosh/danny.htm
Danny's Kid Page.

http://www.interlog.com/~gordo/kids.html
Otis Index: sites for kids.

http://www.informns.k12.mn.us/kamkids/
Creative Kids in Kamchatka.

http://huizen.dds.nl/~ink/
The Kids' Club.

http://www.america.com/~dcop/tudlp
The Ultimate Disney Link Page.

23. Additional Teacher Resources

http://putwest.boces.org/Standards.html
Developing Educational Standards Page.

http://curry.edschool.Virginia.EDU/insite/
InSITE (Information Network of the Society for Information Technology and Teacher Education): a WWW resource for exploring ways in which the Internet can be used both to benefit teacher education programs and as support to K–12 staff development technology initiatives. Includes links to U.S. State Departments of Education.

http://www.heinemann.co.uk/heinemann/elt/elt.html
This is U.K.-based site offering news on educational books, events and technology, guides to relevant sites of use for class and course-work, as well as sample materials to download.

★ http://www.smartpages.com/worldlink/worldlink.html
World Link: monthly newsletter designed to help educators navigate the Internet with tips, updates on projects, and new sites.

http://www.c3.lanl.gov/~jspeck/mini-grants.shtml
Mini-grants, information, and freebies.

http://www.ncrel.org/ncrel/sdrs/pathwayg.htm
Pathways to School Improvement.

gopher://pluribus.tc.columbia.edu/
Teacher's College, Columbia University.

http://www.pacificrim.net/~mckenzie
From Now On: monthly electronic commentary on educational technology issues.

★ http://www.pacificnet.net/~mandel
Teachers Helping Teachers: teacher idea exchange; "one-stop shopping" to useful pointers.

http://seamonkey.ed.asu.edu/epaa/
Electronic edition of Education Policy Analysis Archives.

http://sunsite.unc.edu:80/horizon/
Horizon Home Page: information about emerging trends, potential social and technological developments, and their implications for education. Online counterpart of the newsletter On the Horizon.

★ http://www.ed.gov/pubs/
U.S. Department of Education Online Library: useful resources for teachers.

★ http://www.clark.net/pub/journalism/awesome.html
Well-known list of awesome sites, some educational. Many of the very best resources are included here.

http:// web:107/fia/educate/index.html
K–12 educational links, worldwide.

★ http://www.lib.umich.edu/chhome.html
Clearinghouse for Internet resources; a basic resource for finding information on topics of interest to you and your students.

http://www.halcyon.com/garycres/sshp/startup.html
This site was developed by a group of social studies teachers in Washington called the BESST Team (Building Excellence in Social Studies through Technology).

http://www.ncrel.org/ncrel/sdrs/pathways.htm
A site designed to help teachers access educational research quickly and apply it to school and classroom practice.

http://uu-gna.mit.edu:8001/HyperNews/get/text/guide/index.html
Globewide Network Academy resource collection for online educators: databases, directories, hotlists.

http://camil45.music.uiuc.edu/210/mayfield/welcome.html
This site is billed as a music teacher's fundraising site, but any teacher looking for fundraising ideas will want to visit. Includes links to online fundraising services.

http://www.actrix.gen.nz/biz/cwa/
New Zealand educational site; pointers to further resources.

http://www.scholastic.com/public/Learning-Libraries.html
Scholastic Gopher, with projects.

★ http://www.tenet.edu/education/main.html
K–12 Server from Tenet: contains links to WWW servers at K–12 schools, school districts, departments of education, colleges of education, and miscellaneous educational sites.

http://netspace.students.brown.edu/eos/main_image.html
Education Online Sources.

http://www.cis.uab.edu/info/grads/mmf/EdPage/EdPage2.html
Educators at all levels may be interested in this site, which provides an educational interface to the Internet.

http://www.cs.uidaho.edu/~connie/interests.html
An Educational Guide to the Web.

http://actein.edu.au/acteinnew/help.html
An Australian resource, Actein's WWW page, Internet Help for Teachers, provides helpful tips for getting started on the Net.

http://river.ihs.gov/GrandCanyon/GCrt.html
In the mood for a little vicarious adventure? Check out this multi-media raft trip down the Colorado River in the Grand Canyon.

http://www.microweb.com/pepsite
PEP: Resources for Parents, Educators & Publishers. This site provides an overview of the children's software industry. Includes over 100 pages of information, industry news, product reviews, searchable databases.

http://www.imagescape.com/helpweb
Helpweb: guide to new users of the Internet that covers many basic topics, such as Web searches, e-mail, FTP, and newsgroups.

http://www.artsednet.getty.edu/
More than 250 pages of free lesson plans and other downloadable resources for arts educators.

http://www.byu.edu/acd1/ed/coe/vlibrary/vlibrary.html
The Educator's Virtual Library.

http://www.clark.net/pub/lschank/home.html
Although this page is no longer under development, it is a very good resource for teachers developed by Larry Shank.

http://www.naples.net:80/media/wsfp/lounge.htm
Tools to help teachers use the Internet in the classroom. From the Southwest Florida Public Television program, *The Faculty Lounge.*

http://web.csd.sc.edu/bck2skol/bck2skol.html
Well-developed Internet tutorial.

http://www.netskills.ac.uk/
Another good resource for learning about the Internet.

http://pages.prodigy.com/hstat
Web site from Prodigy that deals with education and telecommunications.

http://cpsr.org/dox/links/educ.html
A good starting point to help teachers and parents, educational software developers, and education activists find resources on the World Wide Web.

http://www.childcybersearch.org/cases.htm
Site for tracking missing children.

http://www.learner.org
Learners Online: from the Annenberg/CPB Project. Home page for

educators that includes a guide to math and science reform, latest funding information, and educational strategies.

http://www.ualr.edu/~coedept/index.html
College of Education Online; developed by the University of Arkansas at Little Rock. Includes links to curriculum areas.

★ **http://www.cris.com/~felixg/OE/OEWELCOME.html**
The Online Educator magazine provides educators with up-to-the minute information about the Internet. This site is worth a visit for sample articles and current and past hotlinks, which are well categorized and annotated.

http://www.ed.uiuc.edu/Mining/Overview.html
The Computing Teacher: collection of excerpts from the book by Judi Harris. The focus here is on using the Internet as a tool for problem solving and collaboration.

http://www.thelinq.net/
Education Station: another list of education-related Internet resources.

http://www.smartpages.com/worldlink/worldlink.html
World Link: monthly newsletter designed to help educators navigate the Internet with tips, updates on projects, and new sites.

http://www.byu.edu/acd1/ed/InSci/Projects/Museums.html
Teacher's Guide to Museums and Exhibits on the Web:

http://uu-gna.mit.edu:8001/HyperNews/get/text/guide/index.html
Teacher's Guide from the Global Network Academy. Resource collection for online educators.

http://www.scri.fsu.edu/~dennisl/resources/resources.html
Middle School Teacher Resource Center.

http://owl.qut.edu.au/oz-teachernet
Australian site providing a calendar of curriculum projects using telecommunications.

★ **http://www.byu.edu/acd1/ed/InSci/Projects/ WWWSubjectGuide.html**
Subject Curriculum Guide: this guide is divided first by curriculum subject areas. It includes resource databases, lesson plans, activities, exhibits, and museums, as well as pointers to broader indexes.

http://www.cardinalpub.com/etr
Educational Technology Resources: an extensive variety of free educational software offerings. Includes new educational software and resources for administrators.

★ http://www.well.com/user/learning
The Well: popular resource for Internet learning, with pointers to further excellent resources.

★ http://www.southwind.net/~lshiney/teach.html
Teacher's Edition Online.

http://tecfa.unige.ch/info-edu-comp.html
Educational Technology Page from TECFA (Training Technologies and Learning) in Geneva, Switzerland.

http://olam.ed.asu.edu/epaa/
Charter Schools 1995: a hypertext resource on charter schools from the Educational Policy Archives.

http://www.montana.edu:80/~wwwxs/
National Teachers' Enhancement Network (NTEN): telecomputing guides for students and teachers; online teaching experiences written by course instructors.

http://www.aspensys.com/eric2/welcome.html
ACCESS (outreach arm of the ERIC system): ERIC resources are used to improve teaching, learning, and education decision making.

http://edweb.sdsu.edu/edfirst/edfirst.html
Education First Application Design Team Page: a HyperCard stack guides users through brainstorming a technology project and creates a HTML, Web-ready project workpage. Includes learning tips and web links.

http://www.caso.com
A Web site that lists more than 700 college courses that can be taken online. This site also has many educational links for the Web, telnet, FTP, etc.

http://wn.apc.org/~pwest/vgc-wel.htm
A virtual organization aimed at providing educational support materials via the Web. Contains career guidance formation and an Internet edition of *Human Resource Management Magazine*.

★ http://www.ed.uiuc.edu/lrs/
Learning Resource Server from the University of Illinois College of Education. Provides links to some of the most exciting uses of technologies for learning on the Internet.

http://www.bham.wednet.edu/default.htm.
Bellingham Public Schools Web: provides ideas for designing collaborative and educational Web-based activities. It also offers a good collection of WWW curriculum resources by subject or grade level, and lesson plans for integrating technology into the curriculum.

http://www.nova.edu/Inter-Links/education/education.html
Inter-Links: resource from Nova University for helping people find their way around the Net. The Education Link is a well-organized set of pointers to key educational sources.

http://www.mbnet.mb.ca/cm
This site is affiliated with *Canadian Materials* magazine and provides reviews of recent educational material with a Canadian focus.

http://www.mbnet.mb.ca/~mstimson/text/rightrack
Parents' and teachers' resources.

http://www.education.lanl.gov/RESOURCES/ OII/OII.html
New Mexico Online Internet Institute: teachers participating in the Institute contribute their favorite Web resources.

★ **http://prism.prs.k12.nj.us/WWW/OII/disc-pub/ novae-group/index.html**
Novae Group (Teachers Networking for the Future): An excellent e-mail update for teaching resources. Contains the archives for Novae Group postings.

http://www.byu.edu/acd1/ed/InSci/Projects/ WWWSSubjectGuide.html
Subject Curriculum Guide: this guide is divided by curriculum subject areas and includes databases, lesson plans, activities, exhibits, museums, and broad subject indices.

http://njnie.dl.stevens-tech.edu/
Teacher-developed curriculum links and other resources for classroom projects.

http://cnet.unb.ca/lotw/
WWW Instructor's Manual—Learning on the Web '96: provides teacher support for using the Web and for creating learning environments on the Web.

http://netspace.students.brown.edu/eos/ main_plain.html#Sources
Educational online sources from Brown University; a first stop for teachers new to the Internet.

★ **http://www.eworld.com/education/resources/**
eWorld: an Apple-sponsored page for the learning community. Includes Apple Education Resource, a K–12 Education Home Page, and School House, which features innovative K–12, college, and campus sites worldwide.

★ **http://galaxy.einet.net/galaxy/Social-Sciences/Education.html**
Links to Adult Education, Curriculum and Instruction, K–12 Education, Measurement and Evaluation, and Special Education.

Notes

Chapter 3

1 How to design an online project that works. *Classroom Connect* (Premier Issue), 5.

2 Moursund, D. (1994). What is the "information superhighway"? *The Computing Teacher*, 22(3).

3 Heide, A., & Henderson, D. (1994). *The Technological Classroom: A Blueprint for Success*. Toronto: Trifolium Books.

4 Liz Tompkins, Massachusetts, USA (personal communication).

5 AUP sites compiled by R. Smith, T. Davidson and B. Stewart for Dr. L. Anderson's Technology Lab Management course, Mississippi State University, May 1995.

Chapter 8

1 Heide, A., & Henderson, D. (1994). *The Technological Classroom: A Blueprint for Success*. Toronto: Trifolium Books.

2 Harris, J. (1994, October). Teaching teachers to use telecomputing tools. *The Computing Teacher*, 60–64.

Bibliography

Classroom Connect Yearbook, Volume 1: 1994–1995. Lancaster, PA: Wentworth Worldwide Media.

Dern, D.P. (1994). *The Internet Guide for New Users*. New York: McGraw-Hill.

The Educator's Guide to the Internet (2nd ed.). (1995). Virginia Space Grant Consortium.

The Educator's Online Resource Guide. (1995). Lancaster, PA: Wentworth Worldwide Media.

Ellsworth, J.H. (1994). *Education on the Internet*. Indianapolis, IN: Sams Publishing.

Giagnocavo, G., McLain, T., & DiStefano, V. (1995). *Educator's Internet Companion*. Lancaster, PA: Wentworth Worldwide Media.

Gilliom, G. (1995, December). When your kids are online. *CompuServe Magazine*, 12–21.

Gilster, P. (1994). *Finding It on the Internet*. New York: John Wiley & Sons.

Harris, J. (1994). *Way of the Ferret: Finding Educational Resources on the Internet* (Rev. ed.). Eugene, OR: International Society for Technology in Education.

Heide, A., & Henderson, D. (1994). *The Technological Classroom: A Blueprint for Success*. Toronto: Trifolium Books.

Honey, M., & McMillan, K. (1994, October). NII (National Information Infrastructure) Roadblocks: Why do so few educators use the Internet? *Electronic Learning*, 14(2), 14.

How to Get Connected to the Internet: Facts and Funding. (1995). Lancaster, PA: Wentworth Worldwide Media.

Hughes, K. (1994, May). *Entering the World Wide Web: A Guide to Cyberspace*. Enterprise Integration Technologies.

Internet Activities Using Scientific Data: A Self-Guided Exploration. (19??). Washington, DC: U.S. Department of Commerce, National Oceanic and Atmospheric Administration, Office of Educational Affairs, & Space Environment Laboratory.

The Internet in K–12 Education. (1993/94). Pittsburgh, PA: John J. Heinz III School of Public Policy and Management, Department of Engineering & Public Policy, & Carnegie Mellon University, Department of Social and Decision Sciences.

Joseph, L.C. (1995). World Link: *An Internet Guide for Educators, Parents and Students*. Columbus, OH: Greyden Press.

Kongshem, L. (1995, September). Data security on the Net. *Electronic School*, A17–19.

Krol, E. (1992). *The Whole Internet*. Sebastopol, CA: O'Reilly & Associates.

Liu, C., Peek, J., Jones, R., Buus, B., & Nye, A. (1994). *Managing Internet Information Services*. Sebastopol, CA: O'Reilly & Associates.

Mageau, T. (1994, May–June). Will the superhighway really change schools? *Electronic Learning*, 13(8), 24.

Minatel, J. (1995). *Easy World Wide Web with Netscape*. Indianapolis, IN: Que Corporation.

Owen, T., Owston, R., & Dickie, C. (1995). *The Learning Highway*. Toronto: Key Porter Books.

Palmer, E. (Ed.). (1995). *The Internet: A Selective Bibliography*. Ottawa: National Library of Canada, Library Information Service.

Pike, M.A. (1995). *Using the Internet* (2nd ed.). Indianapolis, IN: Que Corporation.

Salvador, R. (1994, May–June). The emperor's new clothes. *Electronic Learning*, 13(8), 32.

Sparks, D. (1993, February). 13 tips for managing change in schools. *Education Digest*, 58(6), 13.

The Switched-On Classroom. (1995). Boston: Massachusetts Software Council.

Walker, D. (1995, January–February). *Making an Internet project work*. Multimedia Schools.

Williams, B. (1995). *The Internet for Teachers*. Foster City, CA: IDG Books.

The Teacher's Complete & Easy Guide to the Internet

Index